WITHDRAWN

SUN YAT-SEN

A Portrait

SUN YAT-SEN

SUN YAT-SEN

A Portrait

BY STEPHEN CHEN AND ROBERT PAYNE

AN ASIA PRESS BOOK

NEW YORK   THE JOHN DAY COMPANY

COPYRIGHT, 1946, BY ASIA PRESS

All rights reserved—no part of this book may be reproduced in any form without permission in writing from the publisher.

This book is published on the same day in the Dominion of Canada by Longmans, Green & Company, Toronto.

Designed by Robert Josephy

MANUFACTURED IN THE UNITED STATES OF AMERICA

CONTENTS

PREFACE v

I   THE FORERUNNERS   1

II   THE MAKING OF A REPUBLIC   102

III   THE PRINCIPLES OF A PEOPLE   173

IV   THE SENSE OF GLORY   195

APPENDIX A. A Note on Sun Yat-sen's Ancestry   227

APPENDIX B. Chronological Table   229

Select Bibliography   235

Index   237

PREFACE

THE material for a complete life of Dr. Sun Yat-sen, the founder of the Chinese Republic, was lost when a Japanese bomb wrecked the Commercial Press in Shanghai and destroyed the documents so carefully collected by Dr. Linebarger. These documents cannot be replaced; nor for the moment can we hope to see the papers preserved by the Sun family, which were carefully concealed somewhere in Japanese-occupied territory. A fully documented life of Dr. Sun Yat-sen is therefore impossible, and as time goes on it is likely to prove increasingly difficult. This book is an attempt to collect together, in the shortest possible compass, whatever information remains on the life of a great democrat, using wherever possible the unpublished material which has been thrown open to us by members of the Kuomintang party. We are grateful to Mr. Pan Kung-chan, member of the Standing Committee of the Central Executive Committee of the Kuomintang; Mr. Liang Han-chao, Minister of Information; and Mr. Chang Tao-fan, Minister of Overseas Affairs, for their help. In particular we have to thank Dr. Sun Fo, President of the Legislative Yuan, for his great kindness in suggesting sources and materials on the life of his father. Without his general assistance and careful revision of the completed manuscript, this work would have been impossible.

Stephen Chen
Robert Payne

The Chinese characters, composed by Dr. Sun Fo, are quoted from Dr. Sun Yat-sen's favourite saying from Confucius. Translated literally, *Tien Hsia Wei Ku* means, "The universe belongs to all," but the words imply the full context: "When the great principle has been carried out, the universe will belong to all."

SUN YAT-SEN

A Portrait

I. THE FORERUNNERS

I

CHINA in 1866 stood on the threshold of vast changes. The Taiping rebellion had been quelled only two years before; the imperial armies were still hounding down the last rebels in the mountain strongholds of Yunnan and Szechuan, and though a desultory peace had settled upon the country, and though the Emperor proclaimed in a resonant voice that the "world-wide empire" had been stabilized in equity and justice, the wounds opened by Hung Shiu-ch'uan were still festering and the congealed blood did not hide the mortal sores.

Young men could still remember the Opium War against England in 1839, and in the village of Choyhung, on the southern promontory of Kwangtung, there were men who had heard the sounds of the bombardment between British and Chinese warships in the waters off Macao one sultry day in November, when the wind blew from the east and the puffs of the cannon balls hung like white streamers against the gray clouds. But the treaty of Nanking which the emperor Tao Kung signed reluctantly on the advice of his ministers had opened the five ports Canton, Amoy, Foochow, Ningpo, and Shanghai to foreign traders; the desolate island of Hong Kong was ceded to the British, and only a few scholars in high places realized that the Ch'ing dynasty had passed its meridian and was in a decline.

The Taipings were not alone in rebelling against the empire. Throughout the first half of the century there were sporadic revolts—the Nienfei attacked yamen runners in the north; the Moslems in Yunnan took the opportunity of the absence of a provincial governor to rebel against their non-Moslem neighbors with the aid of the aboriginal inhabitants of the hills; the Northwest was restless; there were revolts nearer Peking, where taxgatherers were found beheaded in ditches and the arms of the soldiers disappeared mysteriously. Gradually the old unquestioning beliefs in the sanctity of the "Heavenly Prince" were disappearing, and with the collapse of the Japanese shogunate and the advance of the West there came a new spirit of criticism—in part a legacy of the revolutionary fervor of the Taipings and in part an understanding of the great gulf which divided the people from their Manchu lords.

One day in Fontainebleau, Napoleon had pointed to a globe and said: "China is a vast slumbering lion, which will astound the world when it awakes." But the night of the lion was longer than anyone had imagined, and no one had yet seen the animal awake.

The lion stirred in its sleep and whisked a few flies with its tail. So large and ponderous a lion could rest a few more years without interrupting its slumber. The small ships cannonading against the coast, the demands of foreign merchants, the new knowledge creeping through the customhouses, the vast antiquity of a culture which was in need of new blood, above all the new spirit of self-criticism were beginning to make themselves felt, and in the place of the old stoicism there arose gradually and intermittently the belief that the Ch'ings must be destroyed. It is the inevitable fate of all ruling families to grow up from childhood to adolescence and so from maturity to decline; but the Ch'ing empire had begun in a blaze of glory with K'ang Hsi and Ch'ien Lung, and the precocious child in his old age was showing all the signs of epilepsy and ungovernable autocracy. Meanwhile the lives of the small villagers went on much as usual; men wore their hair in long-hanging braids; women were foot-bound; slaves were bought or exchanged; incense smoke rose in the temples, and small clouds of smoke rose over opium pipes; the yamen runners asked for military escorts, and the magistrates built iron gates to their doors; and from every yamen there flew the serpentine dragon with pointed claws—a symbol of domination resented by the intelligent, and occasionally beloved by the credulous, who added the "Heavenly Prince" in Peking to their store of incredible legends.

It was a world startlingly similar to Kafka's *Castle*. Far in the north lay the mysterious city of Peking, whence orders were transmitted to the yamens by yellow-coated messengers. The governors and the bannermen repeated the orders, wrote reports, attended ceremonial festivals and worshiped the gods of the clouds and rain, built earthworks and practiced calligraphy, conceived plans for the amelioration of the crops, and attended the exasperating and continually increasing trials of the malcontents, and had no idea what they were doing, and possessed no means of understanding the minds of the people. Rigorous in obedience to the laws, they substituted a code for the practice of living, and they were so accustomed to conspiracy and corruption that they annotated the laws with fixed scales for corruption and introduced a formal code even into the labyrinths of conspiracy. And though the taxgatherers were adamant and torture was barefaced and used without discrimination, there were many small villages which did not feel their power—villages which were not even marked on the maps and which lived their secret lives almost exactly as men lived four thousand years before on the Yellow River.

The village of Choyhung—Blue Thriving Village in the Kwangtungese dialect—lay in a nest of hills, with the purple mountain of the Plowshare in the distance among marshes and rich grazing land, about forty miles from

Canton and thirty miles north of Macao in the great delta of the West River, which coils through Kwangtung and Kwangsi and has its source near Yunnanfu in Yunnan. Kingfishers dived over the river: their blue feathers and the blue reeds of the marshes were exported to Peking, and it is from these that the village derives its name. From here the sea was invisible, and only the great waterways and the fields of rice stretching halfway up the mountains could be seen from the whitewashed bamboo-and-mortar houses.

In a small house at the northern end of the village, a house with a beaten earth floor, some tables and wooden beds, with a paved threshing floor and a barn where the winter rye and summer rice were stored, Sun Yat-sen was born on November 12, 1866, the sixth day of the tenth moon of the fifth year of the emperor T'ung Chih. His father, Sun Tao-chuan, was a small holder plowing eight or nine mu of land, sufficient to keep his family of six children, three daughters and three sons, well fed and reasonably well educated in the village school. When he was younger, he had made the journey to Macao, but homesickness or failure in the tailoring trade overcame his spirit of adventure and he returned to the small farm, married one of the handsome daughters of a neighboring farmer named Yeong, and with a little carpentry and painting to increase his earnings set about raising a family from the produce of his farm. He was short and slender, with one of those squat, eager faces which are common in Kwangtung, a farmer hardly to be distinguished from the other farmers in the district, though he was the descendant of a duke who had come down from the north during the oppressions which followed the extermination of the Ming emperors. He was liked by the villagers, but he received no official post and his whole life was bound up with the farm. Like all the other wives in the village, his wife was foot-bound and wore the drab blue gown of Chinese peasants.

Sun Yat-sen was the youngest son. Sun Mei or Teh Chang, the eldest son, had been born twelve years before; Ching-ming, the eldest daughter, born in 1856, died three years later; the second son, Teh Yu, died mysteriously in youth; and there was a daughter born a few years before Sun Yat-sen; another five years later. The parents were already old—Sun Tao-chuan fifty-four and his wife thirty-nine when Sun Yat-sen was born. Besides the old parents and the young children there were two widowed aunts in the family, whose husbands had deserted their farms and set out for California during one of the periodic gold rushes in the middle of the nineteenth century. By 1850 fifty thousand Chinese laborers were working in the mines of California and Peru, and more thousands on the plantations of Cuba and British Guiana; much of the emigration took the form of "contract labor," and recruiting was often by violence or fraud: a sudden descent upon an unsuspecting village with posters and maps, bribes for the officials and measureless wealth promised and assured; but when the contracts were read carefully it was seen that the contractors were as much pirates as the Portuguese frigates which hovered along the Kwangtung coast. By that time, however, it was too late; the emigrants were already battened down in the holds; and it was rare for any news to percolate from the Americas. Some years later the Sun family discovered that one of the brothers had died at sea, another had died in California in the year after Sun Yat-sen was born; and before the family altar a solemn covenant was made that no further sons should be allowed overseas.

Sun Yat-sen grew up like all the other children in the village. He became bronzed by the tropical sun; he attended the festivals of the village; obediently worshiped the idols in the temple of the god of autumn and burned incense before Kuan Ti, the god of war; watched the kitchen god riding to Heaven on an ant's back during the festivals for him between the twenty-third and twenty-fifth day of the twelfth moon; and on New Year's Day, as the youngest child of the family, he would be allowed to post the dragonlike gate gods on the door panels. He lived happily and unthinkingly, sometimes accompanying his father over the hills, from where he could see clearly, in the transparent light, the wharves of Ching-hsing Kuan, the port of the Gold Star, with the white sails of the high-prowed sampans floating across the deepwater bay. Or else he threw pebbles in a fire and watched them explode or change color, or made pipes out of reeds, or followed the mountain goats over the passes, or caught white stickle-backs in the river, while the kingfishers dived overhead and the smoke from the village fires rose above the white houses, until at last he returned home drowsy with sleep, rolled his queue into a pillow and spent a restless night listening to his mother comforting the sister who was already complaining bitterly of the cruelty of foot-binding. And once, when he was asked what he wanted most as a boy, he replied: "I want a bird—a real singing bird!"

In later years Sun Yat-sen, usually reserved about his private life, would speak of his childhood as an unbelievably happy period in a life of continual strain. He particularly liked to tell the story of how he listened, during the long summer afternoons when school was closed on account of the heat, to an old soldier who had taken part in the Taiping rebellion. With a long pipe in his mouth, and with a stick to draw the progress of the battles in the dust, the old soldier recounted how Hung Shiu-ch'uan, a Hakka born in a village less than two hundred li from Choyhung, had set out from Chingtien in Kwangsi with no more than a handful of followers and in less than three years his armies swept through all the provinces of the south and at last the "Great Peace" Emperor had been enthroned in Nanking, believing himself to be the "Heavenly Emperor" and his kingdom to be a "Kingdom of Peace and Heaven." For fifteen years the Taipings remained in power. They worshiped a cross, they believed that men and women were born equal before God, denounced the buying and selling of slaves, forbade concubinage, and after devastating some of the fairest sections of the Yangtse Valley announced a new system of landownership which would give the people a more equitable tenure of the land. For more than ten years the Taipings held Nanking, aided by the secret organizations of the "Triads," a revolutionary society which sought to restore the Ming dynasty to the throne, until Tseng Kuo-fan, a scholar with no experience of warfare, and General Gordon, a soldier with great pretentions to scholarship and biblical criticism, combined by a series of harassing attacks along the Yangtse valley to destroy completely the Taiping capital at Nanking.

Twice before, in the history of the Ch'ings, there were famous massacres—the ten days' slaughter in Yangchow and the "thrice wanton massacre" of Chiating in Kiangsu were still vividly remembered, thought they had occurred at the beginning of the Ch'ing dynasty in 1645, for broadsheets describing the injustices of the Ch'ings had been scattered far and wide by the Taipings before they fell; but the sack of Nanking and the desolation along the Yangtse valley reverberated even upon near-by Canton, a city which had seen so many dynasties pass that it usually remained unruffled. But now less merchandise came along the great waterways which connect Canton with the Yangtse Valley, and the thunder of the guns on Nanking and the massacres of "the Worshipers of Shang Ti" were reflected in the bills of lading, and no one knew what punitive measures were in store for the South, which had assisted the Taipings throughout all the years of Hung Shiu-ch'uan's assumption of the kingship. As he listened to the stories of the old soldier, Sun Yat-sen may have foreseen that another revolution, more carefully related to the needs of the people, was to come; but he could hardly have foreseen his own position in the revolution, or the disproportion between the forces of the Taipings and his own.

At banquets, when all the speeches had come to an end and the rancor inseparable from all revolutionary movements was dissolved in quiet comradeship, he would tell the story of how he hated the senseless repetition of characters in the village school, his nervousness when he was compelled to stand with his back to the teacher and recite *The Three-Character Classic* to the tune of continual blows with a cane on his head. One day, when he had suffered enough, he so far forgot himself as to turn round at his teacher and shout: "Sir, we have a great deal of this book, but we cannot understand one single word of it. Have the goodness to explain it to us. I don't see any use in memorizing such nonsense!" Accustomed to obedience and even to reverence, the schoolmaster exploded: "You young rebel! Do you dare to criticize the sage's teaching? —nothing could be more unfilial in the world." "I am not rebelling," Sun Yat-sen answered quietly, "but I want to know what the characters mean." On another occasion he told the story of how his father planted some trees, which were stolen by the neighbors. His father asked him whether he would help to get them back, and Sun Yat-sen replied: "Not now, but when I grow older I will get them back for you." But it was the story of the schoolmaster which he remembered more vividly, and to the very end of his life he remembered the name of his teacher—Chang.

Piracy was still common in the waters off Kwangtung. For a time foreign ships, usually Portuguese, undertook to "convoy" Chinese merchant craft along the coast, ostensibly as a protection against pirates, but in reality either in order to practice a thinly veiled form of blackmail or in order to trap the vessels in the pirates' lair. The pirates were not satisfied with their toll in merchant shipping; like the Norsemen, they advanced along the rivers, pillaged the rich houses of the merchants, and disappeared downriver as quickly and silently as they came. Sun Yat-sen would tell the story of how he watched the pirates, sword in hand, attacking the fortified house of a merchant in Choyhung who had returned from overseas. The house was built of cement, and the doors of iron, but the pirates broke through the walls with battering rams and the merchant fled. For a long while the pirates could not discover the hidden treasure, the iron-hooped casks and small reticules of chain metal which represented the merchant's life savings; but when they found the treasure they burst into intoxicated laughter and even forgot to hunt down and slit the throats of the merchant and his family. To Sun Tao-chuan the incident must have offered one more proof of the inadvisability of merchants' traveling abroad; but Sun Yat-sen would say that it was at that moment that he recognized the weakness of the Manchu dynasty, which extracted taxes and put men to the torture but was incapable of guaranteeing a safe existence for the people.

One more tragedy, which occurred in the village, left a vivid mark on Sun Yat-sen's impressionable mind. Three brothers named Li, returned sugar planters from Hawaii, built a house with a large garden which they carefully tended and to which they invited the children of the neighborhood. One day when Sun Yat-sen was playing in the garden, some Manchu soldiers and lictors armed to the teeth rudely awakened its peace and carried off the three brothers. They had committed no crime and they were highly respected in the village, but nothing was heard of them. The soldiers established themselves in the house, and the carefully tended garden was allowed to relapse into decay. Some days later it was learned that the three brothers had been arrested on the false accusation of one of the Manchu officials and immediately beheaded. In later years Sun Yat-sen was to relate that he never heard Peking mentioned until he reached the age of fourteen and was about to leave for Honolulu. It may be true, for geography was not taught in the village school, and the name of the capital was known only by a sobriquet. But he was not a rebellious boy—rebellion grows in a harder school than the pleasant vicissitudes of life in Choyhung—and he was of an age when even the murder of three brothers on a neighboring farm might bring no more than a pleasant escape from the monotony of helping his father in the fields.

A more exciting event was to come later when his elder brother, now known as Ah Mei (*Ah* being a term of affection in Kwangtung, like *liao* in the north), returned to Choyhung from Hawaii, bringing not only sufficient capital to rebuild his parents' house but a fund of information about life in the islands of the Pacific. He had left his native village when Sun Yat-sen was six, and no news was heard from him until a year later, when a Chinese merchant chanced to pass through Choyhung. Thereafter there had been a desultory correspondence; the letters were taken to the village letter writer and read aloud, for neither Sun Yat-sen's father nor his mother was literate, and it was not until Sun Yat-sen himself had learned to read and write that they discovered the abundant wealth of Hawaii. Many years later he would recall how the whole family sat around him while he read out a letter describing the islands which to the Chinese, since traders imported enormous quantities of sandalwood from Hawaii, were known as the Sandalwood Mountains, and Ah Mei described the yellow beaches and fertile land with its grapevines, orchards, palms, citrus groves, and terraces of pineapples in the terms of a lover who was glad to escape from the prospect of small holding even in the Blue Thriving Village.

Ah Mei was among the first to cultivate the rich lowlands in the region of Pearl Harbor. He was a careful farmer, industrious, provident, and not a little avaricious. He lived frugally, sent money to his parents, and invested his capital in the land. In 1877 he returned to China, but only for a brief visit—long enough to acquire a bride and to set the tongues of the village wagging on the unaccountable prosperity of Hawaii—and returned, leaving Sun Yat-sen disconsolate. Perhaps Sun Yat-sen was unhappy because he was lonely for his elder brother's companionship, for he seems to have been a quiet and rather secretive child; but though he implored his father to send him abroad, the fate of his two uncles was too recent to be easily forgotten, and he was retained in the house, a hostage to the adversity of his uncles.

Two years later he appeared mysteriously on the passenger lists of the S.S. *Grannoch,* a British ship of two thousand tons, which sailed from Macao to Honolulu with the usual cargo of indented laborers for the sugar plantations. No one knows how he obtained his parents' permission to leave Choyhung, and it seems likely that he left without their permission and made his way to Macao alone, after first receiving his brother's approval. He was fourteen, sturdy and bronzed, with a high forehead and a sensitive mouth, a little taller than most Cantonese for his age. If he had secretly corresponded with his brother and disobeyed his parents' objections, and in so doing broken the supreme law of filial conduct, he was doing no more than thousands of youths a little older were doing at the same time. In spite of the rumors of barracoons in Cuba and harsh treatment in the Philippines, the provinces in the south of China were gradually being depopulated by eager youths determined to make their fortunes overseas.

In later years Sun Yat-sen vividly recalled the small, cramped engine room with the steel gratings, and the transverse beams which held the ship together; he remembered the steam belching from the cylinders, and the red faces of the stokers, and he would say that his profound admiration for Western progress began with the long journey across the Pacific when he was fourteen. He recalled too that a sailor died and his body was wrapped in a sack and covered with a Union Jack and then placed reverently on the fo'c's'le deck, while bells tolled and a bearded captain read from the burial service. When the last amen was sounded, the sack weighted with lead was tipped overboard. Sun Yat-sen was no more imaginative, perhaps, than most boys of his age, but he was struck by the absence of all those ceremonies which are traditionally associated with burial in China, and he surveyed the prospect of similar burial with horror. There are worse ways of learning about foreign civilizations than through their burial customs, and fifty years later, when he lay dying, he gave orders that his body should be embalmed and buried near the last Ming emperors in Nanking, and perhaps his determination to avoid a precipitate burial arose from the dim memory of having once watched the body of an English sailor disappearing in the Pacific. But when he leaned over the taffrail and looked out upon the islands of Hawaii, with their white beaches, green palm trees, and mountains disappearing under thick clouds, there came to him no presentiment of the future, and his brother Ah Mei treated him as he would treat any new arrival from the homeland. The twenty days' journey across the Pacific taught Sun Yat-sen many things he would remember later in life, but the death of the sailor was soon put aside in his memory.

When he stepped ashore at the old King's Pier at Honolulu, he asked his brother whether he could send a letter to Kwangtung, and he was shown the post office—a small red-brick building with a long counter and the inevitable clockface on the inevitable steeple—and a letter was solemnly posted to Choyhung. At that time Honolulu was still undeveloped; buggy carriages drove from the pier to the municipal offices past timber shacks and vegetable gardens, and there was so much dust in the air that the horses wore a special kind of filtering nose bag. Only the area round the pier with the huge warehouses was developed.

Ah Mei took the boy in hand, and after a few days of exploration they drove to the small farm in the Pearl Harbor area where among low-lying marshes, tapioca trees, sugar plantations, and the ever-recurring palms Ah Mei kept a general store in a small village called Ewa, though he worked for the greater part of the day on his rice plantation two miles away. In the dimly lit store, among rice sacks, fly whisks, brushes, sweetmeats, and medicines, Sun Yat-sen learned a smattering of the Hawaiian language, plied the abacus, posted his accounts, and discovered the limitations of a small village store which attempted to supply the inexhaustible demands of the tenant farmers and coolies in the neighborhood; until at last, tired of the musty smell of gunny sacks and molasses, he begged his elder brother to send him to school. There were the inevitable delays. His brother thought he had acquired a good assistant; the boy thought he was being imposed upon.

As usual, when he had determined upon a course of action, he succeeded, and the local diocesan college, founded by Bishop Willis of the Church of England at a time when the Church of England was opening schools all over the world—in India, South Africa, Canada, and the West Indies—welcomed the young Chinese boy whose brother had acquired fame as one of the richest and most enterprising rice planters. The diocesan college lay just outside Honolulu in a long white rambling house facing the beach. It was evidently a school for the more affluent—the boarding fee was a hundred dollars a year, equivalent to eight or nine hundred gold dollars at the present time—and Ah Mei was rich even by Honolulu standards. Sun Yat-sen entered the school after the summer vacation of 1879 under the name of "Tai Cheong." There in the uncomfortable, drafty classrooms, among English, American, Chinese, and Hawaiian boys, he learned the first steps of English, physics, mathematics, morality, and—most enticing of all—biblical history. All the masters were English except the Rev. Solomon Meheule, who took charge of the first year English course, though he was a native Hawaiian. Everything in the school—the textbooks, the methods of teaching, the syllabus, even the refinements of punishment—was English; and English history and the genealogies of English and Jewish kings were taught on this solitary mountainous island in the Pacific as a matter of course. Sun Yat-sen knew no English when he arrived at Iolani (the name by which the school was generally known) except the few words he had learned from his brother. For ten days he listened to the curious low running sounds of English, so unlike the clipped and rather high-pitched utterance of the Cantonese; and on the eleventh day he began to stammer out a few phrases. These ten days' silent observation did him good, and in later months, when he had grown more resourceful and was taking a greater part in the affairs of the school, singing in the choir and serving in the fire brigade, it was noticed that he was always cautiously silent before making up his mind to perform any given course of action. He was known as a resolute assistant in the fire brigade, perhaps because he had once watched his own bamboo-and-mortar village reduced to ashes.

According to Bishop Willis he was a devoted assistant at

Bible classes, and duly attended daily morning and evening prayers. In later years Sun Yat-sen admitted that he enjoyed the distinction of a surplice and walking in procession from the school to St. Andrew's procathedral in Honolulu. Though athletics were encouraged and Sun Yat-sen was fond of swimming, the deliberate atmosphere of Anglican Christianity with its wax tapers and interminable Sunday rituals produced the inevitable effect of making him more self-conscious and at the same time more of a recluse. When he visited Ah Mei his pronounced Anglicanism met the solid rock of idol worship and the more conservative ritual of the Chinese. They were soon at odds; Sun Yat-sen admitted that he had been baptized; the elder brother could not always control his temper. With the fire of a recent convert, Sun Yat-sen laboriously explained the mystery of the sacred Trinity only to discover that his brother was incapable of understanding even the significance of the Ten Commandments. Both brothers possessed hot, sultry tempers. Ah Mei wrote home to Choyhung that Sun Yat-sen was getting out of hand; he was disobedient and spoke disparagingly of the ancestors and was becoming more Western than the Westerners. Worse still, he had been baptized and was talking seriously of becoming a colporteur or a missionary.

All Ah Mei's sense of outraged decency came to the fore, and on the plea that the younger brother must return to China to find a bride—Sun Yat-sen was nearly eighteen and of an age when many of his school friends in China were already married—arranged to have him shipped back to Canton. But before he could begin the journey, Dowager Queen Emma and Princess Liliuokalani of the royal house of Hawaii came to attend the prize-giving at his graduation ceremony in the summer of 1882, and it was in this blaze of royalty that he received from the hands of King Kalakaua, who was already suffering from the delusions of grandeur which were to make his name notorious later, the second prize in English grammar—a book on missionary life in China and a Bible bound in pigskin. On the open dais overlooking the beach and the palm trees, the young boy wearing shorts and with a queue hanging down his back shook hands with the monarch, smiled nervously and happily and walked backwards from the dais.

He was tall for his age, more sunburned even than when he was at Choyhung, and there was now seldom any nervousness in his manner. Like nearly all children born late in their parents' life, he had grown to maturity early. But already the foundations of his life had been laid, and it was a self-assured young student, still wearing a pigtail and still carrying the pigskin Bible, who sailed back to China in the summer of 1883 in search of a wife.

II

HE HAD learned many things at Iolani, and not the least important was his contact with European life. On the fertile soil of Hawaii, American opportunism and English traditionalism had formed a basis of government; for though power resided actually in the hands of the monarch and the whole island was soaked in monarchism, the royal family was as informal as the Dowager Empress of China was unapproachable; and already there were the first signs of a democratic government with elected officials and advisers chosen for their special knowledge of Hawaiian affairs. King Kalakaua was later deposed, but the seeds of his tyranny were not yet evident.

In this atmosphere Sun Yat-sen spent the most formative years of his youth, constantly and perhaps unconsciously comparing the orderly progress on the island with the static obscurantism of Kwangtung. He discovered, as all

Chinese at that time must have discovered, that once transplanted from the homeland a Chinese farmer assumes the character of an Occidental. Though Ah Mei still lit tapers and bowed reverently three times before the family altar, there were thousands of Chinese who were slowly casting themselves adrift from the dominance of the Manchus and leading the frugal lives of foreign settlers. The laundrymen, the small-town butchers, the restaurant keepers, the sugar planters and coolies who were later to become his allies were the products of the first contact between East and West on foreign soil. Among them Sun Yat-sen lived as a brother, and indeed to this brotherhood between the revolutionary and the expatriate Chinese was due the success of the revolution.

He was nearly eighteen when he returned to China, a stocky youth with a sensitive mouth and the hardened manner of a rebel who knew only too well what was in store for him. His brother's letters to Choyhung described a youth who was rebellious and needed firm handling, and Sun Yat-sen might have fallen in with his parents' wishes but for the accident that the sand junk which brought him from Hong Kong to Canton fell among piratical officials. In later years he recounted the episode with great gusto. As the sand junk approached the little island of Cap Suy Mun at the mouth of Hong Kong harbor where the customhouse was established, the captain warned the passengers to prepare gifts for the customs officials. These officials, wearing the Manchu livery of black brocade gowns, silver belts and swords, and caps with blue buttons, descended upon the sand junk and demanded the customary levy. No sooner had they left than a new flotilla of officials descended upon them, saying that though customs duty had been levied by the first officials, they were levying *likin,* a tax originally devised to meet the cost of suppressing the Taipings. Once more the baggage was examined, and once more the duty was paid. Then a third flotilla set out from the customhouse, demanding duty on imported opium, and it was only on the arrival of a fourth flotilla demanding a duty on imported petroleum that Sun Yat-sen completely lost his temper and refused to open his baggage. The captain and the passengers begged him to remain silent, and even wanted to offer him bribes; but while the inspectors searched the passengers' baggage, the boy's voice could be heard complaining bitterly against the exactions of the Manchus. When the inspectors came to the place where he was standing, Sun Yat-sen in spite of the pleadings of the captain refused to open his baggage, and the inspectors decided to execute a warrant against the sand junk and attach her until the next morning, when she was allowed to sail up to Ching-hsing Kuan, with Sun Yat-sen still standing on the prow and declaiming against the corruption of the officials and the decadence of the Manchus.

This is the story as it was related in after years, and there is little reason to doubt its truth. Nearly all Chinese returning from abroad must have found the exactions of the officials exorbitant, and Sun Yat-sen was not the only expatriate to voice his displeasure. Accustomed to the freedom of Hawaii, where taxes were almost nonexistent and the schedules of customs duty were worked out on the same scale as customs charges in European ports, he must have found the Cantonese inspectors unbelievably exacting. Worse was to follow. Trained as a Christian, with the ardor of a recent convert, he had seen idolatry disappearing in Hawaii, but he had only to see the painted gods on the bridge of the sand junk to realize that idolatry was still in existence in China. It was an unruly and rebellious youth who jumped ashore at Ching-hsing Kuan and drove to Choyhung, a youth with a pigtail and a Bible: the one a symbol of all that he was beginning to detest with the fervor acquired from the knowledge of a greater freedom; the other a symbol of the iconoclasm which in the space of thirty years was to shake China to her foundations.

Ah Mei was right. The boy was unruly and unresponsive to village life. He especially hated the village idol worshipers. There was a small temple near his old school with a tiled roof and paved courtyard; in the darkness of the temple interior there were three plaster idols, gods of a long-forgotten fertility cult, whose obscene purpose, though known to the village elders who derived their authority from them, was inconceivable to the illiterate farmers in the neighborhood, who performed at the festivals with the mixture of concern and disinterestedness which is still common among Chinese temple worshipers. Pei-ti, the god of autumn, Ti-ho his wife, and Wang-mo his mother belonged to the third order of the gods approved by the Manchu ordinance along with the gods of the walls and moats and the god of fire.

On one of the festival days, probably in the autumn of 1883, with the help of Lu Ho-tung, a friend two years younger, Sun Yat-sen decided to put his iconoclasm into action, and while the worshipers filled the temple, he climbed on the pedestal supporting Pei-ti and began to harangue the villagers with a torrent of righteous abuse. According to one of the villagers who still remembered the occasion, he addressed them in a high-pitched, screaming voice: "I could forgive you if you offered me a single reason for worshiping this idol! Is he strong? Can he protect you? Why do you kneel before him and offer incense candles, when he cannot even protect himself—" and with these words, he broke off the god's arm, revealing the hollow core and the sacking stuffed into the arm by the idol makers. Then, after mutilating the virgin and her mother, he stepped down from the pedestal and walked quietly away through the throng of silent, appalled worshipers.

He, who had been so studious in his youth, had returned from abroad only to mutilate the country's gods! No penalty fell from heaven, no sudden blight destroyed the harvest. The honor of the gods and the temple guardians, however, was impugned and a council of village elders assembled to pass judgment on the crime. All Sun Yat-sen's rebellious animadversions against concubinage, footbinding, opium smoking, bribery, and corruption were solemnly discussed, and it was remembered against him that he had gone round the village asking everyone to translate the Manchu inscriptions on the coins issued by the Imperial Board of Revenue—and everyone had failed. He had even asked the unsuspecting villagers whether the Prince of Heaven, the emperor Kuang Hsu, was Chinese or Manchu, and he had laughed in their faces when they said he was Chinese.

The punishment for rebellion was death by decapitation or by being buried alive in a pit. It was a time of savage punishment—"death by the thousand knives" was still customary in Peking, and adulteresses were burned in oil—and only the respect in which his father was held in the village saved him from the village elders. The boy was summarily banished and the father was ordered to repair the idols. In this atmosphere of suppressed rebellion and indignation, Sun Yat-sen left Choyhung, a vagabond with no plans for the future except to vindicate his rebellion.

He reached Hong Kong late in the autumn of 1883, possessing no valuables except those that his parents had secretly saved for him, for banishment entailed that the victim should leave the village with only the clothes he wore and the tools of his trade. In Hawaii he had been given letters of introduction to the teachers of the diocesan school of the Church of England in Hong Kong; he may have corresponded with them even before he left Choyhung. We know that he spent a month at the school immediately after his banishment and left no definite impression upon the teachers; and for the next three or four months nothing further is known of him. He may have gone to Shanghai, where Lu Ho-tung was then living. Rumor and conjecture have concluded that he may have returned to Choyhung on the serious illness of his father or to attend the family councils during the negotiations for his marriage to a young farmer's daughter of the neighboring Lu family. But in April 1884 he entered Queen's College, at that time the best school in Hong Kong, and on the thirteenth of the fourth moon of the tenth year of the emperor Kuang Hsu—that is, on May 7, 1884—he married.

At Queen's College he studied seriously, attended Bible classes, and appears to have been baptized a second time; he improved his knowledge of the Chinese written language and maintained his correspondence with Hawaii. He met the pastor of an American evangelical mission and helped to organize missionary activities in Macao and along the West River. On holidays and week ends he returned to his wife and family at Choyhung—the idol-mutilating incident seems to have been forgiven—and he succeeded in converting two students from the school to Christianity.

Meanwhile events were occurring in Annam which were to change the whole course of his life. During 1883 and 1884 French pressure on Annam resulted in open hostilities against the Chinese government, which retained nominal suzerainty over the vassal state, receiving annual tribute from its emperor. The French launched attacks by land and sea, penetrating the frontiers of Yunnan and raiding the Chinese coast as far as Amoy and Formosa. Defeated off Fukien, the remnants of the French fleet sailed through the archipelago of Chusan and entered the Yangtse estuary, where their superior gunpower proved to be completely successful. The French admiral Courbet ascended the Min River to the Fuchow arsenal and in seven minutes of cannonading destroyed the Chinese fleet of eleven huge wooden war junks. The Chinese were successful in Yunnan, where the battles of Chen-nan-kuan (South Frontier Gate) and Cool Mountains showered glory on General Liu Ying-fu's "Black Banner Regiments." A long-sword regiment which recaptured the Cool Mountains after a long winter siege is remembered in Chinese history because it was the first Chinese army equipped only with lances, battle-axes, and swords to hold off an enemy equipped with bayonets and rifles. But though the French armies retreated in a disorderly rout from Yunnan, and the French government fell when the disaster at Cool Mountains (known as the battle of Liangshan in Chinese and Langson in Annamese) was known, Annam was lost; and by the Franco-Chinese treaty of Tientsin in 1885, the Chinese government through the viceroy Li Hung-chang recognized the French protectorate over Annam and freedom of trade between Tongking and the adjoining Chinese provinces, but refused to pay the indemnity which the French had demanded.

Ever since the emperor Shih Huang Ti had brought Annam under the administrative control of the Ch'in empire over two thousand years before, Annam had remained a vassal state of China, regularly offering tribute and sending envoys to Peking. The loss of Annam shocked China out of her complacency, and when a French cruiser coming down from Formosa put into Hong Kong dockyard for repairs, Sun Yat-sen joined the students in encouraging the shipyard workers to down tools.

The Franco-Chinese war and the loss of Annam proved to be a greater shock than idol worship or corruption in high places. For the first time Sun Yat-sen saw visibly enacted before his eyes the weakness of the Manchu regime in the face of foreign aggression. In his later writings he alluded to this war as the critical moment which determined his life as a revolutionary.

His early revolutionary activity, however, was cut short in the following year by an urgent summons from his brother in Hawaii. Appalled by the idol-breaking incident and the rumors that the young revolutionary was defiantly attacking the Manchus from the safety of the British colony of Hong Kong, Ah Mei threatened to stop all financial assistance to the family; and when even this threat failed to have any effect, he asked Sun Yat-sen to come immediately to Honolulu on the plea that documents concerning the sale of various properties in which the younger brother had an interest must be signed immediately. Once again Sun Yat-sen sailed for Honolulu.

The quarrel between the two brothers was remembered long afterward. Sun Yat-sen indignantly refused to give up his Christianity in return for a regular allowance. Just before he left Honolulu, in March 1885, he said: "I am sorry to have disappointed you, but I regret still more the fact that I cannot follow in the footsteps of our forefathers. I cannot abide their old customs. I thank you for your generosity—and with all my heart I can only return the money to you. Money will never make me betray Christianity, and indeed money is a curse in China, a source of corruption and a burden to the people."

The tone of this speech to his brother, if it is accurately recorded, suggests a kind of Christian anarchism; but it contains also a note of desperation, as though he was already schooled in adversity. He returned by way of Japan and Shanghai, his passage money defrayed by a group of friendly Chinese Christians who saw in the young convert a promising preacher of the gospel. But there were no theological seminaries in Canton or Hong Kong at the time; many of his friends were missionaries with medical training, and after some months of acute poverty and inactivity he determined to study medicine as the first step toward dedicating his life to the ministry. A photograph taken at the time shows him wearing the long black gown and black skullcap of a student, with a firm chin, a wide, sensitive mouth, and oddly dreaming eyes—the face of a boy who has already discovered in himself a sense of dedication.

The Pok Tsai hospital in Canton rivaled the Victoria Hospital in Hong Kong in the excellence of its facilities for studying medicine. Crowded with outpatients who gathered from every corner of Kwangtung, it grew out of the patient advocacy of a Scotch missionary, Dr. John Kerr, an old man remembered for his white beard, his stocky manner, and a legendary facility with the surgeon's knife. In this atmosphere Sun Yat-sen was perfectly at home. The gruff Christianity of the Scotsman delighted him; the white-robed nurses and the shining medical instruments in the hermetically sealed glass cases spoke of a world in which the discoveries of the West could be put to an infinite number of services. He spent the year 1886-1887 working as an assistant in the hospital, studying in the laboratory and looking on while operations were performed. But the most useful periods were spent in the large library which Dr. Kerr had assembled through more than forty years of practice.

He was not alone in Pok Tsai. He boarded with a friend who shared his own interests and who entered the hospital at the same time. Cheng Shih-liang was a Cantonese and already a member of the Triad Society (San Ho Hui), also known as the Hung Men or the Society of Heaven and Earth. The original aim of the society was to upset the Manchus and restore the Ming dynasty, but in the years following the Taiping rebellion it had degenerated through lack of a coherent plan, and like the Red and the

Green Societies had become an organ for the prosecution of family feuds and for the assassination of corrupt officials. Cheng Shih-liang's interest in the society was aroused when his father died brokenhearted as the result of an unsuccessful lawsuit against a local magistrate who refused to pay his debts. The magistrate bribed the judge, and shortly afterward Cheng Shih-liang's father, after a bout of one of those ungovernable tempers which the Chinese call *ch'i*, died, leaving to his son the duty of avenging his honor. Both students were popular at Pok Tsai, and within a few months Sun Yat-sen was initiated into the Triad Society.

Sun Yat-sen possessed a genuine affection for his sworn brother and corresponded with him when he left the Canton Hospital in 1887 and entered the Alice Memorial Hospital in Hong Kong, founded during the same year by a wealthy Chinese merchant, with Dr. James Cantlie as one of the co-founders. Sun Yat-sen was the first pupil to enroll, in October 1887, and among the first to graduate five years later. In the Alice Memorial Hospital, named after the English wife of Sir Kai Hokai, he studied botany, zoology, and chemistry, in addition to the purely medical subjects.

In his autobiography he wrote: "All the years between 1885 and 1895 were like one day in my hard fight for national liberty, and my medical practice was no more to me than a means to introduce my propaganda to the world." The arduous life of a medical student was not made easier by continual journeys from Hong Kong to Macao for revolutionary purposes. Once more Sun Yat-sen found himself in an atmosphere entirely suited to him. The work was hard, but it was made endurable by his friendship with three students, Chen Shao-pai, Yu Shao-huan, and Yang Hao-ling. The four of them received the derisive nickname of "the Four Big Brigands" for their revolutionary activities.

But though these revolutionary activities nearly always ended in failure, and there were few converts, his work at the hospital was highly praised by the doctors and his marriage was a complete success. In October 1891 his only son, Sun Fo, was born. In the autumn of 1892 he received the certificate of proficiency in medicine and surgery—the highest degree that the hospital doctors could offer him.

He was twenty-seven; he was married; he had spent most of his life wandering from one city to another, and it might be expected that he would settle down, practicing surgery during the day and continuing his revolutionary activities and connections with the secret societies at night. He worked for a while in a hospital at Macao, where Dr. Cantlie occasionally visited him, marveling how the relatives and friends of the patients would crowd round the operating table where Sun Yat-sen, wearing rubber gloves and with a white mask over his face, looked oddly out of place among the crowds of peasants; and Dr. Cantlie noticed that they were particularly interested in the operation for removing stone from the gall bladder. More than once Dr. Cantlie refers to his distinction of manner, which made the quiet-voiced student immediately respected by men of widely differing views. But neither his skill as a surgeon nor his popularity among the Chinese patients prevented the Portuguese government from banishing him from the colony, ostensibly on the grounds that only doctors with Portuguese degrees could be allowed to practice in the colony, but more probably because the Portuguese government had received a note from the Manchu government requesting that he should be extradited. Sun Yat-sen packed his bags and set off secretly for Canton, where his friend Lu Ho-tung was waiting for him. Shortly afterward they decided to brave the anger of the Manchus and journey to the north.

He was always restless, and for the next thirty years he was never to stay more than six months in a single city. Like many men bred on quiet farms, he possessed a strange wanderlust, a curious obstinacy for travel in the wildest places and among the poorest people. With Lu Ho-tung, he decided to travel due north and east.

At Tientsin they would interview the old viceroy Li Hung-chang, who had been one of Tseng Kuo-fan's most redoubtable assistants in the suppression of the Taiping rebellion, but who was now regarded as foremost among the progressives, for he had created in the capital of Hupei a vast new nucleus of institutions of higher learning, among them a medical college, which may have been—though no details of the journey are available—one of the objects of their visit to the north, since they were both anxious to pursue their medical studies. Together they had prepared a solemn memorial addressed to the old Viceroy, a long and fervent testament on the political and social situation in China which seems never to have been delivered, though it was printed in installments a year later in the Shanghai newspaper *Wan Kuo Kung Pao*. The terms of the memorial included many arguments which were later incorporated in the famous *Three Principles of the People*. It advocated the urgent necessity of developing Chinese education, agriculture, mineral resources, and the circulation of commodities; demanded the establishment of an increasing number of schools and adequate facilities for encouraging promising pupils, the introduction of scientific methods in agriculture, the development of industries, a complete reorganization of the transport system, the elimination of trade barriers and superfluous taxes, and protection for the merchants. The memorial was carefully documented; but it could hardly have succeeded in attracting attention at a time when China was more concerned with foreign affairs, and the two friends returned to the south through Wuchang and Hankow having accomplished a part of their mission, but having failed entirely to convince the old Viceroy.

They reached Canton during the days of stress immediately preceding the Sino-Japanese War which broke out in the summer of 1894. Interference of Japan and China in Korean affairs made the war inevitable. Originally the war was due to the influence of a secret society called the Tong Kaks, which demanded complete autonomy for Korea. The Emperor of China, on the advice of Yuan Shih-kai, a protégé of Li Hung-chang and at that time stationed in Seoul, asked for Chinese reinforcements to quell the rebellion of the secret societies. The Japanese, fearing that their influence would disappear under a Chinese invasion of Korea, immediately sent powerful landing parties, took possession of the palace, captured the monarch, and issued in his name a proclamation calling upon the Japanese to expel the Chinese troops. The struggle was brief and full of humiliation for China. By the treaty of Shimonoseki, China was constrained to acknowledge the independence of Korea and to cede Formosa, the Pescadores Islands, and the Liaotung peninsula to the Japanese.

To Sun Yat-sen the news came as no surprise. Convinced that defeat was inevitable, and that it was still too early to begin the revolution, he left once more for Hawaii, where he inaugurated a new chapter of the Hsing Chung Hui (Revive China Society), a secret revolutionary organization which had been started some years before in Macao. In the formal declaration of the society he wrote:

"When the people are united together with one heart and one purpose, and are willing to go through all manner of trials with indomitable courage, the country can be saved, however perilous its position. The people are the foundation of a country, and when the foundation is strengthened, the country will be secure. When the Chinese people were striving for selfish ends, they did not realise that they were neglecting the fundamental problems of government. They did not know that the loyalties and virtues of the people were being sapped and held in open contempt by foreigners."

The new society grew slowly. A secret ritual was introduced, and all members had to swear allegiance to the society on an open Bible. To Sun Yat-sen's surprise Ah Mei became a convert, and more and more wealthy sugar planters joined the society under his influence. A considerable program for advancing the aims of the society was introduced; schools were to be opened, newspapers were to be established, plans were prepared for increasing trade between China and Honolulu. Meanwhile Sun Yat-sen lectured incessantly, opened new chapters of the society on the Hawaiian islands, and in the name of the party sent a long series of proclamations and pronunciamentos to Peking demanding urgent reform. These proclamations, however, were left unread, and Sun Yat-sen was to declare regretfully that it was at this moment in his life that he realized that peaceful measures were in vain and revolution inevitable.

The headquarters of the society were in Shanghai, but the most important field of operations lay in Kwangtung. Among the articles of the society may be found the statement that it was formed "to unite all patriotic Chinese, to cultivate the arts of wealth and power, for the purpose of reviving China and securing her unity." The real aim of the society was less diffident; it was to overthrow the Manchu regime by force. The society was organized in small groups of about fifteen men; the entrance fee was deliberately made as small as possible—five dollars—and rich members were asked or ordered to subscribe to the limit of their purses. The society grew slowly until, as it became affiliated with the other secret societies south of the Yangtse, it began to possess increasing authority. The memorials which Sun Yat-sen sent to Peking were not the outpourings of small, unorganized societies, but the first intimations of revolt; and there is some evidence that Peking recognized the danger and did everything in its power to attack the society.

Suddenly, from Shanghai, came a message of recall. Soong Yao-ju, who was later to become famous as the father of three alarmingly beautiful children, was at that time a prominent member of the Methodist Church, a wealthy millowner and one of the leaders of the society in Shanghai. The defeat of the Chinese troops in Korea produced the inevitable result of prolonged rioting as large bands of armed soldiers retreated slowly over the western frontier; and in this atmosphere of defeat and intellectual despair, Soong Yao-ju saw a favorable opportunity for revolt. Accompanied by a close friend and sworn brother, Tung Yui-nan, Sun Yat-sen immediately returned from Hawaii and made plans for a revolutionary offensive against Canton as the first step toward a national revolution.

Various factors had contributed to the choice of Canton. It was a place well known to the leaders of the capital; it was far from the capital; it was one of the most important centers of the secret societies south of the Yangtse; it was near Hong Kong and therefore in comparatively easy communication with the outside world. Cheng Shih-liang, the student who had befriended him at Pok Tsai, was placed in charge of the bluejackets and the defense corps, and he also acted as liaison officer with the secret societies. Together with Lu Ho-tung he was given control of a "scientific agricultural station" in Canton: in reality an office of propaganda and a munition depot situated inside the city walls. Chen Shao-pai (one of "the Four Big Brigands"), Tung Yui-nan, and Hwang Yung Hsueng kept the "Chien Hung store" in Hong Kong, which later became their headquarters.

American chemists were engaged for the manufacture of bombs; pistols, rifles, and dynamite were bought chiefly from the Philippines and secretly unloaded by stevedores belonging to the secret societies; complete plans of Canton were drawn up, and dossiers concerning the Manchu officials, their whereabouts and the most minute details of their daily lives, were compiled. An elaborate code of secret signals, a timetable of operations, and a new flag completed the preparations which continued over a period of six months. To the tailors who were set to make the flags, Lu Ho-tung, their designer, would explain that they were bedcovers for a younger sister, and the white, twelve-pointed sun on a blue sky represented "mutual love throughout the twelve hours of the day," though in fact the blue sky and white sun represented the universe in its eternal brilliance. In an essay on the meaning of the national flag, Chiang Kai-shek, Sun Yat-sen's successor as generalissimo, wrote: "Using the blue sky and white sun to represent our country, Sun Yat-sen wished not only that our country will, like the blue sky and white sun, live on in the universe in eternal brilliance, but like the sun shining in the sky, our country will radiate its light all over the world, making it bright everywhere and at all times—a new world of culture and peace with justice for all and freedom and equality. The white sun's twelve rays symbolise the day's twelve hours and the year's twelve months. The meaning is that we must, like the rotating earth, continue to seek after progress ceaselessly, according to the old saying, 'As Heaven proceeds vigorously, so the superior man must incessantly strengthen himself.'" The blue and white flag was to be the signal of revolt.

September 9, 1895, was the day chosen for the insurrection. On the previous day five columns were concentrated on the approaches of Canton. At dawn on the ninth, information reached headquarters that a powerful Hong Kong detachment was out of contact with the five columns, and six hundred pistols shipped in seven casks of what appeared to be cement had failed to arrive at their destination on the S.S. *Tai-an*. The insurrection was about to begin, and the leaders were anxiously looking at their watches when Sun Yat-sen hurried up with the information that a message had been received from Hong Kong saying that the pistols would be two days overdue.

The revolutionary forces were compelled to retire. So far there had been no fighting. With the mysterious delay in the arrival of the six hundred pistols, the revolutionary armies were hopelessly outgunned. Sun Yat-sen, from his secret headquarters somewhere in Kwangtung, sent an urgent message to Hong Kong to delay the shipment of the pistols still further. No reply was received, and it was not learned that the guns were already in the hands of the Maritime Customs in Hong Kong.

Worse followed. It was learned that a traitor had visited the yamen at Canton on the previous night and that all their plans, including the position of the headquarters, had been revealed. Lu Ho-tung immediately ordered the revolutionary forces to retire, and with Sun Yat-sen escaped to a previously arranged hiding place. On the way Lu Ho-tung remembered that the membership book of the secret society had been left behind in the headquarters. Fearful of the result if the membership book was found, he returned alone to headquarters and burned the book with other incriminating papers, only to find that a few minutes later the headquarters were surrounded by imperial troops. With four others he was arrested and publicly beheaded. He was the first Christian and revolutionary to face the Manchu executioners since the fall of the Taiping kings. He died bravely, bitterly assailing Manchu corruption in the "confession" written on the night before execution.

He was not the only victim. Many of the soldiers in the revolutionary army were rounded up, and forty sailors on the S.S. *Tai-an*, which had slipped into Canton too early owing to the breakdown of communications between the insurgents outside the city and those who were preparing to take up arms within the city walls, were arrested. Their officers were summarily executed, and the rest died of slow starvation in jail.

On the principle that the best hiding place was the one where he was least likely to be found, Sun Yat-sen made his way to Canton. Once he heard a police spy interrogating his own chair coolies; but his fame had spread among the secret societies in which the coolies played a preponderant part, and when the police spy asked where Sun Yat-sen was living, the coolie replied that "though there was a Doctor Yin, there was no Doctor Sun in the place." Ten days later, on the nineteenth of September, he gained a friend's house, and at night he was let down over the city wall and with Cheng Shih-liang traveled south through the maze of creeks in the Pearl River delta, now hiding in canal boats, now seeking the shore when soldiers came to search the boats for refugees. A few days later he reached Macao, where he found posters on the walls announcing a reward of ten thousand taels for his capture. Twenty-four hours later he reached Hong Kong.

The first revolutionary attempt had failed, but there were others to follow. He had pinned all his faith on the success of this insurrection; he had spent interminable hours discussing the objectives, the combat forces, the affiliations with the secret societies, and the raising of funds, and he was in no mood for defeat. In this predicament he decided upon a course of action which was to have far-reaching consequences. He decided that he would no longer control the affairs of the party from Hong Kong, but instead he would travel continuously abroad soliciting help from the expatriate Chinese.

The Manchu dynasty was largely supported by the money orders of market gardeners, laundrymen, and coolies in foreign countries—their annual contribution to the national exchequer already reached the fantastic total of two hundred million taels. These expatriate Chinese alone possessed the financial resources, the liberty of action, and the political consciousness to decide the course of Chinese history; and in allying himself with the progressive Christians, the secret societies, and the expatriates Sun Yat-sen was doing no more than following the path of historical least resistance. An English medical missionary, a rich sugar planter in Honolulu, and a leader of an immensely influential secret society in Shanghai became in the course of time his closest associates, and the movement which he inaugurated still preserves its Christian influence, owes much of its power to the old secret societies, and still includes in its government a high proportion of returned students from abroad.

The failure of the first revolutionary struggle was reflected in an increased uneasiness among the revolutionaries. Some of this uneasiness may have been communicated to Sun Yat-sen, but there is no record that he ever expressed the least sign of despair. After a few days in Hong Kong, where he visited Dr. Cantlie and took counsel with a solicitor who urged immediate flight "since the arm of the Manchus is long," he sailed by a Japanese ship to Kobe and Yokohama accompanied by Chen Shao-pai and Cheng Shih-liang.

As a sign of his complete emancipation from the Manchus, he cut off his queue, an act which he justified in his reminiscences:

"At Kobe, whither I fled from Hongkong, I took a step of great importance. I cut off my queue, which had been growing all my life. For some days I had not shaved my head, and I allowed the hair to grow on my upper lip. Then I went out to a clothier's and bought a suit of modern Japanese garments. When I was fully dressed I looked in the mirror and was astonished—and a great deal reassured—by the transformation. Nature had favored me. I was darker in complexion than most Chinese, a trait I had inherited from my mother, for my father resembled more the regular type. I have seen it said that I have Malay blood in my veins, and also that I was born in Honolulu. Both these statements are false. I am purely Chinese, as far as I know; but after the Japanese war, when the natives of Japan began to be treated with more respect, I had no trouble, when I let my hair and moustache grow, in passing for a Japanese. I admit I owe a great deal to this circumstance, as otherwise I should not have escaped from many dangerous situations."

The act of cutting off the queue was to have far greater consequences in the future, and was followed by many expatriate Chinese. Originally the Manchu headdress, it had become a symbol of Manchu dominance, though the provinces in the south continually objected to it and petitions asking for its removal were constantly being sent to Peking. The Taipings abolished it; many members of secret societies wore false queues, which they removed in private; but it was left to Sun Yat-sen to make cutting off the queue a signal of revolt against the Manchus.

He did not stay long in Japan. Leaving Chen Shao-pai in Yokohama, and sending Cheng Shih-liang to China to direct operations in Kwangtung, he returned secretly to Honolulu to enlarge the Revive China Society. Here he was joined by his widowed mother (his father had died in 1888), his son aged four, and one young daughter, who had all escaped from Choyhung in the company of a young sugar planter returning to Hawaii after his marriage. The whole family settled down on Ah Mei's cattle ranch on the island of Maui on the slopes of Haleakala, an extinct volcano ten thousand feet high, the old mother bitterly complaining that she could not understand why her youngest son had brought so much misfortune upon the family, while the elder son had brought nothing but good.

By a curious coincidence Dr. Cantlie, who was returning with his family to England by way of America, met Sun Yat-sen in the streets of Honolulu and failed to recognize him at first in his European dress. They spoke for a few minutes under the palm trees and promised to meet again in London; and this brief encounter, heavy with the weight of destiny and forgotten almost as soon as it occurred, settled the fate of the Ch'ing dynasty forever. There have been luckier accidents in history, but the moment when Dr. Cantlie gave the young revolutionary his address in London is one of the most curious and significant.

Sun Yat-sen soon grew tired of Hawaii. In June 1896 he left Honolulu in an American liner for San Francisco, where he remained a little more than a month, and then wandered slowly across the continent, continually shadowed by detectives (who were aided by a photograph Sun Yat-sen incautiously had taken of himself in San Francisco), addressing small meetings of Chinese, talking earnestly and slowly amid the smoke of laundries and among the greenhouses of market gardeners about the crisis in Peking, the corruption of the Manchus, and the necessity of a fundamental national reorganization. He received little sympathy during the journey, and he records in his autobiography that though he worked hard, there were few who paid any attention to him; perhaps a dozen or so in each city he visited.

1896 was a year of comparative peace for China. The Franco-Chinese War had come to an end in June 1895 with a modification of the frontier between Yunnan and Annam; three new ports were opened on the Chinese-Annamese frontier, and French manufacturers and engineers were given prior rights in building railways in Yunnan, Kwangsi, and Kwangtung. The powers took breath. It was not until February 1897 that Great Britain obtained a rectification of the frontier between China and the British possessions in the south. In November of the same year the murder of two German missionaries in Shangtung gave the German government a pretext for seizing Kiaochow on the Shangtung coast, and a few days later the Russian government obtained a twenty-five-year lease on Talienwan, now known as Dairen.

There were other reasons for Sun Yat-sen's lack of success. The reform movement under Kang Yu-wei and Liang Chi-chao—Kang Yu-wei's famous pamphlet *Reform China and Save Her* had been published in 1885—was gaining ground, and there were signs that under a vigorous program of reform the Manchu dynasty might yet weather the storm. Sun Yat-sen remained critical of these reforms. The Manchu dynasty had had abundant opportunity to bring about reforms, and as early as 1866, the year in which he was born, the Imperial School of Interpreters, the Tung Wen Kuan, was enlarged into a college and the opportunity was taken to issue the following memorial:

"Not only do the nations of the west learn from each other the new things that are daily being produced, but Japan in the Eastern Seas has recently sent men to England to learn the language and science of that country. When a small nation like Japan knows how to enter upon a career of progress, what could be a greater disgrace than for China to adhere to her own traditions and never think of waking up? . . ."

In Sun Yat-sen's eyes the glove had been thrown down even before the Taiping rebellion, and no one had had the courage to accept the challenge. In cheap lodging houses in America, the young man who resembled a Japanese and wore dark glasses and whose mustache was a little too carefully trimmed warmed himself with the thought that the time would come when a violent revolution would turn China adrift in the world of scientific progress, and he himself with his surgeon's scalpel and hermetically sealed medical instruments would take the part of the emperor Meiji.

III

WHEN the S.S. *Majestic* sailed from New York on September 23, 1896, the skyscrapers were shrouded in a faint mist and the sea was choppy. A white wind came from the north, enveloping the waves in sea drift. It was the first time Sun Yat-sen had traveled on a great modern liner. He knew no one on the ship; he was exhausted after the long, wearisome tour of America; and at night, when the ship rocked heavily in the midautumn gales, there would come to him occasional doubts about the progress of the revolution in Kwangtung. Where was Cheng Shih-liang? One of his friends had died under merciless torture; the other might even now be dead. "The long arm of the Manchus"—so a lawyer had spoken in an office in Hong Kong. But how long was this arm, and how much longer would the feudal state of China exist in the competitive world of the powers?

He carried as usual the seals of the Revive China Society, and the membership book, at the bottom of his trunk. The ship's spies followed him; he was conscious of a hundred eyes. Far beneath the ship, in the depths of the sea, the cables were announcing his journey. The Chinese minister in Washington had cabled in advance to the legation in London, suggesting that the British government should be asked to extradite him on the grounds that he was a dangerous political criminal, and giving his description, the date of sailing, the name of the vessel, and the number of his ticket.

Here he could no longer disguise himself as a Japanese, and after reaching Liverpool and taking the night train to London and putting up at Haxell's Hotel in the Strand, he called upon Dr. Cantlie, who jokingly suggested that the Chinese Legation was almost next door and he should pay a courtesy visit, and Mrs. Cantlie, struck by the expression on his face, replied: "Don't go near it! They'll catch you and ship you off to China!"—advice that was repeated to him some days later by Sir Patrick Manson, who had once been his professor at the Alice Memorial Hospital in Hong Kong.

His loneliness, or perhaps some curious kind of attraction, brought Sun Yat-sen on the morning of Sunday, October 11, into the neighborhood of the Chinese Legation. He was on his way to join the Cantlies for the morning service at the church of St. Martin's-in-the-Fields, but he could easily have avoided the legation by going a more roundabout way. Suddenly he was overtaken by a Chinese who asked him casually in English whether he was a Chinese or Japanese. Sun Yat-sen replied that he was Chinese, whereupon the stranger began an excited conversation, asking him what part of China he came from and introducing himself as a fellow Kwangtungese.

A moment later Sun Yat-sen found that he was being escorted by two Chinese—another had appeared from nowhere—and they were trying to drag and push him up the white steps, past two Corinthian pillars, into a palatial house overlooking a square. He caught sight of the well-tended gardens in the middle of the square, a few nursemaids pushing perambulators on a quiet Sunday forenoon, and then found himself inside the house, the door bolted, Chinese servants in livery carefully bowing to the two individuals who had escorted him into the house.

In Sun Yat-sen's account of the incident, written a few months later, it is quite clear that he was conscious of a dreamlike atmosphere of events during the famous Sunday: he was like Alice in Wonderland who fell into a tunnel and found everything subject to strange, unexpected laws. He did not know where he was, and no one thought of informing him. For some reason he was escorted round the building; he saw the Kang Hsi vases, the Chinese paintings on the walls, the thick carpets, but he had no idea what was happening until he was taken to a room on the third floor overlooking a dark alleyway, a room with a fireplace and bars over the window, and—but at that moment the door was snapped to and he found himself alone.

He was alone. He felt in his pockets: there were no important documents on him. It was still early in the morning, and he could hear the churchgoers in the street below. The Cantlies would be waiting for him; in a few minutes they would decide that he had been unavoidably detained, and they would drive to church alone. He was not sure whether he was awake or dreaming, and he was still less sure when the door opened silently and in place of the Chinese torturer he had expected, he saw a tall, silver-headed Englishman with a beard and a calm, deprecatory manner, wearing a striped morning suit.

The Englishman explained hesitantly that this was the Chinese Legation; they had received notification that a certain Sun Wen[1] had sailed from America and the Chinese government had therefore asked the legation officials to treat him with particular kindness, since the viceroy Li Hung-chang approved entirely of the memorial presented to him, and much more to the same strain. The tall, silver-haired Englishman was Sir Halliday Macartney, English counselor to the legation, and as he continued speaking, Sun Yat-sen, now lean and wiry, began to wonder whether he could break the window bars and jump down three stories. Sir Halliday Macartney left the room, but a moment later his place was taken by Chinese servants, who watched Sun Yat-sen continually through the keyhole or simply entered and watched him in the room.

As the morning passed, he grew more desperate and unhappy. The Cantonese who had taken his arm in the street whispered that he would be shipped back to China. As he thought of all his failures, his betrayals, and constant, searching doubts, his despair became complete, and he derived comfort only from prayer. He asked to be allowed to write. Macartney had suggested that he should write to his hotel (the Cantlies had found him comfortable lodgings in Holborn), but at the last moment he remembered the membership book and the seals in his trunks and he refused to write. A letter to Sir Patrick Manson was left undelivered. He tried to throw notes into Weymouth Street. When the attendants were not looking, he wrote on small scraps of paper and on his torn handkerchief, throwing the messages weighted with coins out of the window, where they fell on the eaves of the opposite

---

[1] Sun Yat-sen possessed, like nearly all Chinese, a bewildering number of names. His childhood name was Deh Ming; at Iolani he was known as Sun Tai Chu; at Queen's College, Hong Kong, as Sun Tai Tseung. In Japan he was known variously as Nakayama and Hayashi, Nakayama having the same characters as Chungshan (Central Mountain), the name by which he is now known. Since his death his native district, Heungshan, has also been called Chungshan. Sun Yat-sen is a deliberate anglicization, Sun, his family name, meaning descendant, Yat, leisure, and Sen, immortality.

houses and were not found until some weeks later. He begged the two English servants who brought food and coal every morning to help him. One of them informed the legation officials.

Tung—only the surname of the Chinese who trapped him into the legation is known—spent many hours with Sun Yat-sen, who argued that his detention was a violation of international law and of English customary law; and then he learned that Peking had ordered his removal to China in a steamship chartered from the Glen Company with orders to sail for Hong Kong, where the prisoner would be transferred to a Chinese gunboat. Under threats he was made to write a confession admitting that he had entered the legation of his own free will. He knew that time was running short. If his messages were undelivered, no one could save him. Perhaps Dr. Cantlie was out of London; perhaps Sir Patrick Manson had failed to remember him; perhaps the messages he sent through the window were picked up by the legation officials. He described his state of mind in a book, *Kidnapped in London*, written both in Chinese and English, and published shortly after the incidents occurred:

"My despair was complete, and only by prayers to God could I gain any comfort. Still the dreary days and still more dreary nights wore on, and but for the comfort afforded me by prayer I believe I should have gone mad. After my release I related to Dr. Cantlie how prayer was my one hope, and told him how I should never forget the feeling that seemed to take possession of me as I rose from my knees on the morning of Friday, October 16th—a feeling of calmness, hopefulness, and confidence, that assured me my prayer was heard, and filled me with hope that all would be well."

That morning he had appealed to one of the boys for the last time, saying that "just as the Sultan of Turkey wished to kill all the Christians of Armenia, so the Emperor of China wished to kill him because he was a Christian, and one of a party that was striving to secure good government for China. My life is entirely in your hands. If you let this matter be known outside, I shall be saved. If not, I shall certainly be bound and beheaded. It is in your hands whether my life is saved or taken from me. Would you be faithful to God or to your master? Would you obey the fair and just British government or follow the evil ways of the Manchu Emperor?" In the face of such an emotional appeal, the English boy at last agreed to help, and notes began to pass backward and forward through the coal scuttle.

It was only just in time. Desperate remedies were necessary, for Chinese police measures under the Manchus savored of the Gestapo. Sun Yat-sen could look forward, as he said later, to "having my ankles crushed in a vice, and broken by a hammer, my eyelids cut off, and finally being chopped into small fragments, so that none could claim my mortal remains." From this day dates his horror of torture and his refusal to use it in the governments under his command.

At eleven on the night of Saturday, October 17, Dr. Cantlie found a letter pushed through his letter box. He opened the door, but the messenger had vanished. He read:

"There is a friend of yours imprisoned in the Chinese legation here since last Sunday; they intend sending him out to China, where it is certain they will hang him. It is very sad for the poor man, and unless something is done at once he will be taken away and no one will know it. I dare not sign my name, but this is the truth, so believe what I say. Whatever you do must be done at once, or it will be too late. His name is, I believe, Sin Yin Sen."

The same night Dr. Cantlie called on Sir Halliday Macartney at 3 Harley Place, but he was informed by the constable on duty that the English counselor to the Chinese Legation was then living at the Midland Hotel and it was impossible to find him at that hour. Dr. Cantlie then went to Scotland Yard, where it was explained that the whole matter was *ultra vires* and the police could do nothing for him.

The next morning, exactly a week after Sun Yat-sen's imprisonment, Dr. Cantlie called upon his friend Sir Patrick Manson and found the English boy at the door with two visiting cards from the legation on which was written:

"I was kidnapped on Sunday last by two Chinamen, and forcibly taken into the Chinese Legation. I am imprisoned, and in a day or two I am to be shipped off to China on board a specially chartered vessel. I am certain to be beheaded. O! Woe is me!"

The two doctors immediately went to Scotland Yard, but received the same reply as before. A visit to the Foreign Office was equally unfortunate—it was a Sunday, and all the responsible officials were in the country.

Haunted by the prospect that Sun Yat-sen might already have been removed to a new hiding place, they decided to act quickly, and while Sir Patrick made inquiries at the Chinese Legation, Dr. Cantlie visited a firm of private detectives and arranged that a watch should be kept on the legation building by a private detective in a hansom cab. At ten o'clock that night Dr. Cantlie called upon the *Times* office in Printing House Square and made a statement. For some incredible reason this statement was left unpublished until Sun Yat-sen's release.

On Monday, Dr. Cantlie formally sought the advice of the Foreign Office. It was discovered that the Glen Company had in fact been approached by the Chinese Legation and a steamship had been chartered by them. The Foreign Office began to show a discreet interest, and a message was sent to Scotland Yard advising a close watch on the legation building. On October 22 a writ of habeas corpus was made out against the legation, but it was thrown out by the judge at the Old Bailey. The legation officials professed to have no knowledge of the affair, and Dr. Cantlie began to imagine that it was already too late for any successful action.

By Thursday morning it seemed that the sands were running out. All means of rescuing the prisoner had been exhausted except the press. In desperation Dr. Cantlie gave a long and detailed interview to a *Globe* correspondent, and Londoners streaming out of their offices that same evening were surprised to see posters bearing the words: "CHINESE REVOLUTIONARY KIDNAPPED IN LONDON." Within two hours Portland Square was thronged by a crowd of reporters and the inevitable curious sensation-seekers, who gazed up at the windows of the Chinese Legation or stood respectfully aside when Dr. Cantlie drove up to his house in a hansom cab. Other reporters discovered Sir Halliday Macartney at the Midland Hotel. The Secretary for Foreign Affairs, Lord Salisbury, was interviewed by Dr. Cantlie, and after politely explaining that imprisonment without trial was an infringement of British common law, he advised the Chinese minister to surrender the prisoner.

Sun Yat-sen from his third-story window heard an inexplicable hubbub of voices below. He did not know that the legation building was in danger of being attacked by an English mob dressed in high collars, with smokestack hats and carefully creased trousers. English tempers had been aroused. The thought that in the center of London, near the town house of the Duchess of Devonshire, the Manchu government should attempt to shanghai a prisoner—the word "shanghai" was coming into common use at that time—stunned the common people. On Friday,

October 23, exactly twelve days after the arrest, Sun Yat-sen was released by Sir Halliday Macartney with the inexplicable words: "I release this man over to you, and I do so on condition that neither the prerogative nor the diplomatic rights of the legation are interfered with."

Sun Yat-sen blinked as he came out of the dark rooms into the wintry sunlight of a London square, where he was surrounded by reporters and a crowd of well-wishers who deafened him when they suddenly burst out cheering. He looked thin and ill, but obviously relieved. Dr. Cantlie, a Foreign Office messenger, a chief detective, and the released prisoner drove off to Scotland Yard, where a statement was filed; and a little later, when he returned to his hotel, he found a crowd of reporters waiting for him. It was his day of triumph. In the Chinese edition of *Kidnapped in London* he comments: "The reporters drew me into the hotel more forcibly than Tung drew me into the legation building, and they coveted news from me more anxiously than the Manchu government coveted my head." All that night and during the greater part of the next day visitors called at the hotel, and at last Dr. Cantlie had to beg them to give the protégé a rest. On the day after Sun Yat-sen's release a telegraph clerk sitting at Gravesend was surprised to notice a cable from Peking authorizing the expenditure of six thousand pounds by the Chinese Legation to charter the vessel which would have shipped Sun Yat-sen back to China.

He was now a marked man. Wherever he went, he would have no need to introduce himself. The prisoner in the third story had become the subject of legend, mentioned in pantomimes that Christmas. The Cantlie children produced a devastating drama showing the evil Manchus—their faces painted in alarming reds and greens—and the virtuous hero. The future was still dark, but the prisoner had escaped with a profound knowledge of the necessity

THE FORERUNNERS 47

of prayer (a knowledge shared by his successor in Sianfu forty years later), and with the consciousness that he had been saved by grace for some high mission, which was not yet clear to him, though it would become increasingly clear as the years passed. He was not yet thirty; he had taken part in one unsuccessful rebellion, and he had been sensationally kidnaped in the heart of the British Empire and very nearly dispatched to China in the disguise of a madman. But there were many more dangers in store.

Most dangerous, perhaps, was the success of the reform movement. Kang Yu-wei and Liang Chi-chao were publishing manifesto after manifesto against the Manchu government. *Confucius as Reformer,* written to show that Confucius was not a conservative imperialist but a philosopher prescribing essential reforms, was having an unprecedented success. The emperor Kuang Hsu had attained his majority and was surrounding the throne with the most earnest and brilliant of the reformers. Between the peace of Shimonoseki in 1895 and the autumn of 1898, reforms began to be projected by the provincial and national governments on a scale never before attempted. Schools teaching Western subjects were founded, railways were planned, the Board of War was ordered to report on several proposals concerning army reform, a naval college was projected, a bureau for the translation of Western scientific and literary works and textbooks was opened in Shanghai, and government officials were exhorted to address themselves conscientiously to the questions of reform. The tide of progress was moving fast—faster than it had ever moved in China before. As the news of these vast movements reached England, there were many sympathizers who thought that China would grow out of her old feudal customs and follow the road marked out by Japan.

A solitary revolutionary reading in the British Museum reading room or traveling penniless and friendless over

Europe could hardly dare to hope for success. He was to confess later that the next two years were perhaps the hardest in his life:

"The years between 1895 and 1900 were the most difficult time in the progress of the revolution. Since I have failed, the hold on China, my personal work, the position of further operations, and the foundation of revolution built during more than ten years, have all disappeared. Propaganda overseas was without any effect. Just at this time there grew up the pro-monarchist party, which worked for the enemy. Its opposition to revolution and republicanism was greater than that of the Manchu government. At this time the prospect of revolution was dark beyond comparison, and nearly all hope was lost."

In the British Museum reading room, home of so many lost causes that have been miraculously restored, he set himself to read books on politics, law, agriculture, mining, engineering, cattle rearing, military and naval strategy; above all, economics and sociology. He was particularly interested in Henry George and in Karl Marx, whose *Das Kapital* was translated into English in 1887, while a concise introduction to Marxism had been written by Aveling in 1892. It was probably during this period that he met Lenin and the Russian revolutionary exiles, and he makes reference to them in many places in his published lectures and writings. At a banquet during the First National Congress of the Kuomintang he told the members:

"Once I met several Russians at a library in London while I was doing some reading. After an exchange of conversation we knew that we were revolutionary comrades. The Russians asked me, 'How long will it take the Chinese Revolution to succeed?' Confronted with that question, I did not know how to answer. I was then in exile after my first defeat. Although I did not know what was the next thing to be done, I was very hopeful to begin again in a year or two, and wished to succeed. But to those Russians I did not want to give a casual answer, so I told them my most conservative estimate and said: 'Perhaps it will succeed in thirty years.' The Russians were surprised and remarked, 'In such a big country as yours, can you succeed in thirty years?' I asked the Russians, 'How long does it take your revolution to succeed?' They answered: 'If we can succeed in one hundred years, we shall be satisfied, but now we are struggling. Although success only comes after one hundred years, we must struggle now. If we do not struggle now, we shall not succeed even in one hundred years. Because we want to succeed in one hundred years, therefore we must struggle hard at present.' After having heard what they had to say, and reflecting on what I had told them, I felt very much ashamed of myself. It was because that after my defeat I was very anxious for the Chinese Revolution to succeed, and in order to give a guarded answer to these foreigners I made an allowance of thirty years. After I heard what they said, I knew that their project was many times surer and their spirit many times greater than mine."

But he was too accustomed to action to think in terms of hundreds of years, and like the Russian exiles he spent his enforced leisure wandering around Europe. On the Continent he was nearly unknown, and he suffered from a terrible loneliness. His physical stamina was always strong until the later years—he could work twenty-four hours at a stretch and always ate sparingly—and he trained himself to live on a bowl of rice and a few vegetables each day.

There were few Chinese in Europe at the time. Students sent to foreign universities in the seventies had been recalled; legation buildings were still dangerous, and he was beginning to be distrustful of chance-met Orientals for good reasons. His friends and his brother in Honolulu remained loyal, and he was generous to them in this autobiography: "They have never failed me; but then, fortunately, apart from traveling, my wants are few. I have often for weeks together lived on a little rice, and I have journeyed many hundreds of miles on foot." He foresaw the coming revolutions of Europe, and came in contact with the leading members of the Second International. He made a study of social problems and appears not to have been particularly impressed by French democracy, while the social insurance undertaken by the German government through the genius of Bismark appears to have passed unnoticed.

Soon there came the news of the *coup d'état* by which the empress dowager Tsu Hsi reasserted her authority with the aid of Yuan Shih-kai, at that time in command of the Tungwa division of the Peiyang or Northern Ocean army. The *coup d'état* occurred just at the moment when the young Emperor was about to give orders for her imprisonment, but it was the Emperor instead who found himself imprisoned on an island in a lake inside the Forbidden City. Six of the most influential members of the reform movement were executed, newspapers were suspended, and the wonderful series of reforms published during the "Hundred Days of Reform" were canceled outright. An unknown number of reformers disappeared, though Kang Yu-wei escaped on a British gunboat to Hong Kong and Liang Chi-chao made his way to Yokohama on a Japanese merchant ship. Thus the leaders of the reform movement remained to fight their battles on a more auspicious occasion: while the famous "Five Objects of Knowledge" written by Chang Chih-tung, the viceroy of Hunan and Hupeh, were forgotten in the sudden blaze of reaction. They read:

1. Realise the shame of not being like Japan, Turkey, Siam or Cuba.
2. Realise the fear that we may become like India, Burma, Korea, Egypt and Poland.

THE FORERUNNERS 51

3. Realise that if we fail to change our customs, we cannot reform our methods; and if we fail to reform our methods, we cannot utilise modern implements of war.
4. Realise that what is important is the call for men of attainment with a knowledge of the procedures used by foreign governments.
5. Realise, when you are abroad, the greatness of your own country, and when you see strange customs, do not forget the customs of your ancestors and the wisdom of the sages.

Looking back upon China from Europe, Sun Yat-sen could say truthfully that he had realized all the five objects of knowledge, but they had brought him no nearer a solution. He decided to return to China, and in 1898 he sailed from London to Canada by the S.S. *Numidian,* reaching Montreal in July, and thence sailing from Vancouver to Japan by the S.S. *Empress of India.*

At Yokohama he was greeted as he stepped on shore by two messengers sent by his friend Inukai, then leader of the Liberal party but later to become more famous as prime minister of Japan. Later he met Toyama and the old Count Okuma, who were then in power. He lived frugally at 121 Yamachita Cho in the foreign quarter of Yokohama, within a stone's throw of the Chinese Consulate, in a small bamboo-and-paper house which was eventually destroyed during the 1923 earthquake.

Meanwhile the breach between the revolutionaries and the dissident monarchists, which had always been large, widened until they became irreconcilable enemies, Kang Yu-wei founding the Pao Huang Tung (Protect the Emperor Party) with a program of constitutional monarchy and reform which bitterly assailed the Empress Dowager and attempted by all possible means to revive the program of reforms inaugurated by the imprisoned Emperor. And while the Empress Dowager continually exacted her price of revenge, there were still some members of the court circles who continued their subterranean warfare against her person and her reactionary ideas, at the same time urging the strongest measures against revolutionary utopianism. Chang Chih-tung, viceroy of Hunan and Hupeh, became the spokesman of this party, and he insisted repeatedly that a republic, however necessary at the moment, savored too much of rebellion, and "only the ignorant and the foolish will rejoice at the inauguration of a republic, and the present is not the time."

Against these subterranean forces Sun Yat-sen worked by digging deeper. There remained his alliance with the secret societies and the survivors of the Canton rebellion; and still more important perhaps, there remained the Christians and the expatriate Chinese. He had little difficulty in winning over the Chinese merchants in Yokohama, nearly all Cantonese, and there were more Chinese merchants in Nagasaki, Kobe, and Osaka. He sent Chen Saopai, one of "the Four Big Brigands" to Hong Kong to publish the *Chung Kuo Pao* (the *China News*) with an outspoken program of democracy and freedom from the Manchus; and he dispatched Shih Chien-ju to the Yangtse Valley, where the secret societies were once more beginning to show their influence, and set Cheng Shih-liang to organizing the secret societies.

These secret societies were large, numerous, and powerful. The government ruled *de jure*, but it was not altogether untrue to say that the secret societies ruled *de facto*. They were still unorganized and continually quarreling among themselves; but they had begun in nearly every instance as benevolent institutions, and something of their original purpose survived. Their roots delved deep in Chinese life. The Yellow Eyebrows and Yellow Turbans were prominent in civil war in the Han dynasty. The Red Spears, an organization of farmers, held the south of the

Yangtse in fee, while the Association of Elder Brothers was dreaded all over China for its terrible code of revenge. The White Lily and the White Cloud Societies were originally Buddhist institutions founded in the twelfth century, but they too had maintained a consistent attitude against oppression; a rebellion started by the White Lily Society in the southwest in 1796 and another by the Heaven's Reason Society in the north in 1831 paved the way for the Taiping rebellion. Some of the most moving passages in Sun Yat-sen's *Three Principles of the People* concern the history of the secret societies:

"After Shun-Chih had overthrown the Mings and become master of China, the loyal ministers and scholars of the Ming Dynasty rose everywhere to oppose him. Even up to the first years of K'ang Hsi there was still resistance and China was not yet completely subjugated by the Manchus. In the later years of K'ang Hsi, when the veterans of the Ming Dynasty were slowly passing away, a group of intense nationalists who realized that their day was over, conceived the plan of organizing secret revolutionary societies. But just at this time K'ang Hsi inaugurated the *Po-hsueh Hung-tzu* examination which caught almost all the old Ming scholars in the net of Manchu government service. The thoughtful group among them saw that they could not depend upon the *literari* to keep alive the national spirit, so they turned to the lower classes and to those 'who are homeless upon the rivers and lakes.' They gathered these people together, organized them into groups, and gave to them the spirit of nationalism to preserve and perpetuate. Because these people came from the lowest class of society, because of their rude behaviour which made them despised, and because they used a language not spoken by the educated to spread their doctrines, their part in the anti-dynastic struggle attracted little attention. These Ming veterans showed true knowledge and discernment in their plan for saving the national idea. Just as wealthy men, whose treasures have in time of peace naturally been kept in expensive iron chests, when they see looters breaking into their homes, are afraid that the costly chests will be the first things opened, and therefore bury their treasures in places that will not be noticed, and possibly, during times of extreme danger, in the midst of the worst filth, so the Ming veterans, seeking to preserve China's treasure, sought to hide it in the roughest and lowest class of society. And so, when the Hung-men Society wanted to overthrow the Manchus and restore the Mings, why did they not plant their nationalist ideas among the intellectuals and transmit them to posterity through literature, in the phrase of the well-known historian, Ssu Ma Chien, 'store them in famous mountains and bequeath them to worthy men'? Because, when the Ming veterans saw the Manchus inaugurating their examination system and almost all the men of wisdom and learning enticed by it, they perceived that the intellectual class was not dependable, that 'treasure could not be stored in famous mountains and bequeathed to worthy men,' and must therefore be hidden in the lower class of society. And therefore they rallied the secret societies whose organizations and initiations were simple and adaptable, and entrusted to them the preservation of nationalism, not through literature but through the genius of our language."

Sun Yat-sen was still attempting to weld all the secret societies under a single unified command when the Boxer uprising of 1900 broke out. This movement was the result of the propaganda of still another secret society, the I Ho Tuan, or Corps of Righteous Harmony. Arising first in Shantung, where a reactionary Manchu, Yu Hsien, had been appointed governor of the province in 1899, it drew its strength from the antiforeign feeling which was being openly pursued at court. The program of the movement is clearly reflected in the inscriptions which were posted up in all the villages of the province: "Protect the country, destroy the foreigners!" and "Protect the Ch'ings, destroy the barbarians!" The society had the approval of the Empress Dowager, who hoped to distract attention from the internal problems of China by launching sporadic attacks on foreigners; and though Yu Hsien was recalled under pressure from foreign powers when a German missionary was murdered in Shantung, and Yuan Shih-kai was sent to replace him, she received Yu Hsien with marked favors and extolled his virtues in a solemn memorial. By June 1900 the situation had become acute. Yuan Shih-kai was too much of a soldier to be impressed by a cult which performed gymnastics, practiced incantations to make men invulnerable, and believed in the virtues of complicated ritual (which included cock-killing in the dead of night); and the headquarters of the movement spread from Shantung to Hupeh, where Christians, both Chinese and foreign, began to disappear mysteriously, and Christian missionaries were found dead with strange signs tattoed on their chests.

The uprising, which might have suffered the fate of many similar uprisings, became dangerous only when the entire garrison at Tientsin, the gateway of the capital, threw in its lot with the Boxers and besieged the foreign settlements on the afternoon of Sunday, June 17. To protect the foreigners in the city, the Taku forts commanding the approach to the sea were stormed by an international landing party; and it became increasingly clear that the safety of foreign nationals depended upon the maintenance of communication between Tientsin and the sea. Meanwhile at court antiforeign feeling grew out of hand. All the accumulated resentment derived from eighty years of concessions of railways and mining rights, and of the loss of territory, smoldered into a self-righteous conflagration; and if nothing further was needed, there was the railway line between Peking and Tientsin opened three years previously to show the predominant and growing influence of the foreigners. The railway line was partly broken up by the Boxers, an act which sealed the fate of the uprising.

If things were bad in Tientsin, they were worse in Peking. The capital was in a state of continual, exasperating crisis. Against the urgent advice of the grand councilor Jung Lu, who had been her closest confidant and whose resolute action had led to the imprisonment of the young Emperor and the assassination of the reformers, the Dowager Empress continued to offer her protection to the movement. She ordered Tung Fu-hsiang, the unprincipled governor of distant Kansu, who had sworn to drive all foreigners into the sea, to assume command of the uprising. Yu Hsien, now governor of Shansi, exacted his pound of flesh by sending for a list of missionaries and their families in the provincial capital of Taiyuanfu and ordered their removal to the yamen courtyard, where from an upper window he watched with indescribable joy the murder of twenty-three Christians. The Christians however were not alone in suffering martyrdom. On the morning of June 20, the German Minister, Baron von Ketteler, was murdered on his way to the Tsungli Yamen in Peking. Mr. Sugiyama, chancellor to the Japanese Legation, was murdered on the eleventh by Tung Fu-hsiang's troops, though the body was not found until some days later.

In this atmosphere of intrigue and murder, Jung Lu behaved for the first time in his life with perfect propriety, sending message after message to the Empress demanding the cessation of support for the uprising. Meanwhile Li Hung-chang, viceroy of Kwangtung and Kwangsi, used his influence to mitigate the severity of the powers by obtaining their assurance that no state of war existed. Yet it was not until the end of August that an international column fought its way to Peking and relieved the besieged foreigners—and committed the unbelievable stupidity of throwing the most beautiful capital in the world open to looters. The court fled to Sianfu in Shensi. Four months later on December 22, the Empress Dowager accepted the terms of the powers: the punishment of the culprits, the payment of an enormous indemnity of nine hundred million silver taels, provision for the legation guards, the destruction of the Taku forts, the reconstruction of the Tsungli Yamen and the erection by the Chinese government of expiatory monuments in the desecrated foreign cemeteries. Revenge had become more than just; it had been calculated to humiliate, and succeeded only too well, with the result that contact between the Chinese and foreigners became increasingly difficult and suspicious as the years passed.

China had received many humiliations (and foreign governments had received many humiliations from the Chinese) during the nineteenth century, but none ever reached the proportions of the settlement which followed the Boxer uprising. Sun Yat-sen seems to have regarded the uprising with the same detachment with which he viewed the Sino-Japanese War. He believed that the instability of the country was inherent in her historical growth, and only the destruction of the old order and inauguration of a revolutionary government could save her.

There were rumors that Li Hung-chang intended to head a separatist movement in the two southern province with Sun Yat-sen as one of his principal advisers. Though Sun Yat-sen could hardly believe that such a course of events was possible, he sailed for Hong Kong and sent a confidential agent with powers to approach the Viceroy, while he himself sailed for Saigon. The news was too good to be true. Li Hung-chang left for Peking to negotiate on behalf of the imperial court with the foreign powers, and the South was left in the same confusion as before.

Sun Yat-sen returned from Saigon to Hong Kong to learn that all his dreams of an alliance with Li Hung-chang had vanished into thin air. As the result of a military conference held on board ship, he sent Cheng Shih-liang to Waichow, an important market town along the East River in Kwangtung, about a hundred miles due east of the provincial capital, to plan an insurrection. Meanwhile Shih Chien-ju and Tung Yui-nan were sent to Canton for co-operating action, and Cheng Shao-pai was ordered to provide ammunition and supplies. From Hong Kong Sun Yat-sen hoped to worm his way with a small army of foreign militia to Waichow, but the British government refused him a landing permit and he returned to Saigon only to learn that Miyazaki Torazo, who had hurried to Singapore as liaison officer between the revolutionaries and the reform party, had been jailed on the false charge of attempting to assassinate Kang Yu-wei. Sun Yat-sen went to Singapore to effect the release of the Japanese revolutionary; and since it was impossible to return to Hong Kong, he took ship for Formosa, then ceded to Japan as the result of the Sino-Japanese War of 1895. The governor, Kodama Gentaro, sympathized with his plans, and Sun Yat-sen set about engaging Japanese military experts and ordering artillery from Japan and four million rounds of ammunition from the Philippines—ammunition which had been left over after the failure of the Philippine revolution in the winter of 1898.

As time passed, the strategy became broader and he decided to reorganize his forces in the hope that when the whole of the Kwangtung and Fukien seacoast was in his hands, he could take Amoy by storm. As first this second insurrection was successful. The cities along the coast from Sing-an to Waichow and Ping-hai fell to the forces of

Cheng Shih-liang, who was reputed to have marched out with only eighty men and to have mustered ten thousand before he retired owing to lack of ammunition. Once more the commissariat was at fault, and the second insurrection failed for the same reasons that overwhelmed the first.

In Japan a government had fallen. The Japanese liberals, who sympathized with Sun Yat-sen's program of reform and Western democracy, were succeeded by a government headed by Prime Minister Ilto, who ordered the cancellation of the agreements signed by Sun Yat-sen and Kodama Gentaro. Although they had abandoned fighting, the revolutionary forces still had to make their way to their bases. As soon as the news of the Japanese change of cabinet came through, Sun Yat-sen dispatched Yamada Ryosaku to Cheng Shih-liang, who rode through the opposing lines to meet him. A little later, when Yamada Ryosaku was returning to Canton, he lost his way, fell into the hands of the imperial forces, and was summarily executed. He was the first foreigner to die for the Chinese revolution.

In the face of superior forces, Cheng Shih-liang gradually disbanded his army and made his way to Hong Kong. Once more however the lack of good communications, constant treasons, and the strength and loyalty of the Manchu forces worked in their disfavor. A small group had been left behind in Canton under the command of Shih Chien-ju with orders to blow up the Viceroy's yamen as soon as Cheng Shih-liang's relief army appeared. On September 6, 1900, Shih Chien-ju ran down the long tunnel which the revolutionaries had cut through the yamen wall and ignited the long trail of explosives. There was a slight explosion, but only a small part of the yamen was destroyed, and the viceroy Teh Sai (Li Hung-chang was still in Peking) remained unharmed. On the next day, while on his way to join a ship sailing for Hong Kong,

Shih Chien-ju was arrested and tortured. Eleven days later he was executed with the sword.

Sun Yat-sen remained outwardly unmoved. He possessed the sage's capacity for watching the thunderstroke without alarm. Questioned in Japan on the failure of the second insurrection, he replied: "We are not in the least depressed over the result. Quite the reverse, in fact, as it shows us how easily the imperial troops can be defeated, as soon as our men are properly armed and prepared for the great effort." He believed that even if these immature armed attempts failed, they had succeeded in arousing the people to the necessity of revolution, and these failures were perhaps necessary trials to test the strength of the Manchus.

Meanwhile the situation in China was growing worse. The ultimate effects of the Boxer indemnity were still unknown. By the protocol, China was saddled with a large addition to her debt, and the legations in Peking were gradually taking on the guise of armed fortresses. More serious was the lack of intellectual leadership in China herself. The necessity of reform penetrated the mind of the Empress Dowager only in the summer of 1901, and it was almost a year before the court returned to the capital. In August and September of the same year, the startled inhabitants of the capital woke up to find that the famous "Essay with Eight Legs," invented by K'ang Hsi to assure a livelihood for the scholars of the Ming dynasty, had been abolished; there was a new ministry of education under Chang Chih-tung, the viceroy who had compiled the sensationally successful *Charge to Learn* with its insistence on monarchism, Confucianism, and Western science; funds were being set aside for students traveling abroad; education had become the special care and prerogative of the court.

The change of heart was not entirely unexpected, for

THE FORERUNNERS 61

the clamor of the reformers had continued unabated. For the first time in two hundred years the court became the fountainhead of knowledge. Tientsin and Shanghai were selected as the focal points of the new movement; military schools were opened in Tientsin; the Nanyang Technical Academy was founded in Shanghai, and the old imperial university at Peking was reinaugurated among processions of cheering students, who discussed the new era of scientific progress with the same enlightened materialism as their Russian confreres in the University of Moscow discussed the abolition of serfdom in 1865. Materialism, in fact, became the watchword of the movement. Huxley's *Evolution and Ethics,* Darwin's *The Descent of Man,* even Karl Marx's *Das Capital* were translated and discussed by professors who still sat smoking over their opium pipes in the university common rooms. Though it was generally agreed that the era of scientific advancement was at hand, no one quite knew what revelations were about to be produced or what miracles of scientific achievement might be performed in a country which was still feudal, still ruled by a capricious and self-seeking empress, still too much accustomed to Confucian dialectics to understand the spiritual history of the West.

IV

FOR the spiritual history of the West is not easy to understand. From the days of Babylon we have been obsessed with a certain number of ideas which are entirely foreign to Chinese thought. The craggy coast line of Europe and the sands of Mesopotamia and Egypt have combined to create in the typical European a love of rigor, altitude, community, and strength. The impulse which created the ziggurats in the courts of Sumeria is the same impulse which led the brothers Wright to launch their first airplane. The clarity of the Greek coast line and the burning outlines of Egypt have conspired to make men love mathematical accuracy with the fervor of religious converts setting up statues to their gods. Socrates, Pascal, Hölderlin, and Kierkegaard are more foreign to the Chinese mind than Chuang Tzu and Tu Fu to our own; and this is due largely to the vast difference in the spiritual history of the two empires (since Europe in spite of its fratricidal wars remains an empire). The Chinese mists, the bright shimmering of the Chinese sky, the endless deserts and plains, the high gorges and the solitary temples have produced a race with entirely different, and perhaps more lasting, virtues; and in the place of "rigor" the Chinese have elevated to a high degree the conception of wisdom, and in the place of "community" the conception of the family.

It is to Sun Yat-sen's credit that he was one of the few who, in advocating Western ideas, knew something of their spiritual history. Christianity explained much; the British Museum reading room and his contact with cultured Europeans like the Cantlies and Sir Patrick Manson may have explained much more. In his published writings he is continually comparing Chinese and Western history, discovering the points of contact and the more numerous points where they diverge. Chang Po-wan, the military dictator of the Han dynasty, is compared with Robert Clive; the historian Ssu Ma Chien with Thucydides. Though he once confused Francis Bacon with Roger Bacon, his knowledge of Western history is surprisingly accurate; and he made use of his scholar's habit of disappearing among books whenever he was faced with disaster. In Japan he read voraciously, and even began the study of French. An American who met him in exile reported that his room was filled with bookcases which reached to the ceiling. He was temperamentally a scholar, with a scholar's refinement of bearing and a scholar's love of living for the sake of an idea.

In China the first wave of education was giving place to an excited wave of patriotism, which reached even the universities and middle schools. It was realized that China could only be saved by education and unity in the face of the tumultuous dangers outside. Since revolution seemed impossible and might invite foreign interference, it was decided that the future of the country could only be assured by a selfless devotion to the state. A distinction began to be made between the state and the throne.

In 1902 Shanghai saw the first of an almost endless series of student strikes against a reactionary university president, and in the same year Dr. Wu Chih-hui and Dr. Tsai Yuan-pei opened the Ai Kuo Hsueh Shê (the "Love Country Academy"), which attempted to instill a greater sense of responsibility toward the state among students. Dr. Tsai Yuan-pei was later to become president of Peking National University, and later still a member of the Central Executive of the Kuomintang. Wu Chih-hui, after having founded the academy, began to make fiery lectures on reform in the Chang Garden in the international settlement, and he again organized a volunteer corps in response to the appeal of the Chinese students in Japan, who feared that the presence of Russian armies on the borders of the three eastern provinces was the first sign of the partition of China. The Love Country Academy published its own revolutionary journal under the editorship of Wu Chih-hui, Chang Tai-yen, and Chow Yung, and was eventually prosecuted in the Shanghai courts, Chow Yung and Chang Tai-yen being heavily fined and imprisoned, while Wu Chih-hui escaped and took refuge in England. Chow Yung died in prison, but the influence of the academy survived until the revolution of 1911, with an insistence upon revolutionary reform which far outdid the pyrotechnical displays of Liang Chih-chao.

In Yokohama, Sun Yat-sen was an occasional guest at Liang Chih-chao's house. The two revolutionaries would sit over cups of tea, discussing with perfect freedom the opposing revolutionary movements they had founded. They were at once friends and enemies; there seems to have been no rancor between them. The reform movement was now riding the wave of success, but the Manchu government had so successfully borrowed its fire that only by a stratagem could Liang Chih-chao be called a revolutionary leader. Yet the reform party possessed great power abroad, and Sun Yat-sen was compelled to oppose them with every weapon at his command. When he learned that they were deeply entrenched in Hawaii, the cradle of the revolutionary movement, he wrote an open letter to the overseas Chinese in Hawaii:

"You are now accustomed to believing that the revolution and the programme of the reform party are exactly the same, though different in name. You indulge in the belief that the reform party is carrying on the cause of the revolution under the name of protecting the imprisoned Emperor. But I assure you that you are wrong.

"Kang Yu-wei and Liang Chih-chao have founded the reform party in the hope of restoring the Emperor Kuang Hsu to the throne, and for no other reason. If you still doubt my words, read Kang Yu-wei's message to Chinese merchants in north and south America. In his message he advised them never to practice revolution, nor to talk about it, nor even to think about it."

In the same year he wrote a message to a friend giving an account of his struggles with the reform party:

"I have been engaged in a hard struggle against the reform party in the United States, and have overcome them in five or six places. I intend to travel wherever there are

Chinese and I believe that in three or four months I shall succeed in overcoming them all. I do not think it will be difficult for me to do this, because there influence was at its height when Liang Chih-chao was there, but now the movement has gradually lapsed into decadence."

The revolutionaries and the reformers were strange bedfellows. In an edict issued by the Empress Dowager in 1903 all her political enemies were forgiven with the exception of Kang Yu-wei, Liang Chih-chao, and Sun Yat-sen.

After two years in Japan, Sun Yat-sen began to feel that the movement was ripe for a second world tour. Early in 1903 he arrived in Annam, ostensibly the guest of the French government with whom he had been in communication through the legation in Tokyo, but actually as the guest of the rich Chinese merchants in the Revive China Society. The excuse for his visit was the international exhibition at Hanoi. He made inquiries about supplies of ammunition through the acting governor (the former governor had been recalled), and addressed meetings of the merchants with some success. He returned for a few weeks to Japan, and then set out in the S.S. *Siberia* for Hawaii, where he arrived on October 5, 1903. He continued his revolutionary activity and worked on a program of reform not unlike the one formulated by Wu Chih-hui. At the Hotel Street Theater in Honolulu in December he addressed the first mass meeting he had ever held. It was noticed that he had increased in intellectual stature since the failure of the second revolution; long periods of silence punctuated by short periods of intense activity had made him at the same time more of a recluse and more of a man of action; and the success of the meeting was sufficient justification for continuing to spread the gospel of revolution.

The financial resources of Hawaii were limited, and for

the sake of the revolutionary exchequer he decided to leave immediately for America. When Hawaii was annexed by the United States, largely as a result of the increasingly autocratic temper of King Kalakaua, Chinese born on the islands before the annexation were offered the privilege of American citizenship. But Sun Yat-sen had not been born in Hawaii, and the exclusion laws against the entry of non-Americans into the United States were still in force. A stratagem was accordingly planned. On March 9, 1904, six months after his arrival in Honolulu, Sun Yat-sen signed the following deposition in the presence of a public notary:

I, Sun Yat-sen being first duly sworn, depose and say that to the best of my knowledge and belief I was born at Waimanu, Ewa, Oahu, on the twentyfourth day of December, A.D. 1870; that I am a physician, practicing at present at Kula, Island of Maui; that I make my home in said Kula; that my father, Sun Tet Sung, went to China about 1874 and died there about eight years later; that this affidavit is made for the purpose of identifying myself and as a further proof of Hawaiian birth; that the photograph attached is a good likeness of me at this time.

Sun Yat-sen

Three weeks later he sailed on the S.S. *Korea* for San Francisco, arriving on April 6. His first visit to America had been a failure; and no sooner had he left New York and arrived in England than he was arrested by the Chinese Legation. This time he was arrested as soon as he set foot on American soil. An explanation of his arrest appeared some days later, when Prince Pu Lun, a brother of the Emperor, arrived in San Francisco as official representative to the St. Louis Exhibition. The American government and the rich Chinese merchants were naturally afraid of incidents, and Sun Yat-sen was forcibly detained in the customhouse until the Prince and his retinue had left for St. Louis. Even then, a five-thousand-dollar guarantee of good behavior, paid by one of his missionary friends, was demanded before he could be released.

As soon as he was released, he decided to hold a meeting; but the Odd Fellows Hall in San Francisco was not the ideal place for preaching revolution, the auditorium was packed with members of the reform party, and he was heckled off the platform. Further meetings in San Francisco were abandoned when the Chinese consul-general posted a proclamation on the walls of Chinatown:

> There is a revolutionary leader in our midst, who is arousing people by his false statements. The educated element can easily understand that his aim is to collect money, which he will afterwards squander, and I fear the ignorant people will become his victims. As Consul-General, it is my duty to protect them. I advise the elder people, who will not be turned by his false statements, to caution their younger brothers and sons against this man. He will squander your money and get you into trouble.
>
> May 6, 1904   Consul-General Chung

Throughout his second visit to America, Sun Yat-sen was dogged by bad luck. He arrived in New York by way of Philadelphia thin, tired, and exhausted, but "though he often appeared weary and worn in body, he was always enthusiastic for his cause." So said the Chinese pastor Huie, who offered him sanctuary in his home.

His revolutionary fervor had not left him. Among laundrymen, gardeners, laborers, and coolies, he continued to work quietly and efficiently, addressing small gatherings and making contact with the secret societies. Once in Philadelphia a laundryman called at his hotel after a meeting and thrust a linen bag, containing his entire savings, into his hand and then disappeared. Sun Yat-sen never forgot the gift. It was during his second visit to America that he came under the influence of Abraham Lincoln, an influence that was to last throughout his life. "Government of the people, by the people, for the people" became the watchword of the Chinese revolution, at first in the Chinese rendering of "The people are to have, the people are to rule, the people are to enjoy," and later in the pronouncements of the Three Principles of the People: nationalism, democracy, and livelihood. These principles were hammered out, not in the seclusion of the scholar's study, but in continual argument and persuasion. They were the kindling fire which was later to produce the great conflagration. Years later he would say they were as important as ammunition for the success of the revolution, and he did not fail to remember that they had been worked out by a worried and frail-looking man in New York's Chinatown.

He made his first speech on the Three Principles of the People not in New York but in Brussels. Attracted by the cheap cost of living in Belgium and by small subsidies from the Manchu government, Chinese students were flocking to the universities of Antwerp, Ghent, and Brussels. After collecting four thousand Belgian francs, a little over a thousand French francs, and two thousand German marks, some Chinese students invited him to come to Europe and preach the gospel of revolution. At Brussels he addressed thirty students, in Berlin twenty, in Paris ten. He had spent more than a year in America without coming in contact with more than a handful of students, and though the numbers were small in Europe, they were far greater than in America. In his autobiography he wrote:

"After the Boxer trouble in 1900, the ignorance and impotence of the Manchu Court became more and more apparent, while pressure from without grew more urgent everyday. In indignation Chinese students in increasing numbers went abroad for their education to Europe, America and Japan. Simultaneously, within the Empire, the reform party gained in momentum and there seemed to be no way of putting a stop to it. Those who had hitherto looked upon revolution as treason, and avoided it like the plague, were now somewhat reconciled. When I visited Europe for the second time in 1905, the majority of the Chinese students had come to believe in revolution. Thereupon I sounded the clarion call by announcing the Three Principles of the People and the Five-power Constitution, which I had long cherished."

While Sun Yat-sen stayed at the homes of the students, he began to think out the problems of revolution afresh, and gradually he came to believe that the old Revive China Society had outlived its usefulness. In its place there arose the first conceptions of the as yet unnamed Tung Meng Hui—or revolutionary alliance.

The small student circles in Paris, Berlin, and Antwerp were to have an extraordinary effect on the history of the revolution. It was here, rather than in New York, that the blueprints of the future were drawn. America supplied the slogans and the example; the unheated, dusty rooms in the suburbs of Paris and Berlin provided the details. All students, but particularly poor students, are revolutionary material. Sun Yat-sen's stay in Europe had important results. He began to be regarded for the first time as the future leader of the revolution; he found that he was acceptable to the students, and they were completely loyal to him.

One incident of the time has been recorded. A student named Wang, of Berlin University, was warned by a Manchu student that when the news of his affiliation to the new party reached Peking, he would probably lose his stipend, and perhaps even his head. Sun Yat-sen was no longer in Berlin. The two students, thoroughly frightened, followed him to Paris, where they discovered the register of the society in a hotel bedroom. The book was carefully wrapped up and taken to the Chinese minister, but instead of rewarding them for stealing the book, the minister scolded them severely and ordered that it should be immediately returned. The two culprits returned to Sun Yat-sen's lodgings and begged for forgiveness on their knees.

Meanwhile the war between Russia and Japan had come to an end with the virtual defeat of Russia. When the Treaty of Portsmouth was signed in September 1905, Japan was emerging from the feudal state like Athene fully armed from the head of Zeus. The successful conclusion of the war had a pronounced effect in China, and more particularly among the Chinese students, who saw in the rise of their neighbor a vindication of all the reforms undertaken by Kang Yu-wei, and of the revolutionary fervor of Sun Yat-sen. In the Russo-Japanese War, China was the loser, for by a secret agreement with Russia, Japan was offered increasing advantages in Manchuria. The example of the first Oriental nation to defeat a Western power sent Chinese students hurrying into Japanese universities.

It was at a time when Japanese imperialism was at its height that Sun Yat-sen arrived from Europe at Yokohama and a few weeks later, on August 13, 1905, found himself greeted by hundreds of cheering Chinese students who escorted him to the Kojimachi Fujiro, the largest hotel in the city. In comparison with his modest success in Europe, his success in Japan was overwhelming. Nearly thirteen hundred people crowded into the hall, and some hundreds were refused admittance. The influence of Kang Yu-wei was still predominant; and though the hall was crowded and he was listened to with respect, he knew that he had not succeeded in awakening the overwhelming majority of his listeners. Some weeks later he was introduced by the Japanese liberal Miyazaki Torazo to two survivors of the Hunan uprising in 1904—Hwang Hsing and Sung Chiao-jen. The meeting took place at the headquarters of the Twentieth Century Chinese Society in Tokyo, an institution where Chinese students gathered to discuss politics and listen to lectures.

The friendship between Sun Yat-sen and the two Hunanese revolutionaries was to have important consequences. When Hwang Hsing offered to join whatever revolutionary brotherhood Sun Yat-sen cared to form, the possibility of a successful revolution became appreciably greater; and when, a few months before the Treaty of Portsmouth, on August 20, 1905, the first chapter of the Tung Meng Hui was formed, Hwang Hsing assumed the office of vice-president. The full title of the new organization was Chung-kuo Ke-ming Tung Meng Hui, or Chinese Revolutionary Alliance, but it was usually shortened to "Tung Meng Hui" to avoid suspicion. As in all previous societies there was a complicated code and a curious accumulation of secret verbal signals; to discover whether a stranger was a member of the organization, it was necessary to ask him certain questions. "Who are you?" "We are the Chinese." "What is the thing?" "This is the Chinese thing." "What is the matter?" "The universal matter." These precautions may appear childish, but it was necessary to maintain secrecy within the party, and nothing else so fitted the occasion.

The inauguration meeting was attended by many scholars and revolutionaries who later formed part of the executive of the revolutionary movement. Hu Han-min, Wang Ching-wei, Hwang Hsing, and Sung Chiao-jen were present as members of the party, of which Sun Yat-sen was elected president. During the meeting one of the benches at the back of the hall broke down, and Sun Yat-sen remarked casually that this augured well for the downfall of the Manchus. The oath was read out; the objects of the revolution were read out; and as the streams of students from every province of China streamed out of the building into the sultry heat of the evening, it was realized that the work of the revolution was already beginning.

During the meeting, six fundamental principles were enunciated:

1. The overthrow of the present government.
2. The establishment of a republican government.
3. Maintenance of world peace.
4. Nationalization of the land.
5. Promotion of friendship between the Japanese and Chinese peoples.
6. Requests to foreign countries to support the work of reform.

And in one of the declarations of the party—a declaration almost certainly written by Sun Yat-sen—the influence of the French Revolution upon the new revolution which was about to sweep through China is evident:

"Besides overthrowing the Manchus and recovering China, there are the problems of the form of government and the economy of the people. Although these problems are complicated, we must possess the unifying spirit, namely liberty, equality and universal love. So the revolution today is by the people, while formerly it was brought about by the hero. The essence of revolution by the people lies in the fact that all the people possess the spirit of liberty, equality and universal love, and all share in the responsibilities of revolution."

The inauguration of the Tung Meng Hui was the most important step in Sun Yat-sen's revolutionary career. He wrote later: "On the day when the 'Tung Meng Hui' was inaugurated in Tokyo by intellectuals representing the whole of China, I began for the first time to believe that my revolutionary work might be completed during my lifetime." During the first years of struggle, the majority of the revolutionaries had been workmen. Now for the first time intellectuals thronged to the revolutionary meetings, and it was their impetus which led to the founding of new chapters in every province of China. The growth of the movement was phenomenal. "In less than a year the membership reached tens of thousands, and new branches were established all over China, in the Straits Settlements and in America. The revolutionary current became so swift that we began to watch its progress with something like stupefaction."

Like most revolutionary movements, the new party laid special emphasis upon reaching the masses. A monthly publication, founded by a levy of five dollars from each member of the party, was immediately started and placed under the editorship of Sung Chiao-jen with the assistance of Hu Han-min and Wang Ching-wei. The *Min Pao* or *People's Gazette,* founded in January, 1906, acquired a reputation for violently provocative articles, and became the most widely read publication among the Chinese students in Japan.

The times were violent; and just as Lenin waged mortal war with the Mensheviks in *Iskra,* so Hu Han-min and Chang Chih fought against Liang Chih-chao as bitterly as they fought against the monarchy. This violence was reflected in the novel *The Thirty-Year-Old Flower Fades Like a Dream,* written by Miyazaki Torazo, in which Sun Yat-sen appears disguised as the young hero, a doctor who plans assassination in intervals between conducting serious abdominal operations. The sentimentality of the novel, the descriptions of the underground struggle with the Manchus, the tortures suffered and inflicted by the revolutionaries, made the novel immediately popular; and the Chinese minister of the interior ordered that anyone found in possession of the novel should be apprehended and imprisoned. But sentimentality and violence are true bedfellows, and the quarrel between the protagonists of the two movements became more violent as the year drew to a conclusion. When Liang Chih-chao was addressing the students in Tokyo on "the Nature of the Constitutional Monarchy," the hall was packed with agitators from the Tung Meng Hui. A fight broke out between the members of the two parties, and Chang Chih, one of the assistant editors of the *Min Pao,* mounted the platform. Inevitably there were blows. Boots, sandals, rotten food, face towels, and even benches were thrown onto the platform, and in the confusion Liang Chih-chao fled for his life.

Perhaps this violence can be excused by the temper of the times. It sprang from the bitter and often brilliant editorials of the rival journals. And simply because the violence did not result in open warfare, it became more terrible. There were some who said that violence had reached such a pitch that China would wake up one morning to find itself in the throes of a civil war more enduring than the fifteen years of terror which followed the outbreak of the Taiping rebellion; and that in this civil war the forces of the Manchus would be overwhelmed, leaving no single government in control.

Irreconcilable, inflexible, entirely committed to the single pursuit of their own programs, employing different methods and springing perhaps from different sources in the country's history, the revolutionaries and the reformers faced one another in the uncertain light of history, prepared to wage war but undecided as to who would fire the first shot. It was a dangerous, confusing year. Lessons of the Russian Revolution were being learned; perhaps the insistence in the declarations of Tung Meng Hui that power lies in the people was borrowed by the leaders from the Bolsheviks. But the swift tide of revolution was becoming a spate, and already the effects were being noticed in Peking, where autocratic government was beginning to exert itself in a last desperate effort to keep the invaders at bay. "How long shall we have to tolerate these imbeciles?" wrote the Empress Dowager in a minute to one of her ministers. But the "imbeciles" were growing in strength, and everyone knew that the revolution would break out at the touch of a spark.

V

REVOLUTIONS are like flowers that grow where the wind listeth; they arise often inexplicably, as the result of forces which cannot be measured, because they are related to the overtones of the human heart. But the revolution of 1906, which everyone expected, did not break out in the expected form. The revolutionaries desired nothing better than revolution, and at the same time the court circles seemed to have become reconciled to their danger and made plans accordingly.

In the next five years, twelve insurrections of varying magnitude occurred. They sapped the strength of the imperial armies, but they did not succeed in breaking the power of the dynasty. The revolutionaries began to see no hope except in a *levée en masse*. But such a *levée en masse*, though practicable in a small European state, presented difficulties in a country where communications to this day are dangerous and rare. Occasionally it was attempted; secret orders were transmitted to the local organizations, and efforts were made to create a co-ordinated movement over the whole of China. But in practice the movements usually failed for the same reasons that they had failed before—lack of efficient leadership, lack of funds, lack of communications.

To short-circuit the lack of ammunition, Sun Yat-sen made contact with the French military attaché in Tokyo and visited Annam. By 1906 his contacts with the French had grown intimate, and on his return to Japan from a journey in the South Seas he was met at Wusung near Shanghai by a French officer representing the French minister of war. The officer paid tribute to the cause of the Chinese revolution. Sun Yat-sen described the complex revolutionary situation and asked for help. A little to his surprise, help was immediately offered, and seven French military officers stationed at Tientsin were placed at his disposal.

As soon as he arrived in Japan, he sent Liao Chung-kai to act as liaison officer in Tientsin. Shortly afterward the French officers found their way to south China and the Yangtse Valley, reaching Nanking and Hankow, and even penetrating as far west as Szechuan. They compiled reports, visited the revolutionary organizations, and prepared plans for a military uprising. Their efforts were not without danger. In Nanking they made secret overtures to the Imperial Army officers; in Wuchang, a large meeting was held in a church. While one of the French officers was addressing the meeting, it happened that the commander of the Imperial New Army, Chang Piao, entered in disguise and later reported the meeting to the viceroy Chang Chih-tung. Alarmed by the presence of foreigners at a secret meeting, the Viceroy lost no time in communicating with Peking. Notes were exchanged between the Tsungli Yamen and the Quai d'Orsay. The French government does not appear to have been unduly perturbed, but in 1907, when the French government fell, the officers were recalled. One more chapter in the incredible history of China's relations with the powers came to an end; but it was by no means the end of Sun Yat-sen's contacts with French military officers.

In 1906 a revolt broke out in Hunan. It was not the revolution which had been expected among the exiles in Tokyo, but it was an effort sufficiently powerful to make people wonder whether this was not the first of what might become a long chain of revolts in every province of China. Hwang Hsing had been sent to Japan in 1901 by Chang Chih-tung, then viceroy of Hupeh, to study international affairs; he returned to China in May 1903 and began a series of lectures at the Liang-Hu College in Wuchang. In these lectures he vigorously attacked the Manchu regime. Banished to Hunan, his native province, he inaugurated two revolutionary societies, known as Hua Hsing Hui and the Tung Cho, with programs similar to those later incorporated in the Tung Meng Hui. On October 10, 1904, the birthday of the Empress Dowager, he launched an unsuccessful insurrection in Hunan and immediately afterward fled to Japan. He returned in February 1905 to launch yet another insurrection at Hungkiang in the same province, with the help of a fellow revolutionary named Mou Fo-I, who was arrested before the insurrection could break out. Hwang Hsing then fled to Hankow in disguise and shortly afterward made his way to Japan, taking part in the inaugural ceremonies of the Tung Meng Hui.

The insurrection in Hunan on October 19, 1906, was more serious than either of the two previous attempts. A drought in the province made the venture more desperate. The insurrection was carefully planned. Three columns were formed, amounting to about thirty thousand men, a force which included the coal miners of Pinghsiang, the garrison at Lilin, and the secret societies at Liuyang. Although the insurrection had been carefully organized, it was brought about without the aid of the Tung Meng Hui. The attempt began auspiciously with the capture of several villages and small towns; but when the Viceroy ordered the combined forces of the four provinces of Hunan, Kiangsi, Hupeh, and Szechuan to attack the revolutionaries, there was no alternative for the latter but to split up into small groups and make their way through the encircling army as best they could.

In Tokyo, as news of the revolt penetrated the Chinese censorship, excitement ran high, and years later Sun Yat-sen remembered in his autobiography the peculiar exaltation of those days:

"While the revolutionaries were putting up their struggle against the Manchus, the members of the 'Tung Meng Hui' in Tokyo were living in an agony of frustration. Not a day passed but our members thronged the headquarters and clamoured to be sent back to the homeland. Some of the more ardent spirits packed their bags and set off for China without permission; others bitterly complained because they were not allowed to leave. Their patriotism deserves our praise, but the headquarters in Tokyo did not hear anything about the outbreak and therefor could make no preparations."

The revolt failed, not only because it was insufficiently prepared, but also because the forces opposing were overwhelming. The revolutionaries were no match for the combined armies of four provinces, and in knowledge of modern warfare they were still untutored. The revolt, however, had one unexpected effect. The attention of the Manchu government was turned to Japan, where the secret societies had their headquarters; and after an exchange of notes between the Chinese and Japanese Foreign Offices, Sun Yat-sen found himself no longer *persona grata* in Tokyo. Asked to leave the country, he took Hu

THE FORERUNNERS 79

Han-min and Wang Ching-wei to Annam, leaving the *Min Pao* in the hands of his assistants.

The failure of the revolt in Hunan did not affect his determination to lead further campaigns. Already the Manchu government was feeling the strain. Like drops of water falling on rock, the revolutionary process was already changing the shape of the country. In the following five years innumerable uprisings occurred. All failed; but the lessons were being learned, the determination of the revolutionaries increased under successive failures, and gradually the rock began to crumble.

When Sun Yat-sen reached Annam, he set up his headquarters in Hanoi. Shortly afterward another abortive attempt, based on Hanoi, under the leadership of Hsueh Shih-chu, an expatriate Chinese from Singapore, failed because a thunderstorm broke out at a decisive moment. Resumed on April 11, 1907, it was more successful. Volunteers attacked the yamen at Hwang-Kong in Kwangtung, which was captured the following day. Reinforcements of Manchu troops were rushed up, and the revolutionaries would have been put to flight if one of them had not stepped forward in the best revolutionary manner and called upon the attacking troops to die for their country and their children. Wrapping themselves in wet cotton bedclothes and straw mattresses as a protection from bullets, the revolutionaries then took the town by storm, throwing the Manchus into the hills and pursuing them until lack of food and ammunition drove the revolutionaries to disband their forces. The campaign lasted five days. A week later, a single shot fired near Chiniu lake at Waichow was the signal for a further rebellion, but this too failed. With the disturbing echo of a shot fired on the quiet waters of the lake, the fourth attempt at revolution during the year came to an end.

A fifth effort came in July of the same year. In the towns

of Chin and Lien, on the borders of Kwangtung and Annam, there broke out one of the sporadic popular insurrections against Manchu taxes. The Manchu government immediately sent three thousand soldiers under two generals to quell the outbreak. The townsmen sent representatives to Sun Yat-sen asking for help, and Hwang Hsing and Hu I-sen were sent to Kwangsi with orders to lead the struggle or if possible to subvert the forces of the enemy. The two Manchu generals, at a secret meeting, promised their support. French officers were engaged from Annam, and a trusted Japanese lieutenant, Sugano Choji, was sent to Tokyo to facilitate the shipment of the arms and ammunition already purchased by the Tung Meng Hui. Sun Yat-sen calculated that he could form a brigade of two thousand Chinese troops in French territory, and with the addition of volunteers from the two towns he hoped to form a large striking force adequately equipped and armed. "With additional training," he wrote, "we could easily occupy Kwangtung and Kwangsi. From there we could proceed to the Yangtse Valley and join with the modern armies in Nanking and Wuchang. It would not be difficult at all to occupy the entire country."

The perversities of revolution, however, decreed otherwise. For the sixth time the expected ammunition failed to arrive. Sun Yat-sen's troops, numbering only three hundred, penetrated the tax-rioting districts on July 27. The two Manchu generals decided to remain loyal; and the revolutionary forces, faced by this sudden setback, retreated into the mountains. A second invasion was organized shortly afterward. Under cover of night Sun Yat-sen, Hu Han-min, Hwang Hsing, and a number of French officers, with a few hundred troops, advanced against Chengnankuan, the scene of bitter fighting during the Franco-Chinese War of 1885. The town was seized, but the arsenal in the fortress was found to have been denuded of ammunition, and once again the relief troops in the mountain failed to arrive. They had fought in hilly country for seven days and nights without respite; and when their ammunition gave out, there was no course open to them except retreat.

While Sun Yat-sen's troops were retreating through the Cool Mountains, the Imperial Army headquarters in Peking received news that he was operating from French territory, and the Chinese government immediately lodged a protest in Hanoi. Once again Sun Yat-sen found himself banished. He sailed for Singapore, leaving Hwang Hsing in charge of operations from Annam. On February 25, 1908, with only two hundred troops, Hwang Hsing again invaded the tax-rioting districts for more than forty days until the inevitable lack of ammunition forced him back. He had lost two men killed and two others slightly wounded. A month later a more successful raid over the Yunnan border at Hokou took place under the leadership of General Hwang Ming-tung. The commander of the frontier garrison was murdered and several thousand soldiers were taken prisoner; but General Hwang possessed no military training, Sun Yat-sen was in the South Seas collecting money, and an order to Hwang Hsing to go to the help of the revolutionaries failed to reach him, since he had been arrested a few days previously by the French authorities in the belief that he was a Japanese spy. Once more there was a retreat, but this retreat was curiously different from previous revolutionary failures: they returned with five hundred more soldiers than before.

These raids over the frontier were failures, but they were failures with a purpose. Sun Yat-sen believed they would provide the necessary impetus for the reconquest of China, and it was not impossible to believe that a successful raid in Yunnan might one day lead to the downfall of the dynasty in Peking. But such events were rare, and Peking had already taken measures to deal with these sporadic raids over the frontier. Cut off from the rest of China, Yunnan offers small rewards for the revolutionary. Among the high mountains and turbulent rivers of the province, communications even today are difficult and dangerous. The news of a victory on the border would not percolate into the interior for many weeks; and the capture of Chin and Lien, and Hwang Hsing's later investment of Hokou in Yunnan, though important in revolutionary history, offer small consolation to the historian.

Altogether four campaigns were launched from Annam. Though more successful than the campaigns launched in the interior or in Canton, they failed because their success was incommensurate with the needs of the revolutionaries. Something more striking, more startling, was required to shake the Manchus from their pedestals; and from the moment when the fourth campaign ended in failure, headquarters decided that all subsequent movements should begin from Canton. Six hundred of the revolutionaries sailed for Hong Kong, but they were no sooner on board ship than they were arrested and deported to Singapore on the recommendation of the Chinese government. At first the British colonial government refused to accept them, and the prison ship was moored for two nights in Singapore roads before they were allowed to land.

In the early years of the movement an attack on Canton had been comparatively easy. Hong Kong and the mysterious creeks of the Pearl River offered abundant sanctuary; stevedores along the wharves of the British colony were accustomed to unload ammunition disguised as tinned salmon or casks of cement. As the years passed and one revolutionary failure succeeded another, difficulties began to increase. The Chinese government demanded the extradition and banishment of the members of the revolutionary societies, and though extradition was rarely resorted to, banishment became an increasingly useful weapon against the revolutionaries, whose plans for direct action from Hong Kong became almost impossible when the revolutionary leaders disappeared one by one from headquarters. Japan, Annam, Hong Kong, Siam, the British and Dutch colonies in the Pacific refused to give Sun Yat-sen a base for operations in their territory. Realizing that China could be attacked more easily through Europe or America, he set out, leaving Hu Han-min and Hwang Hsing in Hong Kong, for his third and final world tour.

There were to be two more unsuccessful attempts against Canton. The first occurred in January 1910. Attempts had been made to subvert the Imperial New Army, and it was confidently expected that the yamen would be captured without bloodshed; but the revolt broke out prematurely, the imperial troops had not been informed of the date of the outbreak, and in the melee the leader of the revolutionary troops was shot dead.

The discouraging news of the failure of the revolt reached Sun Yat-sen en route for San Francisco. He immediately changed his plans and returned in disguise to Penang, where an important conference of party members was held. For the first time Sun Yat-sen began to realize the distress existing among the revolutionary members, many of whom had come down from the north and after participating in the abortive attack on Canton found themselves penniless and without food or clothing.

Still more bad news reached the members sitting in Penang's Chinatown. During the winter of 1908 the *Min Pao* was suspended by the Japanese government on the grounds that an article entitled "Revolutionary Psychology" was dangerous to the peaceful relations between China and Japan. The party was therefore left without its most influential organ. The Penang merchants subscribed heavily to Sun Yat-sen's request for large sums of money, and a few days later he was able to send to Hong Kong between fifty and sixty thousand dollars, the money to be spent partly in the relief of the revolutionaries and partly to provide ammunition for still another assault on the yamen in Canton.

After the conclusion of the conference, he set out to resume his world tour, and though there is a legend that he traveled through Malaya disguised as a blind vender of trinkets, it is more probable that he left on the same ship that brought him to Penang. The times were desperate. Too many revolutions had failed. In the British Museum reading room, a Russian had once spoken of preparing for a revolution in a hundred years' time; but in a country like China, with its vast antiquity, with its monarchy rooted in the immemorial past, and a people whose inertia acted like a brake on all proposals for reform, it began to be conceivable that there would be no revolution for a hundred years. "We must succeed in a year," Sun Yat-sen told a friend in Penang, "or else we shall fail forever."

VI

AS THOUGH the despair of the times had been visibly communicated to the revolutionaries, the last unsuccessful venture was the most glorious. The revolt broke out on April 27, 1911—the twenty-ninth day of the third moon of the third year of the emperor Hsuan Tung—and resulted in the deaths of seventy-two of the revolutionaries. Between half past four and six o'clock in the afternoon, Hwang Hsing led an assault on the Canton yamen with a hundred and thirty followers, among whom were the flower of the Tung Meng Hui. The attack had been carefully planned. For the first time there were adequate funds available for the purchase of ammunition. The central column under Hwang Hsing had orders to capture the yamen, while nine more columns comprising about eight hundred trained troops were ordered to concentrate on the outlying fortifications. The yamen guards were killed and part of the yamen was destroyed, but the eight hundred troops failed to arrive at the decisive moment, and after an hour and a half of fierce fighting Hwang Hsing ordered his men to retire, for the enemy numbered over two thousand and it was already growing too dark to fight. When the battle was over, it was discovered that forty-three revolutionaries had been killed in battle and twenty-nine had been captured and executed. Hwang Hsing himself escaped with one arm wounded and two fingers missing. Today "the Seventy-two Martyrs of the Yellow-flower Mound" are commemorated on a monument in Canton, and the date of their death has become a national holiday.

With the failure of the tenth insurrection, despair among the revolutionaries reached its height. Hwang Hsing arrived in Hong Kong in disguise three days later, heartbroken by the defeat. Like Yang Sao-jen, who had thrown himself into the Thames after the failure of an earlier revolution, he contemplated suicide. Of this episode Sun Yat-sen said later: "In this battle the flower of the revolutionary spirit was gathered together in a desperate struggle against the Manchus. Unsuccessful though they were, their deaths have struck terror into the hearts of the enemy and paved the way for our final success." A few weeks later Hwang Hsing was once more working on a plan of campaign against the Canton yamen, and the despair, which was so terrible at the time, was accepted, as nightmares are accepted—they are understandable, and yet they can have no great part in our thoughts.

For there is no doubt that the Manchus were beginning to be terrified by the revolts, and they were still more terrified by the wave of assassinations which swept over the country. More than once Sun Yat-sen had given his guarded approval to this form of revolutionary activity. He realized its dangers, but long years of failure had forced him to the conclusion that assassination was a weapon which terrified a whole class. The lessons of the Russian Revolution of 1905 were being learned; and when on September 26, 1905, a bomb was thrown at five high Manchu commissioners as they were starting on their journey to report on the constitutions of the West, it was wrong to assume that the bomb was being thrown by an irresponsible student, though the commissioners included the most enlightened reformers at court. The assassin, Wu Yueh, was killed and the commissioners escaped with light injuries. A more heroic assassination occurred on May 26, 1907, when a young schoolmaster named Hsu Hsih-lin murdered the viceroy of Anhui while he was presiding at the commencement exercises of the Police Institute at Anking. The murder took place in daylight, and the murderer made no attempt to escape. He was arrested, tortured and executed, his heart was cut out and presented to the viceroy's family. His accomplice was his lady cousin Chiu Chin, a member of the Tung Meng Hui. She was arrested shortly afterward, and on the eve of her execution she wrote a poem of seven Chinese characters which has become deservedly famous:

> The autumn wind and the autumn rain
> mortally torments a man.

She was executed with the heavy sword early the next morning; her body was buried in the prison courtyard; the school which she had kept with Hsu Hsih-lin was suspended, and for a while—until the confession written on the eve of execution was found in the library of a junior magistrate—even the one line which has made her immortal was forgotten.

More assassinations followed at a swift tempo. Early in 1910 Wang Ching-wei attempted to assassinate the Prince Regent with the help of three young girls, one of them the daughter of a rich Penang merchant who subsequently became his wife. Wang Ching-wei was a Cantonese, the son of scholarly parents who educated him in an atmosphere of refinement and learning. In 1904 he was sent by the provincial government to study in Japan, where he was introduced to Sun Yat-sen and became an active member of the Tung Meng Hui. In February 1910, he journeyed to Peking and made careful preparations for the assassination; but when the dynamite and bombs were discovered and he was arrested, he made a speech announcing that he had indeed intended to murder the Prince Regent, and according to the rumor of the time it was because the empress dowager Lu Yu was so struck by his audacity that he was imprisoned and not executed.

Meanwhile the tempo of life had been increasing at an alarming rate. The Constitutional Commission returned from Japan and the West in 1906, bringing with it plans for the reorganization of the provincial assemblies and the establishment of parliament under a constitutional government. Many of its recommendations were included in the Imperial Reform Edicts of 1906, but the more important recommendations, including the election of a free parliament, were left unheeded. In consequence by the spring of 1908 petitions for the opening of a new parliament were flowing into Peking. On August 27, 1908, an imperial rescript announced that a nine-year plan of constitutional reform was already in force according to a carefully prepared schedule. But less than three months later, on November 15, 1908, the empress dowager Tsu Hsi died, leaving the state in the hands of a prince regent now known as Prince Ch'un, the infant prince P'u Yi being emperor.

The new reign began inauspiciously with the dismissal of Yuan Shih-kai, the most powerful and at that time the most popular statesman in China. By an imperial edict dated January 2, 1909, Yuan Shih-kai was dismissed on the grounds that he could no longer carry out the duties of his office owing to "foot trouble." The immediate cause of his dismissal was his campaign for the superior claims of Prince Pu Lun to the throne. Moreover, the Prince Regent was the younger brother of the young emperor Kuang Hsu, who died mysteriously the day before the Dowager died. The young Emperor had held Yuan Shih-kai responsible for the failure of "the hundred days of reform," and the new regent was hardly disposed to treat him with favor. Meanwhile Yuan Shih-kai's position in the army was invulnerable, Peking was divided into two camps, and the revolutionaries were overjoyed at the new turn in affairs.

They would have been less overjoyed if they had known Yuan Shih-kai's real ambitions. The Regent was in continual contact with a group of reformers, and it was largely due to his insistence that the provincial assemblies were convened for the first time in October 1909. Though they were predominantly advisory in character, their petitions to the central government were acted upon when pressed with sufficient vigor. Three petitions for the early convocation of parliament were sent to Peking in January, July and October 1910. The first remained unanswered, the second met with refusal, and the third led to the response that the nine-year plan, would be shortened to five years, thus bringing the opening day of parliament to 1913.

Meanwhile the declaration by the United States of an "Open Door" policy toward China led to a decline in the competition for spheres of interest among the powers. But the government's policy of nationalizing the railways and inviting foreign loans had opened up a new era of competition with disastrous results. The Open Door became a series of revolving doors. Though foreign bankers were invited to make loans on the basis of certain fixed apportionments, practice failed to accomplish what theory so much desired; with the inevitable effect that the bankers were compelled to bribe Chinese officials and to resort to intimidating measures in order to hide their accomplices. The provinces struck. They were bitterly opposed to schemes of nationalizing the railways, not only because they were in danger of losing their provincial autonomy, but also because they were in danger of losing their share of the spoils.

The railways were still regarded by the people as messengers of foreign imperialism, a disrupting element, the thin edge of the wedge driven into the heart of China. Their dissatisfaction was reflected in the speeches at the First National Assembly. And though railways were held to be necessary by the more enlightened, the experience of the past had demonstrated that it was not yet perhaps the time for their introduction into a feudal agricultural state. The first railway in China ran out of Shanghai. It was built by foreigners, then bought by the Chinese, who carefully uprooted the rails and shipped them to Formosa, where they were allowed to rust. After the Peking-Hankow line was constructed by a French-Belgian syndicate, many trunk lines fell into the hands of foreign powers: the Tientsin-Pukow railway was owned by Great Britain and Germany, the Shanghai-Nanking railway belonged to Great Britain, and the Chengting-Taiyuan railway to Russia. The story of the early development of the railway was continuously unhappy. The Canton-Hankow railway and the Szechuan-Hankow lines especially were the subject of bitter controversy when Sheng Hsuan-huai, secretary for imperial communications, began to advocate that they should be nationalized out of funds subscribed by an international syndicate including British, American, French, and German bondholders. There had been minor rebellions and disturbances over the railways before; now there were widespread threats. In Szechuan, Hopeh, Honan, and Kwangtung the news of the projected nationalization came at the end of a long period of provincial frustration, and "Railway Defense Societies" were organized. In Szechuan the fear of nationalization was inflamed by riots which broke out at the end of September 1911, and these riots were the precursors of the revolution.

It should have been possible to predict that the final insurrection would break out far from the scene of previous attempts. Wuchang, Hankow, and Hanyang are collectively known as Wuhan. These three cities lying close together straddle the Yangtse River eight hundred miles west of Shanghai. Iron and smelting works, an arsenal, great wharves and granaries containing the rich produce of the Yangtse Valley lie in this triple city, a center which has been famous for its industries for over three thousand years. After the failure of the last Canton rebellion, revolutionary activity had been centered upon the Yangtse Valley; and able revolutionaries like Sung Chiao-jen were busy addressing meetings and establishing book societies in Hankow and the surrounding areas, attempting to subvert the Eighth Division of the Imperial Army stationed in Wuchang and to create the peculiar atmosphere which is inseparable from revolution.

Late in September two regiments amounting to two thousand men were withdrawn from Wuchang to suppress the railway riots in Szechuan. Taking advantage of the fact that the garrison had been reduced in size and was already partly converted to the revolutionary cause, the tenth day after the mid-autumn festival was chosen for the eleventh attempt; but the premature explosion of a bomb in a secret arsenal in the Russian concession at Hankow on the night of October 9 precipitated the outbreak. When the news of the explosion reached the viceroy's yamen, an inquiry was immediately ordered by the viceroy Chen-jui. As a result of the inquiry about fifty revolutionaries were seized and three were executed the same night, while among the documents found were the enrollment registers of the revolutionary brotherhood in the three provinces. The soldiers of Imperial Engineering and Artillery Corps, who were secretly affiliated to the revolutionaries and whose names were recorded in the registers, decided to act quickly. They took possession of an ordnance gun in the artillery park, and for this crime death sentences were passed on eight privates caught by loyal armament guards.

Events followed swiftly. General Hsiung Ping-kuan, in command of the Engineering Corps, ordered an attack on the armament park, and a few minutes later General Tsai Chih-ming, in command of the Imperial Artillery, led his troops to bombard the viceroy's yamen. The viceroy fled. He was deserted by the armed forces of the city, and could rely only on his personal bodyguard. Deriving little consolation from their professed loyalty, he took refuge on a Chinese gunboat moored alongside a British warship. At Hankow messages were received late that night by the consular body to the effect that the viceroy was no longer in a position to afford protection to foreign nationals. By describing the rebellion as antiforeign in nature, he hoped to achieve the singular distinction of coercing foreigners to suppress a rebellion which was aimed at the ruling class of the Manchus, of which he was a member. The guns of the foreign warships in the Yangtse remained silent. M. Réau, the dean of the consular body, a personal friend of Sun Yat-sen, and an authority on international law, replied that interference in internal disputes could hardly be expected from friendly states. His views were upheld by the Russian consul, who added that the viceroy might take the opportunity of reporting to Peking, a task which the foreign powers would be only too pleased to facilitate by allowing him the use of a gunboat to Shanghai.

The tone of the communications between the viceroy and the consular body suggested that the eleventh revolt might be the last. On October 11 the revolutionaries had succeeded in investing Hanyang on the opposite bank of the Yangtse. By capturing the steelworks and the arsenal, they placed themselves in an unexpectedly happy position. Hankow was captured the same afternoon, and by the evening of the twelfth the provincial assembly of Hupeh, sitting in Wuchang, had proclaimed its complete independence from imperial rule and was calling upon all the provincial assemblies to follow its example.

With the triple city and the whole province in their hands, the revolutionaries planned to set up a military government. But who was to be in command? Sun Yat-sen was abroad, Hwang Hsing was trying to reach Hankow but had not yet arrived, and the central direction of the revolution was in the hands of young students and untried officers with no experience of leadership in civil war. It was necessary to appoint a commander-in-chief respected by all the revolutionaries; but no such commander-in-chief was available.

Late at night messengers were sent to the headquarters of Colonel Li Yuan-hung, second in command of the government troops. He was a man of liberal sentiments, popular with his troops, but devoid of superhuman excellence. When the revolutionaries burst into his bedroom, he was found hiding under the bed with only his boots visible. Asked to sign the manifesto calling upon the whole country to unite against the Manchus, he demurred and explained he had no authority to sign such a document.

Besides, he was tired. If the revolutionaries would wait till the morning ... But the revolutionaries could not wait; they were singularly violent, they insisted, they threatened, and one of them drew his pistol, held it to his own temple and threatened to shoot himself if his request were refused. The manifesto guaranteed protection to all foreigners as long as they abstained from actively assisting the enemy, but it also guaranteed the end of the Manchu rule which had lasted for two hundred and sixty years. It was signed by a colonel who had no particular interest in the revolution and whose subsequent history reflects an incredible misunderstanding of revolutionary principles. Yet the three characters of his name at the foot of the proclamation were sufficient to overthrow the dynasty.

Consternation reigned in Peking. The moral collapse of the Manchus was evident in the succession of edicts which were issued from the capital. The viceroy in Wuchang, perhaps the ablest Manchu holding office in the provinces, was at first complimented upon his promptitude in quelling the rebellion, and then—when further reports reached Peking—severely censured and degraded for gross neglect of duty. Orders to the army to attack Wuchang were given and countermanded.

Autumn maneuvers were taking place a hundred miles east of Peking. On October 14 two divisions of the northern army were entrained at Luanchow, the nearest point of the Peking-Mukden railway, under the command of General Yin Chang, the imperial minister of war. Two successive decrees recalling Yuan Shih-kai were issued from the Forbidden City. The first decree appointed him viceroy of Hukwang (the provinces of Hunan and Hupeh) with orders "to direct the suppression and pacification of the rebels"; the second gave him full authority in co-operation with the imperial minister of war to take over military and naval affairs "with a view to the restoration of peace at an early date." Yuan Shih-kai failed to respond to the decrees. He offered the cynical excuse that his old "foot trouble" was not yet completely cured. In Peking there were two schools of thought. The young princes and high officials were determined to fight without him. More conservative members of the government, though recognizing his prestige and probably believing the rumors then current that the Sixth Division worshiped his portrait with greater reverence than they paid to the Emperor, regarded him as the ideal commander and patiently awaited the announcement of his conditions. These conditions were not long in coming. A third edict, issued on October 27, appointed him supreme military and naval commander, with complete independence from the general staff and the minister of war, and unlimited financial assistance.

He accepted. He could not refuse. The position was desperate. The imperial armies were concentrating on the triple city and controlled all the country north of the river with the exception of Hankow, which was being bombarded, and Hanyang, which was being bitterly defended. Yet the revolution was sweeping the country. South of the river, Changsha, the capital of Hunan, and the old northern capital of Sianfu had declared themselves for the revolutionary cause, while the whole bloc of the southern provinces including Kwangtung, the richest and most revolutionary of them all, proclaimed their independence. Nanking held out. The main forces of the Imperial Army were still concentrated at Wuchang. Hankow fell, after twelve days and nights of street fighting, on the afternoon of October 30. In revenge for its arduous defense, the burning city was leveled to the ground by imperial troops led by Feng Kuo-chang.

A few hours before the fall of Hankow, Hwang Hsing arrived to take command of the revolutionary forces.

THE FORERUNNERS

Hanyang was being besieged and in imminent danger of falling. Imperial reinforcements were coming down from the north; revolutionary reinforcements were coming up from the south. Shanghai was captured by Chen Chi-mei on November 4, and a day later a young subaltern named Chiang Kai-shek participated in the capture of the yamen of Hangchow, the capital of Chekiang province, after barely escaping with his life when he landed at Shanghai from Japan.

The revolutionary tide was swift. Nanking held out. A night attack by Feng Kuo-chang's troops on Hanyang compelled the defenders to retreat; but the arsenal was blown up, no ships of the imperial navy were able to reach port, and there were possibilities of its recapture a few days later. The fall of Hanyang gave the imperial forces a larger measure of control north of the river, but the revolution in the south was already a *fait accompli*. But the north was still in a state of turmoil. The generals at Luanchow were in favor of the reform, and taking advantage of the situation in Peking, where sabotage was becoming increasingly violent, they compelled the Prince Regent to accept a complete renunciation of Manchu privileges and threatened to resign unless the nineteen articles of constitutional government proposed by the national assemblies were carried out.

Yuan Shih-kai was formally appointed premier on November 7. Within a month he had dismissed the regent, formed a cabinet which included Liang Chih-chao, introduced a new constitution of nineteen articles, led his army to reinforce Feng Kuo-chang's forces in Hupeh, and made a formal approach to the revolutionaries for a peaceful solution of a situation which was beginning to assume the character of a static balance between the revolutionary forces in the south and the imperial forces in the north. Through the good offices of the British consul-general in

Hankow, negotiations were opened between Li Yuan-hung and Yuan Shih-kai, and an armistice was arranged for December 3. Nanking had fallen to the revolutionaries on the second, when General Hsu Shao-tseng, commander of the Ninth Division of the Imperial Army, joined the popular cause, and with the fall of Nanking the revolutionaries obtained control of the whole of the south and whatever cities and trading stations on the Yangtse remained.

The plenipotentiaries to the peace conference arranged to meet in the City Hall of the international settlement in Shanghai. Yuan Shih-kai appointed as his chief representative Tang Shao-yi, a Kwangtungese born in the same district as Sun Yat-sen. The revolutionaries were represented by Wu Ting-fang, a former minister to the United States. The meetings, which began on December 15, opened in an atmosphere of incriminations and defiance from both sides. The fall of Nanking and the sack of the Tartar City were vividly remembered in Peking; and since Shanghai had already declared itself the headquarters of the republican armies, the danger of further outbreaks of violence increased. The revolutionary party insisted upon the republican form of government, the complete abandonment of the monarchical principle, and the immediate establishment of a national convention. To these demands the northern plenipotentiary could only reply that they were *ultra vires* under the present system of government and he asked leave to refer the decision to Yuan Shih-kai as the representative of the existing tradition. Meanwhile the revolutionaries tried feverishly to get in touch with Sun Yat-sen.

But Sun Yat-sen was still abroad. While the Wuchang revolutionaries were preparing to rise, he was somewhere in the western states of America. He knew that the revolutionary ferment was rising, but he knew neither the date of the revolution nor the detailed plans for the attack of Wuhan. A fortnight earlier he had been handed a coded telegram sent by Hwang Hsing from Hong Kong, but his code book had been sent on with his forward luggage to Denver, Colorado, and he was in no hurry to have it translated. When he reached Denver, he decoded the telegram and was surprised to read: "Chu Chang arrived Hong Kong exWuchang reporting Wuchang revolutionaries urgent need money preparations uprising completed." He could not raise any large sum of money that evening, and as he intended to send a cable urging the revolutionaries to delay the uprising, and moreover was tired from the long journey, he decided to go to sleep. He slept till eleven o'clock the next morning. On his way to a late breakfast he read the headlines in the newspaper: *"WU-CHANG OCCUPIED BY REVOLUTIONARIES."*

The same day he took the train for St. Louis, where he found the newspapers full of accounts of the revolution in China. It was at St. Louis that he read for the first time the news that the revolution had broken out on the orders of Sun Yat-sen, who was to become the provisional president of the Chinese Republic as soon as he could return to China. He immediately sent a telegram telling the revolutionaries why he was late in replying to their cable, and where he was going. When he reached New York he heard that the revolution had broken out in Kwangtung, and in order to save bloodshed he wrote out a telegram to the viceroy Chang Ming-ch'i calling upon him to surrender, and at the same time he ordered the revolutionaries to spare his life.

He was thousands of miles from his own country, and without contacts with the American government; he had to work out a plan of action which would make his services most useful to the infant republic. He knew that he was young and untried in diplomacy; he was seriously out of touch with Chinese affairs. Faced with the problem of how much assistance China could hope to derive from the great powers, he decided that the position of England was the most doubtful, and therefore he determined to make his way as soon as possible to London. Japan, Germany, and Russia were historically pro-Manchu; America and France sympathized with the revolutionaries; but where did England stand? The Anglo-Japanese alliance had recently been renewed, and British policy might be expected to follow Japanese wishes. But the British people were sympathetic, the news of the Wuhan uprising had been greeted with encouraging applause in the great Sunday newspapers, and there remained only the task of ascertaining whether British financial and diplomatic interests in the Far East would be favorable to the republic. He was anxious to seek an immediate agreement on the subject of loans, the prevention of Japanese interference, and the cancellation of the deportation orders made against him by various colonial governments.

He reached London quietly, and immediately conferred with the president of the International Banking Consortium which was handling loans with China, and at a meeting in the Foreign Office an agreement was initialed by which the British government took notice of the changing position in China and provisionally accepted Sun Yat-sen's formal request that no further loans should be granted to the Manchu government, that Japan should be prevented from interfering in favor of the Manchu government, and that the orders of deportation from all British colonies should be immediately canceled. As soon as these agreements were initialed, he slipped away—on November 11—to Paris, where he met Clemenceau and signed a similar agreement with the French government.

His third and last world tour was nearly over. The revolutionary traveling penniless and unknown through America had become transformed, at the age of forty-five, into an elder statesman, with power of life and death over the four hundred and fifty million inhabitants of China. As provisional president of the Chinese Republic, his power was greater than that of the emperor, for it derived a greater measure of assent from the people. He had been gentle and unassuming at all times; at the height of victory, he became still more gentle and still more unassuming.

At Singapore he was welcomed by huge crowds who gathered on the pier and threw flowers and petals at the pony cart which brought him to the house of a rich merchant in Tanglin; at Hong Kong he was allowed to land freely for the first time in sixteen years. He smiled at the cameramen, a little tired after the journey, a little self-conscious under the weight of his new powers; and when he was asked whether he was bringing large sums of money into the exchequer of the new republic, he replied smiling: "What I am bringing back is not money, but the revolutionary spirit."

VII

THE first stage of his pilgrimage was over. The old restlessness had given place to a new assurance, and the young revolutionary who suffered occasionally from the distressing symptoms of men in whom loneliness has become a familiar companion—ill at ease with strangers, nervously fidgeting with his tiepin or smoothing down his hair—had become the inevitable leader of his nation. Those who knew him well say that his outward nervousness was only the sign of an inner serenity; and indeed this serenity became more apparent as the years passed. The natural vehemence of the Cantonese he had mastered early in youth: everywhere he is described as quiet and undemonstrative, continually searching for the roots of things and rarely raising his voice above a whisper when he was angry, or above an even and dispassionate tone when he was talking with his brethern. He was like a surgeon who regards the mosaic of living cells with infinite gentleness, and who makes incisions with a slow, deliberate sweep of the scalpel, pressing the edge of the instrument across the tissues and not into them, or like the instrument maker who spends his life in a constant search for better instruments until he finally emerges as an artist, not an artisan. Sun Yat-sen deliberately regarded his medical training as the first step toward an understanding of the revolutionary processes. The precision of the operating table was perfectly familiar to him; and in the years that followed he was to make increasing use of his knowledge of human pathology.

That a man should live through the revolutionary period of Chinese history and retain these characteristics is sufficiently remarkable, but what is still more remarkable is his consciousness that history passed through him. He had read deeply in the Bible and in *Pilgrim's Progress*. He knew that the Shining Ones carried little wisps of small cord in their hands. The prophets, the chosen vessels of the divine command, were perhaps more closely his models than the revolutionaries who preceded him, and his reverence for the Mings springs from deeper causes than the knowledge that the Ch'ing dynasty was doomed to fall in his hands. In one of his letters, using the biblical language of his childhood, he wrote: "The holy places are darkened—we had to act!" The quiet, almost casual surgeon became almost in spite of himself a genius for action, who failed ten times and succeeded only on the eleventh. "The greatest necessity is to understand the character of the people," he wrote in another letter, and this constant humility is noticeable throughout his life.

Indeed, he was always humble. The descendant of dukes and farmers, he could understand the restraints imposed upon the one and the natural freedom of the other. When he spoke at meetings in Japan, America, and China, he would begin his speeches slowly in a voice that was not always audible above the noises of the auditorium. Gradually, as his voice rose in power and the sweep of the arguments rose to assail existing problems from all sides, leaving no gates open from which sorties could be made, he achieved that peculiar silence among his listeners which is greater than the silence we hear when there is no sound. His voice was low and gentle, the emphasis coming rather from the eyes than from the voice. Many who heard him have recalled "the cold chill in the spine" which accompanied his methodical elaboration of an argument. In the old days Chinese speeches resembled the parallel versification of the Old Testament: a statement would be capped by another vigorously obeying the laws of versification, and differing only from the previous statement in the choice of words while the structure of the sentence remained the same. On this slender tower it was possible to contruct an endless series of antitheses, often meaningless, nearly always illogical. The reform movement had broken the agelong habit; it was left to Sun Yat-sen to speak in the language of the people methodically and logically.

The patient was being wheeled into the operating theater suffering from a malignant tumor of the brain. The silk sutures lay in alcohol in the glass case; the trephine needles were slowly being prepared. Because the anesthetic needle might pick up cancerous cells and start the "seeding" of tumors, the surgeon decided to proceed without any anaesthetic at all. In this interval of silence, while the surgeon raised the scalpel, the world trembled.

II. THE MAKING OF A REPUBLIC

I

"WE HAVE probably had too great an opinion of human nature in forming our Confederation," wrote Washington in a famous letter to John Jay. "Experience has taught us that men will not adopt or carry into execution measures that are best calculated for their own good, without the interference of a coercive force." When the scalpel was lifted and the first incision was made in the skull, the surgeon had promised that he would use the minimum of force. Now he refused to use any force at all.

He arrived in Shanghai on Christmas Day, six days after the opening of the peace conference between the two contending powers. There were conferences everywhere. An assembly of provincial delegates from the provinces which had declared their independence was being convened in Nanking. On December 14 Hwang Hsing had been appointed acting president. On December 29 the delegates met, and by a majority of sixteen out of seventeen votes they elected Sun Yat-sen first Provisional President of the Republic of China.

He remained a few days in Shanghai, seeing old friends and discussing the terms of peace conference with the southern plenipotentiary, and then took the train for Nanking on New Year's Day, 1912. On the afternoon of the same day he entered the city, and shortly after midnight the booming of guns from the ammunition park announced that the oath binding him to the restoration of an early peace had been taken:

"In order to overthrow the autocratic Manchu government and to consolidate the Republican form of government, and to beget blessings upon the people, I, Sun Wen, swear faithfully to obey the popular will of the people, to remain loyal to the nation and to perform my duty in the interests of the citizens, until the time comes when the Manchu rule is dethroned and the disturbances within the nation have been brought to an end and the Republic has been established as a prominent nation upon the earth recognised by all other nations. And furthermore, I, Sun Wen, solemnly declare that I will resign the office of Provisional President as soon as these things have been accomplished."

This proclamation, dated "the first day of the first year of the Chinese Republic" contained a complete break with the past. In the nine characters of the date at the foot of the proclamation, the centuries-old lunar calendar was rejected and the solar system of the West was adopted instead. Further changes were to come. In a proclamation dated January 2, he promised protection to foreigners and regard for China's existing treaties, and under the heading of the "five unities" he continued:

"I say that the foundation of the State is the people. The different races of China, Han, Manchu, Mongolian, Mahomedan and Tibetan, must now be united into one nation. This is what I mean by the unity of the race.

"Since the fighting at Wuchang, more than a dozen provinces have proclaimed their independence. It has now become necessary to form a government to unite all these provinces, and to include Tibet and Mongolia within its sphere of influence. This is what I mean by the unity of our territory.

"When the revolutionary armies began to fight in the

provinces, they were not brought under a single command, nor did they possess a single administrative organisation, though they fought for a common cause. These armies must now be combined under a single command. This is what I mean by the unity of military administration.

"The area of the State is vast and the provinces have their own systems of government. Henceforth every province must be brought under a common central government. This is what I mean by the unity of internal administration.

"Under the Manchu Government many taxes were raised among the poor. Henceforth, national expenditure must be fixed in accordance with the recognised principles of finance in order to maintain the happiness of the people. This is what I mean by the unity of finance."

In January the Provisional President began to form his government. In desperate need of money, he was compelled to borrow from Japan on the security of the ironworks at Hanyang, an act which brought him much hostility later. But the problem of forming a new government out of an impoverished network of provinces was part of a broader problem—the problem of all experience at a state of change. While the new government began to hazard a solution for problems so difficult that generations of emperors had failed even to bring them to the attention of the people, he hoped that a decent eclecticism would solve the issue. Lincoln's conception of the necessary unity of the state, Burke's theory of franchise, the Encyclopedist vision of liberty, Rousseau's social contract, and something of Plato's aristocratic state seem to have been envisaged as the cornerstones of the new China. But the temper of the time demanded more than a decent eclecticism; and in Peking, Yuan Shih-kai was already elaborating a theory of revived autocracy, with the emperor as a divine figurehead working down through his chief prime minister.

In the early days of 1912 China was divided into two armed camps, with two entirely different systems of government. Like Athens and Sparta warring over their respective spheres of influence, the north and the south failed to come to terms. Peking, the northern capital, enjoyed a form of autocratic government; Nanking in the south enjoyed a form of republican government. The emperor was still on his throne. Yuan Shih-kai was premier; and the northern Premier seems to have been outraged by the election of Sun Yat-sen as provisional president before the completion of the peace conference, while the South in its turn was outraged by Yuan Shih-kai's refusal to accept a *fait accompli*. Six route armies from the south were moving rapidly on Peking. The murder of a Manchu official, Liang-pi, in Peking had become known, though widely differing accounts were being received in the Forbidden City. The revolutionaries were beginning to be regarded in the north with something of the same hysterical horror with which the Bolsheviks were regarded on the continent of Europe in 1918.

In order to break the deadlock Sun Yat-sen telegraphed on January 15 to Yuan Shih-kai offering him the presidency on condition that he formally accept the republic and secure the abdication of the Emperor. On January 16, the day after Sun Yat-sen's message, an attempt was made to assassinate Yuan Shih-kai as his carriage was turning into Morrison Street in Peking. The attempt failed, several innocent bystanders were killed, and Yuan Shih-kai demonstrated his undoubted bravery by retaining in his hand the cigarette he was lighting at the moment when the bomb exploded. But once again the tempo of life was moving toward one of these crises which were periodically inflicted upon the northern capital; and with hushed breath the eunuchs whispered to the sounds in the corridors.

The infant emperor was still on his throne. At the winter solstice, carried in the arms of the Prince Regent, he had worshiped under the blue tiles of the Altar of Heaven the original creator of his house. Escorted by princes and the great men of his realm, followed by the Imperial Guards and the dancers and ministers of the court, purified by fasting and anointed with dew, he had climbed the steps of the altar and bowed to the tablets of the imperial ancestors, to the sun and the moon, to the five planets and the twenty-four constellations; and at last he had prostrated himself before the signs of the zodiac, the god of the clouds, the god of rain, the god of wind, and the god of thunder. In the faint light of torches it was observed that the child had been sleeping throughout the ceremony, and that when his childish limbs were folded into the kneeling position, he was seen to yawn and cry out in alarm. Was he drugged? No one knew what auguries the child was invoking from Heaven, but it was certain that he had cried out in alarm. The eunuchs were disquieted. Perhaps the sounds they heard in the corridors were the sounds of rats' feet, and the ghosts of the disemboweled Manchus hurled from the walls of Nanking.

For a month there was silence. Then the telegram, signed by General Tuan Chih-jui, and by forty-six generals of the modern army, precipitated the abdication. On February 12, while mourning bells pealed from the temples, an edict of abdication and a valedictory message were sent to the nation:

"From the preference of the people's heart," said the edict of abdication, "the will of Heaven is discernible. How could we oppose the desires of millions for the glory of one family? Therefore we, the Dowager Empress and the Emperor, hereby vest the sovereignty in the people.

THE MAKING OF A REPUBLIC

Let Yuan Shih-kai inaugurate with full powers a provisional Republic and confer with the Republicans as to the ways in which we can assure peace to the Empire, thus forming a great Republic which will include the territories of the Manchus, Chinese, Mongols, Mohamedans and Tibetans."

"In ancient times," began the valedictory decree, "the ruler of a country emphasised the important duty of protecting the lives of the people, and as their shepherd could not have the heart to cause them pain."

With these words there passed from the Dragon Throne the imperial house of Ta Ch'ing which had failed in the beginning of the twentieth century to bring either peace or purity to the immense country over which it ruled.

II

THE dangerous age was beginning. The task of the emperor's successors was more dangerous than ever before. In the days when couriers rode in ten days from Peking to far distant Szechuan, government progressed satisfactorily in an era of dilatory achievement. But the age of the telegraph, an age of nervous apprehension and sudden visitations by green-clothed messengers from the Post Office, had brought in its train violent changes of government and a complete absence of those benevolent delays which made government so satisfactory in the early nineteenth century. The Morse code has had more influence than the Mosaic code: it is more compelling, and no casuists can avoid the severity of its coming. While the emperor lived in the seclusion of the Summer Palace, the telegraph wires between Peking and Nanking hummed continuously with messages of denunciation and good will, invitations, and threats, and it was as though all the detritus of the old empire were being canalized and drained away along the thin, tenuous wires between the two capitals.

Immediately after the abdication Yuan Shih-kai sent a telegram announcing the end of the dynasty and the inauguration of the republic. The telegram was addressed to President Sun and Vice-President Li Yuan-hung, the National Assembly, and the ministers in attendance at Nanking:

"A Republic is the best form of Government. The whole world admits this. That in one leap we have passed from autocracy to republicanism is really the outcome of many years of strenuous effort by you all, and is the greatest blessing to the people. The Ta Ch'ing Emperor has proclaimed his abdication by Edict countersigned by myself. The day of the promulgation of this Edict shall be the end of the Imperial rule and the inauguration of the Republic. Henceforth we shall exert our utmost strength to move forward in progress until we reach perfection. Henceforth, forever, we shall refuse to allow monarchical government in our China. At present the work of consolidation is most difficult and confusing. I shall be most happy to go to the South and listen to your counsels on methods of procedure. There are, however, immense difficulties facing me in the North, among which must be counted the difficulty of maintaining order, the existense of a large army requiring control, and the fact that the popular will of North and East is not yet united together, so that the slightest disturbance will affect the whole country. All of you who thoroughly understand the difficult situation will realise my difficulties. You have studied the important question of establishing a republic and have formed definite plans in your mind. I beg you to inform me of your opinion of how we may best cooperate in the tasks before us."

THE MAKING OF A REPUBLIC

On February 14 Sun Yat-sen telegraphed a reply in which he stated that it was an intolerable position, when a republican leader accepted a republic as a gift from the emperor:

"Tang Sho-yi [the representative of Yuan Shih-kai at the peace conference in Shanghai] has telegraphed to me the news that the Ch'ing Emperor has abdicated, and that you will support the Republic. The settlement of this great question is a matter of the utmost joy and congratulation. I shall report to the National Assembly that I agree to resign office in your favor. But the republican government cannot be organised by any authority conferred by the Ch'ing Emperor. The exercise of such pretentious powers must surely lead to trouble. As you are already aware of the needs of the situation, you will not of course accept his authority. I cordially invite you to Nanking to fulfill the expectations of the people. Should you be anxious over the maintenance of order in the North, I beg you to inform the Provisional Government by telegraph the name of the man whom you recommend to be appointed with full powers to act in your place as the representative of the Republic. I expect an early reply to this telegram, and once again I extend you a cordial welcome to Nanking."

Having sent the telegram, Sun Yat-sen immediately announced his intention of resigning on condition that Yuan Shih-kai assumed office in Nanking, which was henceforth to become the national capital. On the same evening, looking very worn and thin after a long session, he submitted his resignation to the National Assembly in a solemn valediction:

"Today I present to you my resignation, and request you to elect a good and talented man as the new President. The election of the President is the right of the citizens, and it is not for me to interfere in any way. But according to the telegram which our delegate Dr. Wu Ting-fang was directed to send to Peking, I was to undertake to resign in favor of Mr. Yuan Shih-kai when the Emperor had abdicated, and Mr. Yuan has declared his political views in support of the Republic. I have already submitted this proposition to the honourable assembly and obtained your consent. The abdication of the Ch'ing Emperor and the union of North and South are largely due to the great exertions of Mr. Yuan. Moreover, he has declared his unconditional adhesion to the national cause. Should he be elected to serve the Republic, I am sure that he will prove himself a most loyal servant of the State. Besides, Mr. Yuan is a man of political experience, upon whose constructive ability our united nation looks forward for the consolidation of its interests. Therefore I venture to express my personal opinion and to invite the honourable Assembly carefully to consider the future welfare of the State and not to miss the opportunity of electing one who is worthy of your election. The happiness of our country depends upon your choice. Farewell!"

On the next day, February 15, the National Assembly at Nanking elected Yuan Shih-kai provisional president of the republic. The election took place in the afternoon. During the morning, accompanied by his ministers, Sun Yat-sen had paid a ceremonial visit to the tomb of the emperor Chu Yuan-chang, the first emperor of the Ming dynasty, which lies on the wooded slopes of the Purple Mountain outside Nanking. Under a gray sky the long procession, headed by the President and his cabinet, walked up the avenue of the kings, where the tombs lie under green mounds of earth, among stone images of elephants, warriors, and fabulous animals. The first representative of the new republican government was performing a solemn rite at the shrine of an old, imperial race and of the emperor Chu Yuan-chang, who was the founder of the last Chinese dynasty. This procession, which slowly and mournfully wound its way through the long avenue of kings, was coming to inform the spirits of the dead of the changed climate which had swept over China. The prayer, written by Sun Yat-sen to the spirits of the royal ancestor, begins with a violent impeachment of the Ta Ch'ing dynasty:

"Of old the Sung Dynasty became effete, and the Liao Tartars and the Yuan Dynasty Mongols seized the occasion to throw this domain of China into confusion, to the fierce indignation of gods and men. It was then that Your Majesty, our founder, rose in your wrath from obscurity and destroyed those monsters of iniquity, so that the ancient glory was won again. In twelve years you consolidated the imperial sway, and the dominions of the Great Yu were purged of pollution and cleansed from the noisome Tartar. Often in history has our noble Chinese race been enslaved by petty frontier barbarians from the north. Never have such glorious triumphs been won over them as Your Majesty achieved. But your descendants were degenerate and failed to carry on your glorious heritage; they entrusted the reins of government to bad men, and pursued a short-sighted policy. In this way they encouraged the ambitions of the Eastern Tartar savages, and fostered the growth of their power. They were thus able to take advantage of the presence of rebels to invade and possess themselves of your sacred capital.

"From a bad eminence of glory basely won, they lorded it over this most holy soil, and our beloved China's rivers and hills were defiled by their corrupting touch, while the people fell victims to the headsman's axe or the avenging sword. Although worthy patriots and faithful subjects of your dynasty crossed the mountain ranges into Canton and the far south, in the hope of redeeming the glorious Ming tradition from utter ruin, and of prolonging a thread of the old dynasty's life, although men gladly perished one after another in the forlorn attempt, Heaven's wrath remained unappeased, and mortal designs failed to achieve success. A brief and melancholy page was added to the history of your dynasty, and that was all. . . .

"Although these worthy causes were destined to ultimate defeat, the gradual trend of the national will became manifest. At last our own era dawned, the sun of freedom had risen, and a sense of the rights of the race animated men's minds. In addition the Manchu bandits could not even protect themselves. Powerful foes encroached upon the territory of China, and the dynasty parted with our sacred soil to enrich neighbouring nations. The Chinese race today may be degenerate, but it is descended from mighty men of old. How should it endure that the spirits of the great dead should be insulted by the everlasting visitation of this scourge?

"Then did patriots arise like a whirlwind or like a cloud which is suddenly manifested in the firmament. They began with the Canton insurrection; then Peking was alarmed with Wu Yueh's bomb. A year later Hsu Hsih-lin fired his bullet into the vitals of the Manchu robber chief, En Ming, Governor of Anhui. Hsiung Cheng-chi raised the standard of liberty on the Yangtse's banks; rising followed rising all over the Empire, until the secret plot against the Regent was discovered, and the abortive insurrection of Canton startled the capital. One failure followed another, but other brave men took the place of the heroes who died, and the Empire was born again to life. The bandit Manchu court was shaken with pallid terror, until the cicada shook off its shell in a glorious resurrection, and the present crowning triumph was achieved. An earthquake shook the barbarian court of Peking, and it was smitten with a paralysis. Today it has at last restored the Government to the Chinese people, and the five races of

China may dwell together in peace and mutual trust. Let us joyfully give thanks. How could we have obtained this measure of victory had not your Majesty's soul in Heaven bestowed upon us your protecting influence?

"I have heard that in the past many would-be deliverers of their country have ascended this lofty mound wherein is your sepulchre. It has served to them as a holy inspiration. As they looked down upon the surrounding rivers and upward to the hills, under an alien sway they wept in the bitterness of their hearts, but today their sorrow is turned into joy. Your legions line the approaches to the sepulchre: a noble host stands expectant. Your people have come here today to inform your Majesty of the final victory. May this lofty shrine wherein you rest gain fresh lustre from today's event and may your example inspire your descendants in the times which are to come. Spirit! Accept this offering!"

But there was no answering voice from the Emperor. The old Manchu general Nurhachi, who captured Mukden in 1621 and waited patiently for sixteen years until the whole of China fell into his hands, was followed by a surgeon who waited less patiently over a longer period of time and who was no less successful, though he held office only for forty days. At the tomb of the Ming emperor all the errors of the past were erased; and there was no reason why the new China should not grow with the same splendor which characterized the Mings.

III

ON APRIL 1 Sun Yat-sen laid down the seals of office and left Nanking, exhausted by the ceremonies in the National Assembly, and still more exhausted by the interminable arguments over the site of the capital. He had insisted that it should be in Nanking, which had been a capital at various times during the Ch'ing and Ming dynasties, but the continued presence of Yuan Shih-kai in the north and his desire that the old imperial capital should be maintained, made it difficult for the provincial delegates to come to an agreement. If Yuan Shih-kai could have accepted the invitation of the South, all suspicions would have been removed.

It was with the object of persuading the Provisional President of the necessity of visiting Nanking that delegates were sent to the north. When they reached Peking on February 26, they were received with royal honors, and the gate which was traditionally closed for all except the emperor was opened for them. Shortly after their arrival they interviewed Yuan Shih-kai, who did not insist that he should remain in the north, and even promised to come to the south as soon as he could find someone capable of maintaining order in the north. But already there were rumors that there would be outbreaks of violence as soon as he left the capital. The envoys thereupon suggested that Peking or Tientsin might be regarded as the temporary capital, but the provisional president should be inaugurated in Nanking.

Unexpectedly rioting broke out at eight o'clock on the night of April 29 outside the Chien Men, the central and most important of all the gates in the Tartar City. The rioting, which appears to have been instigated by Yuan Shih-kai on the accepted model of the time, had the effect of sending the envoys into undignified hiding places. They had good reason to be afraid. Yuan Shih-kai was not noted for clemency toward his enemies. His messages to the outgoing president were by now regarded as transparently insincere, and a *coup d'état*, with perhaps a reinstatement of the deposed boy emperor, as a mask for his personal ambitions, was expected. The next morning the rioting

THE MAKING OF A REPUBLIC

Peking of two prominent revolutionary leaders, Chang Cheng-wu and Fang Wei, on August 15 suggested that the visit might end in the massacre of all revolutionary leaders in the North. Hwang Hsing decided to turn back.

Sun Yat-sen determined to brave the lion in his den. It is interesting to examine the reasons which prompted him to continue his ill-fated voyage. There is no doubt that he was physically brave and self-reliant. His life work was completed. Many explanations could be given for the deaths of the revolutionary leaders, and not all of them proved that Yuan Shih-kai was out of sympathy with the republic. He believed in Yuan Shih-kai's good will, and at the same time he was indifferent to his own powers. Above all he was confident that the second president would not prejudice his career by murdering, openly or secretly, the man who had caused the collapse of the dynasty. And since innocence is always the best disguise in the lion's den, and still more valuable a weapon when it is not a disguise but a state of mind, he proceeded by steamer without Hwang Hsing, whose nervous, unstable character in any event would have been a hindrance to the carrying out of his plans.

On arrival in Peking in August he was lodged in the great reception rooms known as Shi Jen Foo Tung. He was banqueted by Prince Pu Lun, a direct descendant of the emperor Tao Kuang, whose arrival in San Francisco eight years before had caused him to be detained in the customs shed. The emperor's chariot brought him from the Peking railway station to the presidential palace. The child emperor P'u Yi's mother, the dowager empress Lung Yu, who had signed the abdication, sent messages politely inquiring about his health, and he was asked to address Chinese Christians in the American Congregational Church. He spoke in southern Mandarin, admitting the influence of Christian teaching upon his life as a revolutionary:

"Men say that the revolution originated with me. I do not deny the charge. But where did the idea of revolution come from? It came because from my youth I have had intercourse with foreign missionaries. Those from America and Europe with whom I associated put the ideals of freedom and liberty within my head and heart. Now I call upon the church to help in the establishment of a new government. The Republic cannot endure unless there is that virtue—the righteousness for which the Christian religion stands—at the centre of a nation's life."

Virtue, however, is rarely the emblem of autocracy; and when Sun Yat-sen visited Yuan Shih-kai in the presidential palace, the atmosphere of autocracy surrounded him on all sides. During one of the evening talks in the President's private room the lights suddenly went out. Unexpectedly Yuan Shih-kai took the visitor's hand and comforted him, saying: "Don't be afraid." Long years of surgery had given Sun Yat-sen's hands no disposition to tremble at sudden emergencies; and the President was compelled to conclude that the visitor's personal courage stood no further need of testing. Henceforward the lion sheathed its claws.

The conversations between the adversaries lasted well into September. Almost everything concerning the destiny of China was discussed. From the Six-Power Loan and the teaching of social science in the schools, they passed to the disposal of government mines, the organization of political parties, the prospect of opening large areas of agricultural land for settlement, and the administration of provincial loans. When Sun Yat-sen finally left the palace, he publicly announced that they were in substantial agreement on all major issues. As a result of their conversations, the President issued an eight-point political program, which was said to have been agreed upon by Sun Yat-sen, Li Yuan-hung, and Hwang Hsing, who changed his mind and reached Peking in September. The feeling between the protagonists in the drama was never better, and at a banquet given by Yuan Shih-kai, Sun Yat-sen is reported to have said: "If Your Excellency remains President of China for ten years and if you can raise a million soldiers, then it will be possible for me to cover China with a network of railways ten thousand miles long."

On the subject of railways, always the project nearest to Sun Yat-sen's heart, they appear to have been in complete agreement, and shortly afterward the former president was appointed director-general of railway development, a post which he appears to have coveted more than any other. His only instructions were to draft plans for railway development throughout the whole of China and to submit them to foreign financiers. The center of mineral wealth lay in the north, and he immediately set out on a tour which comprised Kalgan, Taiyuanfu, Tsinan, and Tsingtao. A month later he returned to the Yangtse Valley and set up a bureau of railway development in Shanghai, having made plans to construct 75,000 miles of government railway in ten years at a cost of three billion dollars gold. From the headquarters of the new bureau he wrote an open letter to "the Friends of China in the United States of America," in which he hoped to dispel the rumors of fresh outbreaks in the interior and to induce foreign financiers to advance capital for his projects. In this letter his attitude toward Yuan Shih-kai appears to be one of the utmost friendliness:

"President Yuan is the head of the nation, the strong worthy leader of his people, and I am not authorized to speak for him, for his Cabinet or for the National Assembly; but I believe I am voicing the sentiment of a united and unanimous people when I warn trouble-makers at home or abroad, that the Chinese nation has joined the great family of republics to remain a member thereof at whatever cost or sacrifice. . . . Now that the country is again at peace, except in certain remote and unimportant districts, I look for a big increase in commerce. With people everywhere working, with peace at north, south, east and west, the country is bound to be prosperous and the Government stable and substantial."

He now imagined a vast network of railways which would penetrate deep into the remote provinces of Kansu, Szechuan, and Yunnan. He was perfectly sincere in the belief that China could only be unified through communications. At Shanghai, near the Office of Railway Development, a temple to the Queen of Heaven had been erected by popular subscription on the ruins of a railway station destroyed by superstitious wreckers. By the populace in the remote interior the railway train was regarded with suspicion and horror still. Sun Yat-sen publicly deplored this attitude in his countrymen. Just as Lenin was to say later that revolutionary reconstruction would remain unfulfilled until the day when every village possessed electric light, so Sun Yat-sen insisted that the first principle of reconstruction lay in communications, and particularly in railways. If the whole of China could be opened out to foreign and internal trade on a scale never envisaged before, the livelihood of the people would automatically increase and the revolution would have accomplished its final aim of giving everyone sufficient wealth and security to live peacefully with his neighbor. But this mood was not to last very long. Some time later, when the early promises of Yuan Shih-kai remained unfulfilled, he was to write in a mood akin to desperation:

"At the birth of the Republic I exerted myself to advocate that the goal of the revolutionary programme should consist in revolutionary construction. But most of my comrades did not think that my ideals were likely, and though I reassured them, and argued with them over and over again, it was still in vain. They considered my ideal too high. But sometimes I wonder whether my ideal is too high, or their intelligence too low."

In his autobiography he reveals his disappointment still more clearly:

"Unfortunately the Revolution was scarcely completed when the members of our party turned out to be of a different opinion from myself, considering my ideals too elevated and unobtainable for the reconstruction of modern China. Some of my comrades even began to entertain doubts concerning the realization of our programme. So it came about that my programme had less chance of being realised when I held the position of President than when I was the leader of the party preparing the Revolution. On the other hand my party comrades cannot escape the reproach of insufficient conviction and effort in the realization of our revolutionary ideals and the carrying out of our revolutionary programme."

It was not until 1914, when Yuan Shih-kai's assumption of the dictatorship finally brought parliamentary government to its knees, that it became generally realized within the Kuomintang that the revolution had failed, not by overstating its case but by underestimating the idealism of the Chinese masses. A letter written by Chen Chih-mei to General Hwang Hsing at this time reveals the discordance between revolutionary effort and revolutionary pretensions:

"Before the Revolution of 1911, men were accustomed to say that Sun Yat-sen was an idealist and even today there are people who hold this opinion against him. But with the evidence of past events before us, let us look back and ask ourselves who it was who brought our party to such a train of reverses. Was it Sun Yat-sen by his idealism, or those who thought his ideal too high and therefore opposed him? Because formerly we mistook his idealism for something else, we were defeated; and we shall continue to be defeated until we return to a programme of idealism according to his original ideas."

To the lasting despair of the Director-General of Railway Development, no railways were built during his period of office. The revolution had been accomplished, pigtails had been cut off, the Manchus had been deprived of their hereditary power, the Emperor lived in seclusion in the Summer Palace, and many plaster-cast gods had been thrown by a still-superstitious populace from their pedestals in the temples. The revolution was incomplete. The livelihood of the people was still insufficient for their needs. And now, in the full tide of reaction, the throne of the Ch'ings which had been overthrown was pieced together and a new emperor, consecrated by bankers and reactionary officers, climbed shakily into the seat.

IV

WITHIN six months of abandoning the presidency, Sun Yat-sen saw the revolutionary party of the Tung Meng Hui become the politically ineffective Kuomintang. The new party held its inaugural meeting in Peking on August 25, 1912. Sun Yat-sen was not entirely in favor of the new organization, which had been welded together from many parties with divergent principles by Sung Chiao-jen; and from the beginning he appears to have feared the emergence of a nonrevolutionary group. When revolution is exchanged for politics, the vision perishes. And though he gave the new movement his blessing at the inaugural meeting, and accepted the presidency of the new party (a post which was little more than titular), he began to hope that something more startling might emerge, either as a result of his own efforts or from the momentum the old party had gathered in its years in the wilderness. The keynote of the new movement, however, was sounded in its manifesto, wherein nothing remained of the old arduous comradeship and sacrifice of the original revolutionary members:

"We declare that we shall adopt as our principles the idea of social service as a preparation to the introduction of socialism in order to facilitate the better the standard of living, and to employ the powers and strength of the government quickly and evenly to develop the resources of the country."

No more drab manifesto could have been written. The impulse which brought the revolution into being had disappeared, and in its place there existed only the threat of an exalted bureaucracy. But Sun Yat-sen could do nothing. He had alienated many by his criticisms of the lack of revolutionary spirit among the officials; he was pleased when the old guard of the Tung Meng Hui organized a Tung Meng Hui club in Shanghai in the vain hope of preserving the revolutionary character of a party which had died, and could only come to birth again on the emergence of a new revolutionary spirit.

Sun Yat-sen remained in Shanghai at the office of the Railway Development Board until the end of the year. In February 1913 he sailed for Japan, ostensibly to study industrial conditions and railways, but more probably to study public reaction to the new regime in China. As director-general of railway development he was offered the use of a private coach on the Japanese Imperial Railways. When he arrived at the Tokyo railway station on February 14, he was greeted by more than three thousand wildly clamoring Chinese students, who threw flowers on his path, presented him with scrolls, and demonstrated their affection for the first president. Accompanied by his wife and by E-ling Soong, the eldest daughter of Charles Soong, acting as his secretary, he attended banquets and received deputations and made a few speeches, in which he was clearly at pains to show his loyalty to Yuan Shih-kai. He was impressed with the method by which the Japanese had been able to build railways out of domestic loans, and suggested that a similar procedure might with advantage be followed by the Chinese. When he left the port of Moji on March 18, he was busily preparing a report on railways for presentation to the chief executive. It was while he was still at sea, three days off from Shanghai, that a murder took place in China which was to alter the political structure of the state more profoundly than any dynastic murder in the past.

Sung Chiao-jen, the Kuomintang candidate for the premiership, was shot dead at ten o'clock at night just as he was about to board the night express for Peking. The North Railway Station in Shanghai was beflagged in honor of his arrival. He was seen talking with General Hwang Hsing, he held a cigarette to his lips, and suddenly the cigarette fell on the platform, and it was some moments before it was realized that the tall, bald-headed intellectual lying on the railway track had been shot dead. The situation was ugly. The murder of Chang Cheng-wu and Fang Wei the previous year was still remembered. Yuan Shih-kai's complicity in the assassination was readily believed by Kuomintang members. Sung Chiao-jen had been one of the most uncompromising advocates of parliamentary reform; he was the organizing genius of the party and a stern critic of the reorganization loan which Yuan Shih-kai was seeking to raise on the international market. His death was the signal for violent attacks on the President among the Kuomintang newspapers, who accused the Peking government of direct responsibility for the murder and implicated a high official of the ministry of the interior.

A few days after Sung Chiao-jen's assassination Sun

THE MAKING OF A REPUBLIC

Yat-sen arrived in Shanghai, where he received an ovation. He was the only man who could restore the constitution, and he was powerless. He immediately wrote a manifesto urging the revolutionaries to rise against Yuan Shih-kai, but Hwang Hsing opposed him, insisting that the republic had been established on a basis of law, and nothing would be gained by a course of violent action, for the murder was still *sub judice* and the country was sick of violence. Against this argument Sun Yat-sen knew himself defeated. Later he even intended to sail for Kwangtung and declare its independence himself; he also ordered Chen Chih-mei to declare the independence of Shanghai; but the revolutionaries had lost their fervor, and even when the northern navy came to negotiate with the revolutionaries, the latter were so much at odds among themselves that they procrastinated until it was too late. Sun Yat-sen lost all hope in Yuan Shih-kai.

The National Assembly was to open on April 8. Though numerically stronger than any other party, the Kuomintang failed to achieve a majority. And while the debates in the chamber continued, Sung Chiao-jen's death and the position of Sun Yat-sen in the struggle became inevitably less important than the immediate problem of the reorganization loan. The debate was becoming increasingly bitter. The vice-president of the senate, Dr. C. T. Wang, hotly opposed the loan at a meeting of the consortium group held in the splendid offices of the Hong Kong and Shanghai Banking Corporation in the legation quarter of Peking. The power of the National Assembly to assert itself was being put to an ultimate test. Money was needed by the republic. A million pounds sterling from a Belgian banking syndicate had been sufficient to tide over the difficulties of the spring of 1912, but they were absurdly insufficient for China's needs. A loan floated in the autumn by a member of the London stock exchange provided a further five million pounds sterling for the winter.

In spite of these loans, Yuan Shih-kai was in the position of a chief executive with an exchequer unreasonably disproportional to China's potential wealth; and in despair of domestic loans, he began to make overtures for a far larger loan from an international consortium of British, American, French, German, Japanese, and Russian bankers. On March 16 President Wilson announced that the United States government could not approve of American participation in the loan on the grounds that the conditions attached to it compromised the independence of China. The Six-Power Consortium became the Five-Power Consortium, and in defiance of the majority decision of the National Assembly a loan of nine million gold taels was pushed through.

In a last effort to avoid what came to be considered as a mortgage upon all the movable property in China, Sun Yat-sen sent a telegram to Dr. Cantlie in London imploring the British government to use its influence to prevent the issue of a loan which would give Yuan Shih-kai the moral support of the powers and sufficient ammunition and weapons to provide his model army for many years to come. The telegram read:

"Cantlie 140 Harley Street London. Submit on my behalf following appeal to British Government, Parliament, Governments of Europe, and give same widest publicity in all Press. To Governments and peoples of foreign powers. As a result of careful investigation by officers appointed by Government to enquire into recent murder of Nationalist leader Sung Chiao-jen in Shanghai, the fact is clearly established that Peking Government is seriously implicated in the crime. Consequently people are extremely indignant, and situation has become so serious that nation is on the verge of most acute and dangerous crisis yet experienced. Government, conscious of its guilt and enormity of its offense, and realising strength of wave of indignation sweeping over the nation as direct result of its criminal deeds and wicked betrayal of trust reposed in it, and perceiving that it is likely to lead to its downfall, suddenly and unconstitutionally concluded loan for pounds 25,000,000 sterling with quintuple group despite vigorous protests of representatives of nation now assembled in Peking. This high-handed and unconstitutional action of government instantly accentuated intense indignation which has been caused by foul murder of Sung Chiao-jen, so that at present time fury of the people is worked up to white heat and terrible convulsion appears almost inevitable. Indeed so acute has crisis become that widespread smouldering embers may burst forth in devastating conflagration at any moment. From date of birth of Republic I have striven for unity, peace, concord and prosperity. I recommended Yuan Shih-kai for presidency because there appeared reasons for believing that by doing so unification of nation and dawn of era of prosperity would thereby be hastened. Ever since, I have done all I could to evolve peace, order and government out of chaos created by revolution. I earnestly desire to preserve peace throughout republic, but my efforts will be rendered ineffective if financiers will supply Peking Government with money that would or probably will be used in waging war against people. If country is plunged into war at this juncture, it will inevitably inflict terrible misery and suffering upon people who are just beginning to recover from dislocation of trade and losses of various kinds caused by revolution. For establishment of republic they have sacrificed much and are now determined to preserve it at all costs. I appeal to all who have lasting welfare of mankind at heart to extend to us in this hour of need their moral assistance in avoiding unnecessary bloodshed and in shielding my countrymen from sad fate which they have done absolutely nothing to deserve."

To Sun Yat-sen's arguments, the financiers in Peking could respond that the revolutionary had performed exactly the same disservice to China when he mortgaged the Hanyang ironworks to Japanese financial interests. Money had to be raised; the government had to go on. But how was the money to be raised? There was no question but that the consortium loan was, in principle, wrong. Nor was there any doubt that the revolutionaries, had they been in effective power, would have spent some part of the money on enlarging and modernizing their army. But by May 21 the loan had been oversubscribed, and on that day the break between Sun Yat-sen and Yuan Shih-kai became complete. The storm rose over a country still suffering from past wounds. Both men played for position. When rumors of unrest in the Yangtse Valley reached Peking, Yuan Shih-kai replaced revolutionary commanders with his own men and began a campaign against Sun Yat-sen, by pamphlet and newspaper reports, which was equaled in virulence only by the campaign which Sun Yat-sen waged against him.

The "Second Revolution," however, was not the product of the antagonism between two men. In all revolutions, a second revolution is inevitable. It did not come at once, but grew gradually out of the conflicting loyalties of the time. The dismissal in June and July of three provincial governors of Kiangsi, Kwangtung, and Anhui, all members of the Kuomintang party, led to scattered outbreaks of violence in the provinces, but it was only on July 2 that Sun Yat-sen sent an ultimatum to Yuan Shih-kai:

"Formerly you were invited to the presidential office to bear the heavy responsibility of the country, and now you should leave this office in order to save the country from disorder. If you follow my advice, I will persuade the

THE MAKING OF A REPUBLIC

soldiers and the people of the South to lay down their arms. If you reject my advice, I shall adopt the same measures against you which have been used to overthrow the absolute monarchy. I have made up my mind. This is my last word, and I hope you will take it to heart."

The ultimatum had been preceded by a warning. On April 9 a short message was telegraphed from Shanghai: "You are betraying your country. I must oppose you in the same way that I opposed the Ch'ing dynasty."

The dismissal of the three governors, Li Lieh-chun, Pao Wen-hui, and Hu Han-min, was not so much the signal as an occasion for the renewed outbreak in the south. A few days after his dismissal Li Lieh-chun declared the independence of the province of Kiangsi. Later the same day Pao Wen-hui declared for the independence of Anhui, and on the next day, July 13, Chen Chiung-ming proclaimed the independence of Kwangtung. On the fifteenth Hwang Hsing proclaimed the independence of Nanking, and five days later Hsu Chung-chih and Sun Tao-jen came out with the independence of the province of Fukien. More declarations of independence followed. Tan Yen-kai in Hunan and Chen Chih-mei in Shanghai followed almost immediately, and similar outbreaks were reported in various towns of Szechuan and Yunnan. On the twenty-third Sun Yat-sen received a telegram announcing his dismissal from the post of director-general of railway development on the grounds that he was financing rebellion with funds advanced for the construction of railways.

The declarations of independence had not been made without bloodshed. On the twentieth fighting broke out in Shanghai. Chiang Kai-shek was about to leave for Germany, when a hurried conference called by Chen Chih-mei led to an attack on the arsenal. The telegraphs were captured; the arsenal remained impregnable. Heavy fighting broke out on the afternoon of the twenty-second, when the revolutionary troops assembled at Lunghua and advanced under a clear sky against the heavily defended walls of the arsenal. After sunset searchlights playing from the gunboat *Haichuan* onto the attackers enabled the defenders to repulse the attack. Fighting continued until the evening of the twenty-ninth, but the battle was already lost. The combined effect of the superior gunpower of Yuan Shih-kai's troops and of the enfilading fire from the gunboats proved too strong for the attackers, and the revolutionaries retired the same evening. Meanwhile Nanking held out, and it was not until September 1, when the last outposts of the revolutionaries in the outskirts of Nanking were rounded up, that the revolt came to an end.

At the beginning of the rebellion and on the advice of Chen Chih-mei, Sun Yat-sen escaped from Shanghai on a German cargo vessel in the hope of reaching Canton before serious fighting broke out. The vessel discharged at Foochow and he was held up until it was too late. By the time he reached Hong Kong, the revolt had failed and Chen Chiung-ming was on his way to Singapore. Sun Yat-sen sailed for Formosa and later for Tokyo, where he was followed by Hwang Hsing and a few of the more important revolutionary leaders from the south.

The second revolution had failed completely, yet the National Assembly, sitting in the Temple of Heaven in Peking, still retained a strong and influential body of Kuomintang members determined to curtail the powers of the President. The committee was working on a permanent constitution based on the electoral system, and by October 26 a proclamation and a complete constitution were already in existence. If Yuan Shih-kai had accepted the constitution, he might have been able to carry a united China with him, but by fighting against the constitution with the same ruthlessness with which he fought the revolutionaries, he alienated the sympathies of the people. His government was not yet recognized by the powers; he was still provisional president, and until he was formally elected by the National Assembly, he would remain in exactly the same position as Sun Yat-sen when he returned from London in 1911.

Early in September a flood of telegrams from governors and high officials began to arrive at the National Assembly demanding the election of Yuan Shih-kai as president of the republic. Many of the telegrams were forged; others were sent in good faith by high officials who had no idea that their messages would have the effect of forcing an issue which could only be determined by the assembly acting in freedom. To make matters worse, Yuan Shih-kai organized a citizens' corps to maintain order in the neighborhood of the Temple of Heaven. At the third voting, the combined influence of the flood of telegrams and menaces from high officials and provincial military governors, and the threats of the carefully chosen and disreputable citizens' corps, secured the election, and on October 6, 1913, he was proclaimed for the second time "Great President" of the republic, taking the oath of office four days later. As the result of an election brought about by intimidation, bribery, and corruption, the new republic was recognized by the powers.

Profound cleavages in parliament and internal administration are not solved by bribery; and since the growth of a state follows organic laws, a solution imposed from without only postpones the day of reckoning. On October 26 the constitution known as the "Constitution of the Temple of Heaven," because the legislators met in the temple, was laid before the new president. The articles describing the powers of the president offended Yuan Shih-kai, who is reported to have declared: "In my work I am conscious only of serving the country's best interests. Then why do you hamper me with these absurd restrictions?"

Once more a flood of denunciatory telegrams arrived from the provinces. The National Assembly stood firm, with the result that eight Kuomintang members were arrested on October 31, and shortly afterward the Kuomintang party was dissolved by proclamation. Three months later, in January 1914, there were three hundred vacant seats in the National Assembly, and no effort was being made to elect new members. A new political council, known as the Yo Fa Hui, consisting of fifty-seven members appointed by the government, was summoned, however, to take its place.

Autocracy rode high. With the Kuomintang banned, many of the leaders in prison, and a new constitution enlarging the term of the presidency to ten years, Yuan Shih-kai could look forward to a period of tranquillity and autocracy, the tranquillity made still more tranquil by the absence of an opposition, and the autocracy made absolute because the ruler was no longer compelled to obey the traditional codes of the emperors. The wheel had turned full circle. The fifty-seven members of the new council contained four representatives from Peking, two from each province, eight from Mongolia, Tibet, and Sinkiang, and four from the chambers of commerce. In a country where a single province like Szechuan may contain a population equal to that of France, no more unrepresentative council could have been chosen. And it was in this climate of autocracy, where the autocrat himself was unconscious of any opposition (for all manifestations of disloyalty were hidden from him), that China entered upon the fatal year 1914.

What were the causes of the failure of the second revolution? Chen Chih-mei held the view that the failure had arisen because the revolutionaries confined their attention to the South. He introduced the slogan: "We must capture the North." The revolutionary foundations should have been laid among the traditional centers of Chinese culture, along the Yellow River, in the northeast of China and more particularly in the area around Peking. Yuan Shih-kai had stationed loyal troops at every strategic point in the south. Other reasons for the failure, the lack of ammunition and trained military leadership, the insufficiency of the original revolutionary ardor, the bureaucracy of the revolutionaries once they had attained power, were also brought forward, but it was left to Sun Yat-sen to point the moral of the failure. In a letter to General Hwang Hsing he wrote: "A small group of revolutionaries from the 'Tung Meng Hui' succeeded in overthrowing the Manchus in a few years, but hundreds and thousands of Kuomintang members remained impotent in the face of Yuan's aggressions. Why is this?" Part, perhaps the greater part of the blame, he laid on the anarchic tendency of the Chinese to split into warring groups; their habitual dissidence had failed to produce order because they prized freedom so highly that they refused the slightest compulsion. In *The Three Principles of the People* written twelve years later, he said:

"In the second year of the Republic Yuan Shih-kai contracted large foreign loans without the consent of Parliament, killed Sung Chiao-jen and did everything possible to injure the Republic. I urged all the provinces to rise immediately and punish Yuan, but because everyone in the party was talking of freedom, there was no unity. In the south-western provinces, for example, from divisional commanders and brigadier generals down to privates, everyone was talking about his own personal liberty. None would work together. Then this liberty was extended to the provinces, and each province insisted on its own freedom and refused to cooperate with other provinces. The southern provinces, which were enjoying some of the left-over glory of the Revolution of 1911, displayed great enthusiasm on the surface, but the party within was split to pieces and could not agree upon orders. As for Yuan Shih-kai he had the old six-army defence organization of the Peiyang Party; the divisional commanders, brigadier generals and all the soldiers in these six armies were under splendid discipline, and subject to one command. In a word Yuan Shih-kai had a firm organisation, while we in the Revolutionary Party were a sheet of scattering sand. . . . This shows that a principle that suits other countries does not necessarily suit China. The revolutions of the West made use of the struggle for liberty, but the Chinese Revolution cannot be said to aim at liberty. If we declare that we are fighting for liberty, we shall remain a loose sheet of scattering sand * and we shall never be unified, we shall never attain the desired end of our revolution. . . . The Europeans fought for individual liberty, but today we have a different use for liberty. How shall the term 'liberty' be applied. If we apply it to a person, we shall become a sheet of loose sand; on no account must we give more liberty to the person; but we must give greater liberty to the State. The individual should not have too much liberty, but the nation should have complete liberty of action. When the nation has complete liberty of action, then she will be strong, but in order to make the nation free, we must each sacrifice our personal freedom. Those students who practise rigorous discipline are able to work diligently day after day, and thus they spend time and effort upon learning: when their studies are completed, their knowledge is enlarged and their powers have been multiplied, and they are of service to the nation. Soldiers who sacrifice their personal liberty are able to obey orders, and thus they repay their country with their loyalty and assist the nation to achieve its freedom. If students and

---

* This term, which was later to become famous, was first used in the Confucian classic known as the *Shu King*, II, i.

soldiers spoke only of freedom, they would be in a state of continual licence. Schools must have rules and armies must have discipline. What kind of a school has no rules? What kind of army has no discipline?"

But the lack of discipline, as he realized, was deeply planted in the people. It was a herculean task to make order where there was no order before, and he knew the penalties of failure. Henceforward it became his task to make a block of granite out of the loose eddies of scattering sand.

V

THE revolutionary leaders, meeting in Japan, were faced with a crisis. The failure of the second revolution involved the failure of the first, for there can be no advantage in destroying one autocracy for the purpose of instituting a second. The power of Yuan Shih-kai had never been greater. His term of election was now increased to ten years, and he possessed supreme authority over finance, the armed forces, the declaration of war, and the conclusion of treaties. In January 1914 the last remnant of parliament had been dissolved and the new "Constitutional Pact," an arrangement by which Yuan Shih-kai could still speak of his constitutionally appointed powers, gave him a favorable position in the eyes of foreign powers.

Against such an autocracy desperate measures were needed, but means for enforcing them were still being disputed when Sun Yat-sen, on July 18, 1914, inaugurated his fourth revolutionary party at the Tsukichi Seiyonen hotel in Tokyo under the name of the Chinese Revolutionary Party (Chung Hua Ke-min-tang). There was no longer any reason to hide the revolutionary character of the party, and though the new party resembled the old in many ways, it refused to countenance bureaucracy in its own camp. At last the lessons of the second revolution were being learned. Once more candidates for membership had to be introduced by two members; they were asked to make a solemn pledge of loyalty and sign the register with their fingerprints. The new party distinguished itself from the three previous parties in its increasing rigor. In the letters written at the time Sun Yat-sen shows how he was appalled by the disunity and bureaucracy which prevailed in the Kuomintang party, and sought every means to combat it. In a letter to a friend overseas he wrote: "The Kuomintang appeared to be powerful and influential, yet disunity and disorganisation prevailed within it. Furthermore the members were blinded by the theory of equality and liberty, and set the orders of their leaders at defiance. Thus the leaders were mere puppets and the members were no less scattered than sand." And in his autobiography written many years later, he said: "The state of affairs became so discouraging that I made up my mind to fight single-handed. Therefore I organised the 'Chung Hua Ke-Min-Tang' on the strictest principles with the object of removing all social and political evils and restoring the supremacy of law."

He began to grow frightened of the example of France, of whom a distinguished German had said: "France is drunk with liberty. When she has raved and screamed, she will fall down dead drunk, and when she wakes up she will find herself in prison." Now more than ever he grew afraid of liberty. Rigor! Rigor! Rigor! In all his speeches and conversations of the time can be heard the whiplash descending on friend and foe alike.

The natural anarchic tendency of the Chinese to live behind high walls, their desire for freedom from all interference however just and necessary, their arbitrariness and willful destruction and sabotage of the law must be extirpated for all time. The high walls must be broken down; the whole course of Chinese family life, with its intimate and abiding loyalties transcending all others; their latent fatalism, their instinctive seeking for a refuge, encouraged by the three religions of China—all these must disappear, and in their place there must be implicit obedience, not to the elders or to the ancestors, but to the urgent tasks of reconstruction ahead. The old adage, "The Emperor stands at the center of the world like the hollow of a whirlpool which creates everything," must disappear, and in its place there were four hundred and fifty million emperors striving actively for a new revelation. Again and again he repeated from Mencius: "The work of man can change Heaven." But men must be guided, they must be ruled, they must obey with the same lack of self-consciousness as the soldier at the front; and in this mood of terrible earnestness, demanding discipline from all men, Sun Yat-sen began the reconstruction of the party.

It was perhaps time. Already men were comparing the state of China to the period of the Wars of the Three Kingdoms—a state of unbridled opportunism, assassination, and heroism. This state of anarchy could not endure indefinitely. Yuan Shih-kai himself had realized its dangers, and for this reason assumed autocratic power; but he failed to perceive that the greatest danger was his own ignorance of the nature of the dangers he was compelled to fight. He was no longer the spiral hollow of a whirlpool, but a silent wedge driving into the heart of the people. Anarchy increased. When the newspapers are muzzled, when prices are rising, when free criticism is taken from the people and autocracy reigns in ignorance of what is passing through the minds of the people, then there grows among the people a tendency towards obstinacy and sabotage. This was the position in which Yuan Shih-kai found himself.

There were strong forces at work, not only among the foreign capitalists, to put an end to a situation which had persisted with one brief, heroic exception since 1876; and Sun Yat-sen was too much of a politician not to know that final victory might depend upon small increments of fortune. A statesman like Yuan Shih-kai might have saved the situation by making terms with his adversaries. He was still popular in the army, though his popularity derived from his exertions in the past and not from his influence at present. He surrounded himself with relatives who held important government posts. Newspapers edited by his son were already being issued in two versions: one for consumption in the Presidency, the other for consumption by the people. He was riding high, but like the heroes of Attic tragedy, he knew no means of measuring the distance of his fall.

Sun Yat-sen, like a mole burrowing deep underground, knew that he could undermine the adversary only if he was armed with a party in which implicit obedience was obtained. With such a party under his control, it might not even be necessary to create a great revolutionary army. The revolutionaries in 1911 had destroyed the army from within: their faith had destroyed a mountain. But the seed of revolution had been deeply sown, and by the time the party had come to power, a casual opportunism rather than faith characterized the minor revolutionary leaders. This lack of faith was castigated by him with no attempt to hide his bitterness: "Formerly, when the revolutionary party overthrew the Manchu Government, it did away with the 'Great Emperor.' When the 'Great Emperor' was gone, there grew up a host of small emperors. These small emperors were as despotic as usual, and compared with the 'Great Emperor' were more tyrannical."

THE MAKING OF A REPUBLIC 139

Under this new tyranny democracy was impotent, and Sun Yat-sen's proud boast that the revolution of 1911 had "demolished the monarchy and produced a situation from which democracy could rise anew" was sadly at odds with the real situation in 1914, a situation which has been described by the poet William Blake:

> The hound of Vengeance found the Bed
> To which the Purple Tyrant fled;
> The iron hand crush'd the Tyrant's head,
> And became a Tyrant in its stead.

Rigor must become the watchword of the new order; and though Sun Yat-sen was forced to watch Wang Ching-wei's defection to France and Hwang Hsing's disappearance to America, neither approving of his assumption of autocratic power within the party, he could see no other way out.

From the Tung Meng Hui the new party took over the conception of the three stages of revolutionary development: military government, government by party tutelage, and constitutional government by the people. From Chen Chih-mei the party derived the conception of a northeastern rebellion centered upon Peking. Chen Chih-mei and Tai Chih-tao were accordingly sent to Dairen to establish revolutionary organs and to arrange for simultaneous uprisings against the dictatorship. They returned to Tokyo six months later with favorable comments on the conditions at the port, but they insisted that the Manchurian gendarmerie were equal to the task of stamping out a rebellion. A little later conditions in Manchuria grew more favorable, and in June 1914, shortly after the inaugural meeting of the new party, it was reported that two of the commanders of the army in Manchuria were anxious that Chen Chih-mei should proceed to the north and lead a rising. Chen Chih-mei was unable to go, and Chiang Kai-shek and Ting Kung-liang were sent instead.

The new mission was dangerous. Chiang Kai-shek spoke indifferent Mandarin; he had no personal knowledge of Manchuria and no followers in the northeastern provinces; and the towns it would be necessary to visit—Harbin, Tsitsihar, and the region of Heilungkiang—were known to be heavily garrisoned by loyal troops. In spite of these difficulties, he stayed six months and returned to Tokyo to make a comprehensive report on the situation, relating that he saw little hope of rebellion and Chen Chin-mei's theory of attack would have to go by default. Once again the conspirators were faced with the problem of discovering the Archimedean point by which they could move the amorphous weight of China; and it is significant that with the exception of a small uprising in Hunan in 1915 and an attack upon the arsenal in Shanghai during the same year, the remaining revolts occurred in the south. The city of Canton, where Sun Yat-sen spent his early years and where his son was later to be mayor, remained the revolutionary center of China. He sent Chen Chih-mei to Shanghai and hoped for further rebellions in the Yangtse Valley, but he still dreamed of conquering China from the South. Chen Chih-mei's theory was only temporarily shaken; the importance of the northeast still retained its primacy, and thirteen years later, when Sun Yat-sen was dead and civil war had laid the country prostrate, the old theory was revived in another form when Chiang Kai-shek set out from the south on his final expedition against the northern warlords. This time victory was complete; but of its three protagonists, only one remained.

VI

"I HAVE made up my mind to fight single-handed," Sun Yat-sen wrote after the failure of the second revolution. But like most men who fight singlehanded, he felt the mortifications of loneliness: against these superb engines of destruction he knew himself powerless. Hwang Hsing and Wang Ching-wei had left Tokyo and taken flight in the desert. He, who could command the obedience of most, found himself suddenly confronted with the disagreement of two of his most intimate friends. He, whose intellect was fashioned for the uses of the spirit, could not live on spirit alone. Like all men who create, he was compelled in his loneliness to enter the mystical city where even loneliness is transformed into understanding, and the terrible acedia which occurs at intervals during the lives of all scholars and all creative spirits becomes another kind of blessedness altogether.

But Tokyo in the summer of 1914 was a city of intrigue and renascent imperialism, by no means the city he desired. He was far from his family; his visions had turned to ruins; the loneliness which afflicted him during his youth had increased with age; and he was still undecided about his future plans. At forty-eight, when most men are settled for life and have some accomplishments to show for their struggles, he led the exasperating life of a refugee living under an assumed name with little or nothing to show for his battles. Rigor had become the watchword of the new movement, but it is necessary to realize that this rigor was partly dictated by the defensive mechanism of failure. Rigor! Stubbornness! Optimism! With these weapons the new Christopher Columbus, after long years of poring over maps, and after great suffering, set out on his new voyage to the East. The aim was the greatest prize recorded in history—the conquest of China.

He had hoped, ever since he assumed the presidency, to make bloodless conquests. To conquer a country with an idea is historically more efficient than conquest by the sword. A few months after the revolution a schoolgirl in America had written an article which showed a fervent belief in the new China:

"Five months ago our wildest dreams could not have been for a Republic. To some, even the promise of an early constitutional government was received with scepticism. But deep down in the heart of every patriotic Chinese, were he a politician or a labourer, there was the anti-Manchu spirit. All the sufferings, such as famine, flood, and retrogression in every phase of life were traced to the tyrannical Manchus, and their court of dishonest officials. Oppression was the cause of that wonderful revolution which came as a blessing in disguise.

"The Revolution has established in China Liberty and Equality, those two inalienable rights of the individual which have caused the loss of so many noble and heroic lives, but there is still Fraternity to be acquired. And it may be for China, the oldest of nations, to point the way to this fraternity. In other ways, too, China will take her place in the effort to uplift humanity. A race amounting to one quarter of the world's population, and inhabiting the largest empire of the globe, whose civilisation displays so many manifestations of excellence, cannot help but be influential in the uplifting of mankind. China was the first possessor of a criminal code; her philosophers gave the world some of her noblest contributions to human thinking; while her extensive literature which has delighted and won the admiration of those learned Europeans who spent their lifetime in the exclusive study of China and her exquisite code of Social and Moral Ethics are hardly paralleled elsewhere. For centuries the Chinese have been a peace-loving people. They have esteemed the arts of peace, and neglected the arts of war, worshipped the scholar and slighted the soldier. China, with its multitudinous population, and its love of peace—love in the real essence of the word—shall stand forth as the incarnation of Peace. It cannot but be instrumental in bringing about that humanitarian movement—Universal Peace—when Rights need not be backed by armies and 'dreadnoughts,' and all political disagreements will be, at last, settled by the Hague Tribunal."

Ching-ling Soong, who wrote this essay, was a daughter of Charles Soong and a sister of Sun Yat-sen's secretary, E-ling Soong. Like her sister, she had grown up in an atmosphere of Methodist piety, a little overawed by her Bible-reading mother and the ascetic life of the Soongs in Shanghai. The Soong household was wealthy, deeply religious, ascetic, and revolutionary. At a time when the daughters of rich merchants are expected to know little more than the art of embroidery, she had seen revolutionaries entering her father's house, and she had been able to guess the reasons of his revolutionary fervor. Early in 1908 she left Shanghai and sailed for America. She spent four years at the Wesleyan College, Macon, Georgia, leaving with a B.A. in June, 1913. In America she had been distinguished by her beauty and by her deep love for English literature and revolutionary idealism; and when, after the revolution, her father sent her the new flag of the Republic, she pulled the Dragon Banner from the wall and stamped on it crying: "Down with the Dragon! Up with the flag of the Republic!"

The marriage on October 25, 1914, was kept secret for several months. Sun Yat-sen's marriage to the young university graduate was certain to raise problems, for his first wife was still living and there was every reason to avoid a scandal. The missionaries would accuse him of a crime against the Bible; the revolutionaries would accuse him of violating one of the unwritten laws of the revolution. He never answered these accusations. He had married a younger woman at a time when he desperately needed her help, and he continued to respect and love the first wife who could no longer help him in the arduous tasks ahead.

The marriage with his former wife had been ideally happy, though there were long periods when they saw each other rarely. During the eight years following the marriage, his wife lived in his mother's gray-brick house and saw him only on his rare holidays from Hong Kong and Canton. She bore him three children at Choyhung and remained at the ancestral home until the whole family was compelled to flee to Hawaii after the failure of the first revolutionary attempt in 1895, returning only in 1909 when Ah Mei sold his property in Hawaii and settled down first in Kowloon and later in Kwangchow-wan.

Sun Yat-sen's eldest son therefore received his regular schooling in Honolulu, graduating from St. Louis College. He entered the University of California as a freshman in 1911, hurrying back to China when the news of the revolution and his father's election to the presidency became known. The whole family then proceeded to Nanking, and photographs were taken of Sun Yat-sen in his presidential uniform accompanied by his wife, his three children, and the elder brother, whose services to the revolution were never sufficiently recognized during his lifetime. When Sun Yat-sen resigned the presidency, the family was once more scattered. Sun Fo and the daughters sailed for America, Ah Mei moved to Macao, and Sun Yat-sen took his wife to Shanghai when he assumed the post of director-general of railway development. He appointed Charles Soong treasurer of the newly formed bureau, and when he sailed for Japan in February 1913, he took with him his wife and Charles Soong's eldest daughter E-ling. When E-ling married Kung Hsiang-hsi, at that time a young and promising director of the Shanghai Y.M.C.A., Ching-ling took her place.

But during the spring of 1913 an event occurred in the family which plunged Sun Yat-sen into the forebodings of grief. His eldest daughter, Sun Yen, returned from America seriously ill, and in July, when the second revolution was at its height, Mrs. Sun Yat-sen accompanied the sick daughter to Macao. Here, a few weeks later, Sun Yen died; and in this city, filled with the brown monuments of a decaying empire, Mme. Sun Yat-sen remained, to become famous in the local community of the colony for her charity, her deeply religious nature, and a life of complete self-denial.

At birth Ching-ling was endowed with all the talents. She was beautiful, vivacious, intelligent, and idealistic. When Sun Yat-sen married her, she was young enough to understand the significance of the revolution, and her freedom from the prejudices of an older generation of Chinese women gave her authority to speak for the renascent China now coming to birth. She could read French; her English was perfect; she was possessed with an ardent and revolutionary temperament. She agreed with everything her husband did and said, and was as hopelessly in love with him as he was in love with her, knowing perfectly well that their motives would be misunderstood but conscious that history would forgive and understand them. Several years later, when she first appeared publicly in Canton, she was greeted with an outcry from the missionaries and even from some of the revolutionaries, who regarded her appearance as a direct assault upon the Chinese conception of the family. That Sun Yat-sen should marry again was not in dispute. What was a dispute was his evident desire to give the second wife the same status as the first; and though the quarrel continued until his death, history has already given its verdict, for both wives are now deeply respected by the Chinese and offered the peculiar veneration which is offered only to the humble and the blessed.

VII

MEANWHILE in China the reaction continued. By the end of 1913 Yuan Shih-kai had made himself president for life, dissolved parliament as Cromwell dissolved the Rump, expanded and developed the model army, revived the ceremonies at the Altar of Heaven and appointed his own nominees to all important posts. He was determined to maintain his position, and if China had been an island living in isolation from the rest of the world, he might have been able to maintain his power indefinitely.

Unfortunately for China "splendid isolation" belonged to the past, and that remote, vast island in Asia over which the early emperors once ruled was already perishing in a flood of communications; and now, from every newspaper and wireless mast, and from every neighboring island, power was being wielded more despotically than ever before. Though the power of guns and newspapers was more effective than the decrees which issued from the presidential palace, and though the power of the relatively silent opposition was continually being reflected in the strange restlessness now beginning to attack the people, Yuan Shih-kai could still exert his authority through the army. The dictator of a large state is at the mercy of forces beyond his control. He cannot stand still. He must continually increase his country's sphere of interest. Yuan

Shih-kai failed to do this, with the inevitable result that he was strangled by his own impotence.

When the First World War broke out in the summer of 1914, China stood neutral. Germany had established a naval base and trading station at Tsingtao. Early in November a combined force of Japanese and British troops took it by assault. The task completed, the two British battalions sailed for England and the Japanese battalions were left in control. The Chinese made efforts to regain possession of the base by declaring the abolition of war zone at Tsingtao on January 7, 1915. The Japanese newspapers, with the connivance and perhaps under the orders of the Japanese government, thereupon began a campaign of vilification and defamation against China and the Chinese government.

Late on the night of January 18 a motorcar bearing a Japanese flag entered the gates of the presidential palace. The Chinese guards saluted, and Mr. Hioki Eki, Japanese minister to China, descended, and a few minutes later presented to the chief executive the famous note now known as the Twenty-one Demands. These demands were not only unprecedented in nature, but the procedure of presentation was in total disregard of diplomatic usage. The demands should have been presented to the minister of foreign affairs, not to Yuan Shih-kai. The demands were of the most far-reaching character and were accompanied by an ultimatum.

In twenty-one paragraphs, typewritten on note paper watermarked with dreadnoughts and machine guns, China was asked to accept changes in the administration of the province of Shantung which would lead inevitably to its colonization by Japan, the extension of all Japanese leases and rights in Manchuria to ninety-nine years, control over the main sources of iron and coal supply in the Yangtse Valley, an undertaking by China not to lease to a third power any harbors or islands along the coast of China, and the virtual surrender of railways, mines and harbor works in Fukien province. Negotiations lasted five months, and no conclusions were reached until the final Japanese ultimatum of May 7 compelled China to accept the majority of the demands, or go to war against a country allied to the greatest military powers in the world. Against the formidable strength of Japan, Yuan Shih-kai was powerless. Appeals to the Allies went unheard. Yuan Shih-kai postponed the inevitable surrender as long as possible, but he was in no position to wage war singlehanded with Japan, and when the ultimatum was accepted and he had become the national scapegoat, he was heard to say: "The Japanese are determined to fight us. It is not my fault that they have already won their first battles on our soil."

Yuan Shih-kai was the scapegoat, but it is hardly likely that he would have been able to hold off the Japanese demands, which were peremptory, for five months, if he had been lacking in astuteness. He fought gamely, against great odds, and failed in this through no lack of good faith, but because he was confronted with an overwhelming power. The revolutionaries, however, blamed him for the defeat. As a result, a number of sporadic outbreaks against the government occurred during the summer. Chen Chih-mei returned secretly to the French concession in Shanghai and directed operations. In a desperate effort to hold the Yangtse Valley, an attempt was made to hold Shanghai, and for this purpose it was decided to remove the capable and alert defense commissioner Chen Ju-sheng, who was assassinated on his way to attend a reception at the Japanese Consulate-General on November 10, 1915, in honor of the Japanese Emperor. A more important uprising occurred at the end of the year, when the cruiser *Shao Ho,* commander Captain Huang Ming-shuh, was won over to the revolutionary cause. On December

5, 1915, the *Shao Ho* hoisted the revolutionary flag and opened fire on the Shanghai arsenal, while Chen Chih-mei and Chiang Kai-shek led a small detachment of revolutionary troops against Nantao. Shortly afterward other warships began to fire on the *Shao Ho,* which was compelled to withdraw, and with the collapse of the offensive by the revolutionary forces, this brief revolt came to an end.

Within a week China was a monarchy. The astounding news was greeted by the people with little enthusiasm, though preparations for the change had been continuing for some months. On the advice of Professor Frank Goodnow, his confidential adviser, Yuan Shih-kai had decided that a reversion to the monarchy was necessitated by the internal condition. And who could be a better emperor than himself? With the help of an emergent monarchist party known as the Chou An Hui, or Plan Safety Society, thousands of copies of Professor Goodnow's report on the necessity for a monarchy were circulated. Circulars were not uncommon at the time. Under Yuan Shih-kai hundreds of thousands of tracts against the revolutionaries, and especially against Sun Yat-sen, were dispatched to every province in the country. Though the method was also used by the revolutionaries, it had little to commend it, and it was liable to the same dangers as the press of the time.

The main cause of the assumption of the monarchy may never be known, but the ambitions of Yuan Ke-ting, the President's eldest son, who forged a presidential edition of the Japanese-owned newspaper *Shun Tien Shih Pao* in which reports of mass demonstrations in Yuan Shih-kai's favor were repeated *ad nauseam,* must be considered. On December 12 Yuan Shih-kai signed the decree appointing himself emperor, and on New Year's Day 1916, exactly five years after the institution of the republic, he ascended the

Dragon Throne under the dynastic title of Hung Hsien, or "Era of the Great Constitution."

He had underestimated the strength of popular feeling, and at the same time he had outraged the feelings of the majority of the intellectuals. Before the revolution Liang Chih-chao had urged the retention of the monarchy on the grounds that changes in a governmental system as complicated and delicate as China's would lead to disaster. Now that the upheaval had occurred, he could see no excuse for a reversion to monarchy, since such a change would introduce a second upheaval. Liang Chih-chao's views were upheld by one of his pupils, General Tsai Ao, a young military officer who had accepted office under Yuan Shih-kai and who, like Liang Chih-chao, remained critical of the new regime. As soon as it became evident that Yuan Shih-kai was determined to assume monarchical power, Liang Chih-chao retired to the foreign concession in Tientsin and continued to assail the monarchy with his pen, while General Tsai Ao remained in Peking, ostensibly a loyal servant of the state, but actually carrying on secret negotiations for a rising. Shortly afterward they fled together to the southwestern province of Yunnan. On December 23 they issued an ultimatum to Peking calling upon Yuan Shih-kai to disavow the monarchy. No answer was received to the ultimatum, and on Christmas Day the province rose against the empire, to be followed within a week by the provinces of Kweichow, Kwangsi, Szechuan, and Kwangtung.

The end came swiftly. Realizing that the whole country was against him, and no longer able to count upon the loyalty of his friends, Yuan Shih-kai bowed to the storm. On February 23 the enthronement was indefinitely postponed, and on March 22 the monarchical scheme was abandoned by presidential decree. Thereupon the self-styled Emperor Hung Hsien, after an unconstitutional reign of eighty-three days, vacated the throne.

During this year three men who had played a great role in the formation of the republic died. Yuan Shih-kai died heartbroken on June 6, 1916, having surrendered all his powers to the Vice-President, General Li Yuan-hung. Hwang Hsing returned from America to lead the revolt in Canton, fell ill, and died of consumption in Shanghai on October 31, 1916. Chen Chih-mei was the third. For a long while he had been a thorn in the side of Yuan Shih-kai, who was continually receiving reports of the chronic lack of funds within the party. It was decided to incriminate Chen Chih-mei by means of secret agents who visited him ostensibly to arrange a loan of forty per cent of the capital value of an iron mine. Suspecting a sinister plot behind this seemingly innocent proposal Chiang Kai-shek did his utmost to persuade Chen Chih-mei to have no personal association with the business. But Yuan Shih-kai's agents had adroitly placed negotiations in the hands of Li Hai-chin, a member of the Kuomintang. On May 18 a preliminary agreement was signed, and a few days later Li Hai-chin, accompanied by four assassins in the guise of representatives of mine-owning interests, came to his house and assassinated him.

With the deaths of Yuan Shih-kai and Hwang Hsing, the country lost two of its most powerful leaders. Sun Yat-sen returned from Tokyo in a mood of quiet confidence and in the knowledge that all his prophecies had proved only too true. He realized now that he had underestimated Yuan Shih-kai's reactionary influence; and he remembered his unbounded optimism in the early days when he was director-general of railway development. The failure of the second revolution, however, had taught him a lesson he was never to forget. "The independence of Yunnan and Kweichow," he wrote shortly after his return, "has greatly relieved my anxiety, and it is gratifying to learn that we are not the only men striving for liberty." This tribute to Liang Chih-chao was well deserved, and Sun Yat-sen was perfectly conscious of the role played by the reformers in the movement of liberation. He was never ungenerous. The following months found him in high spirits; he addressed meetings in Shanghai, Ningpo, and Hangchow; and he began to play at first tentatively and then more seriously with the idea of a southwestern federation which might act as a balanced and cohesive force against the continuing reaction in the north.

Yuan Shih-kai had failed because the country was insufficiently prepared to withstand the twenty-one demands of Japan. Under General Tuan Chih-jui, the new premier, China found herself faced with a widely differing problem. On February 4, 1917, President Wilson sent a message to all neutral nations urging them to break off diplomatic relations with Germany as a protest against the German threat of unrestricted submarine warfare. Tuan Chih-jui was in favor of an immediate declaration of war, but he was unable to carry parliament with him. In order to force the parliamentary members into agreement, another citizens' corps was created on May 8, and in the ensuing riots more than twenty members were attacked. Not unnaturally they were angry, and while public opinion made short shrift of the Premier, the military governors, in fear of losing their power, bitterly assailed the constitution. Tuan Chih-jui was finally removed from office on May 23. The military governors who favored the Premier rebelled in retaliation, some declaring the independence of their provinces, others proclaiming open warfare. In despair the President summoned the military governor of Anhui, General Chang Hsun, to a conference in Peking in the hope that his influence would weigh heavily with the remaining *tuchuns*. But the old general, marching into

Peking at the head of his army called upon the President to dissolve parliament; and on June 12 parliamentary government was once more abandoned, while the members of the National Assembly fled in disguise, some to the international settlement in Shanghai and others abroad.

The situation which had been grotesque took a swift turn to the comic. Power had vanished. Peking, which had been the hollow center of a whirlwind for so long, resumed its silent role. Once again the wheel of fortune turned full circle. From the comic, the situation became merely grotesque when on July 1, 1917, in the lull between the battle of Messines and the turmoil of Passchendaele, the old military governor decided that the boy emperor P'u Yi's restoration to the throne would bring peace to the suffering peasants of China. The responsibility for this act lies partly on the shoulders of the old reformer Kang Yu-wei, who was convinced that in a time of desperate troubles no other solution was possible.

The new emperor reigned for less than a fortnight, spending most of the time playing with a toy train presented by the Emperor of Germany. Before the middle of July, Peking was retaken by the premier Tuan Chih-jui with the help of a young brigadier, Feng Yu-hsiang, later to become famous as "the Christian General." Chang Hsun sought sanctuary in the Dutch Legation, the boy emperor disappeared, and the republic was officially restored. On August 14, 1917, China declared war on Germany and Austria.

The logic of events was not lost on Sun Yat-sen and the leaders of the revolutionary party. By entering the war China had opened herself still more to the dangerous subterfuges of the powers, who were more interested in carrying the war to a successful conclusion than in assisting an ally on the point of collapse. The country was split into two compartments. The militarists and the northern group hoped that by entering the war China would regain Tsingtao and the German holdings in Shangtung, while Sun Yat-sen and the majority of the revolutionaries maintained an isolationist position, holding that the greatest problem was to revive the constitutional government. They were not indifferent to the war, but they were desperately in earnest about China. Sun Yat-sen cabled to Lloyd George that he could not understand "the existing campaign to make China enter the war, and to insist upon the sending of Chinese troops to Mesopotamia will lessen England's prestige, for the Chinese people cannot understand why the Allies should have need of them in order to beat Germany." The southern group therefore refused to participate in the war and dissociated themselves from the North. They realized that the revolution had not yet begun, and they were determined to begin it as soon as possible.

Li Yuan-hung refused to resume the presidency, and he was followed by Vice-President Feng Kuo-chang, with Tuan Chih-jui as premier. These men were bitterly hostile to one another, and formed cliques and factions within the government which were to influence the course of Chinese history until 1927. Feng Kuo-chang was the acknowledged leader of what came to be known as the Chihli faction, while Tuan Chih-jui led the Anfu faction named after the street in Peking in which the headquarters of the Anfu Club were situated. A third faction, the Fengtien group (Fengtien is the Chinese name for Mukden) was controlled for many years by the veteran marshal Chang Tso-lin. In the south a fourth party came into being when Sun Yat-sen, accompanied by the northern navy minister and a considerable part of the fleet, sailed from Shanghai to Canton with a few survivors from the constitutional government, after first calling upon Tuan Chih-jui to resign or to revive the constitution. The next ten years are the story of the struggle between these four contending parties.

If Canton could be made into a model city, and if the southern provinces could be governed in accordance with the constitution—for he held the constitution of 1912 still binding—Sun Yat-sen hoped that the rest of China would rise against the war lords and follow his example. A parliament was summoned in August 1917, and on September 1 a beflagged Canton saw the election of Sun Yat-sen as generalissimo, with the two military leaders of Kwangsi and Yunnan, Generals Lu Yung-ting and Tang Chih-yao, as vice-generalissimos. The Generalissimo immediately issued a manifesto against the northern war lords, threatening to organize an expedition against them.

Of the six major provinces in the south, only four had come out openly for the new Canton government. Kweichow and Yunnan were held by Vice-Generalissimo Tang Chih-yao, while Kwangsi and Kwangtung were held by Vice-Generalissimo Lu Yung-ting. Lu Yung-ting was the leader of what came to be known as the Kwangsi faction, a formidable group with headquarters in Kweilin, and continually at odds with the Canton government. Meanwhile Szechuan and Hunan held out under their governors against any form of centralized government, with the result that there were now more than five contending factions, with at least two provinces holding themselves aloof. Upon Sun Yat-sen's arrival General Chu Chin-lan, provincial governor of Kwangtung, voluntarily turned over to Sun Yat-sen the twenty battalions of his army, which were then placed under the command of General Chen Chiung-ming; but the military governor of Kwangtung, who was the agent of the Kwangsi faction, removed General Chu Chin-lan from office and resumed command of the army. The situation would probably have resulted in war if Hu Han-min had not used his good offices to effect a settlement: Chen Chiung-ming was placed in command of the army, which was removed to Fukien province, as far as possible from the borders of Kwangsi. The policies of the two governments, however, remained at variance. The minister of the navy was shot dead, apparently by Kwangsi counterrevolutionaries, and in retaliation Sun Yat-sen led two cruisers upriver to bombard the yamen of the military governor.

The situation was dangerous. It was no longer a question of unifying China, but of preserving the independence of a single province. The influence of the Kwangsi faction began to dominate when a Council of Seven, composed of leading members of the Kuomintang but including several who were secretly affiliated to the Kwangsi faction, assumed control of the Canton government. The Council of Seven included Wu Ting-fang, Tang Shao-yi, and Sun Yat-sen, who once more found himself in a position of power without any means of exercising his power. On May 4, 1919, seeing that his counsels were ineffective, he resigned and sailed for Shanghai.

In the history of China during those tragic ten years between 1917 and 1927, the international settlements played a decisive part. In Europe havens no longer existed, and not even the Vatican City could provide the sanctuary which was offered at all Christian altars during the Middle Ages. The international settlement at Shanghai was the refuge for all defeated revolutionaries, for Manchus, and for retiring war lords. There were some war lords, like Wu Pei-fu, who refused to accept the comparative safety of the settlement, but they were in the minority. And since both sides took advantage of the situation, no side gained any particular advantage. At various times Sun Yat-sen spent a total of nearly three years in the settlement, and it is doubtful whether he would have been able to continue his revolutionary work without the existence of the settlements.

For the revolutionaries the position had been growing increasingly worse during the previous four years. Nothing had been gained by the southern government. The party was powerless, the leader was in exile, the country was developing into a maelstrom of anarchic provincial governments. In a letter dated August 30 Sun Yat-sen wrote:

"I firmly believe that on the fate of the Party hangs the fate of the country, and if our party slackens in its efforts, it is quite conceivable that China will soon be in ruins. So I beg you not to allow our present reverses to prevent you from wholeheartedly struggling for China. Let us pool our forces and steer the ship against the current. Since my return to Shanghai I have continually felt the urgent need of enlarging the party, so as to save the country. Meanwhile I have revised the Party regulations in the hope of pushing our affairs forward."

On September 25 he wrote to a friend abroad: "For the time being I am remaining silent. But pray engage yourself on the task of enlarging the party and thus serve as a source of help to me."

Suddenly, on October 10, 1919, he announced a fourth reorganization of the party, to be known henceforward as the Chung Kuo Kuomintang, or the Chinese Nationalist Party, the title which it still bears. He explained the reasons for the reorganization in a new manifesto in which he outlined thirty-two provisions. On the whole these differed little from the provisions in previous manifestos, but they contained a new emphasis on livelihood. The change in the name of the party was partly due to the fact that the Chung Hua Ke-min-tang lodges overseas still retained the original Kuomintang name, and owing to the difficulty of re-registration in the Philippines and Malaya, no change had taken place when the Chung Hua Ke-min-tang was founded. By reverting to the original name, the party at once assumed a stronger position overseas.

And now at last the future was growing clear. The reformers, the revolutionaries, the monarchists, the anarchists, the dissident Confucianists, and the adventurers who had taken part in the struggle had lost their stakes. Every kind of government had been attempted; all failed. The end of the First World War, which had changed everything else, changed nothing in China, for there were the same powerful forces at work at the beginning and at the end. But gradually, with interminable effort and perhaps with little understanding of what was being done, the people began to grow into an awakening more profound than the awakening of the revolution. The sleeping lion was twitching his tail and giving every evidence of being alive.

VIII

THE end of the World War brought no relief to China. There was still a multiplicity of governments. At the Treaty of Versailles China was represented by emissaries from both the Peking and Canton governments, but only the northern delegates were recognized. At the conference China was impotent. The draft treaty included clauses settling the question of Shangtung in a way favorable to the Japanese. China declined to sign, and the Chinese government eventually concluded separate treaties with Germany and Austria by which Germany lost her extraterritorial privileges, her special concessions, and the unpaid portions of the Boxer Indemnity Fund.

Inevitably the students rose against the treaty, ordering a boycott of all foreign goods in demonstrations which broke out on May 4, 1919. There had been student demonstrations before, notably after the Japanese Twenty-one Demands were accepted by Yuan Shih-kai, but the demonstrations of 1919 were more far-reaching, more terrible, and more insistent than before. The passionate longing for a better world, which seems to reside only in the hearts of students, met a disastrous defeat. China, an ally of the Allies, was being sold to Japan! To the students this statement was one of demonstrable fact: the urgencies of the World War were incomprehensible three thousand miles away from its nearest theater. Now, for the first time, the students realized their power. They could overturn governments, they could appoint ministers of education, and out of their long-suffering poverty they could achieve a philosophy of government. They may have thought a new era was at hand; but the lion was still asleep, they could never entirely agree among themselves, and clever politicians were only too willing to foster disagreement among them. The inherent anarchism of the students, desiring and not desiring, capable of initiating action and rarely capable of carrying it through, was a prey to rumors, propaganda, the influence of parties, and the power of the press. The demonstration came to an end, and the same government was in power as before.

The body politic suffers from most of the diseases of the human body, but there is no name in the medical pharmacopoeia for the herb which will bring scattered limbs together. "China is a sheet of scattering sand," Sun Yat-sen declared after the failure of the second revolution. Inefficiency had produced disunity, and now he determined that efficiency should be restored. Without any army, without a capital, living in exile in the French concession in Shanghai, where the safety of the First President of the Republic was assured by Annamite policemen who fifty years previously might have accompanied the tribute bearers to Peking as slaves, he assumed the role of a prophet of reconstruction.

The successful revolutionary is usually a scholar with a gun. Sun Yat-sen had no army; no wireless station; and —at that time—few faithful followers. But in the small library at 29 rue Molière he began dictating the book which was to serve as a basis for the future Kuomintang party. It was *The Principles of National Reconstruction*, written under three headings—the psychological, material, and social reorganization of China. In the preface to the chapter on psychological reorganization he wrote:

"Shortly after the Chinese revolution, the revolutionaries themselves became the slaves of the theory that action was difficult and knowledge was easy, and since they believed this, they began to regard my plans as utopian, as so many empty words. The theory of the difficulty of action and the easiness of knowledge is my enemy, a thousand times more powerful than the authority of the Manchu Emperors, for the power of the Manchus could only succeed in killing our bodies and could not deprive us of our will. When we truly believe that a plan can be put into practise—to remove mountains or fill up the sea—we can always achieve our purpose. But when we are convinced that the plan cannot be put into practice, even if the plan is only to move our hands or break a twig, we fail in our purpose. Seven years have passed since the foundation of the Chinese Republic, and so great is our belief that action is difficult that we have accomplished nothing at all, and every day my heart aches because we are so inactive."

In *The Principles of National Reconstruction* Sun Yat-sen was demanding from the Chinese an act of faith such as the prophet Isaiah demanded from the people of Jerusalem. Nearly thirty centuries of Confucianism and Taoism, nearly fifteen centuries of Buddhism had taught that knowledge was the sum of wisdom and inaction was the greatest privilege of the wise. "Government should be as simple as the cooking of little fishes," said Laotse. "The superior man preserves his respect by obeying the commands of Heaven," wrote Mencius. "In the wheel of Law, all things are gathered—no one can escape," said Buddha.

The governors and politicians who were traditionally admired were those who were least active in enforcing the laws. To all these religious leaders and politicians Sun Yat-sen replied with a summons to action: "We are living in the world; we must act or perish." Nothing, for example, can be easier than to enforce a workable constitution, nothing can be simpler than to unite China under a single government, if the will is there. "Knowledge is easy, action is difficult" was a theory which paid dividends to inaction (and also to reaction). "Knowledge is difficult, action is easy" is a theory which directly opposes the established principles of the Chinese. If only their principles could be reversed! If only they had a little more faith in direct, spontaneous action, a little more faith in constitutional government, a little more faith in a united China! The possibility of a sudden change of heart was inviting, and he followed it through with the fervor of a prophet looking for the first time on the promised land.

The promised land may have appeared to be near at hand when, in February 1919, a peace conference called between the northern and southern governments in Shanghai failed to come to an agreement. The terms of the conference were vigorously attacked by Sun Yat-sen and Wu Ting-fang in a manifesto issued in June 1920, in which the two governments were described as two robbers intent only on consolidating their spoils. Neither of the two governments was constitutional; both were backed by military power, and military power only. The southern government did not even possess a quorum, for most of the parliamentary delegates, including Wu Ting-fang, had left Canton.

The South demanded as a condition of peace the dissolution of the army ostensibly raised to participate in the World War, and an end to the foreign loans. Tuan Chih-jui, who had extended his military strength during the war, refused; and in the ensuing struggle for power, Chang Tso-lin and two other generals, Tsao Kun and Wu Pei-fu, drove Tuan Chih-jui and the Anfu faction out of Peking. The South remained unmolested. There remained only two contending factions of importance, the North and the South, the North predominating.

The Kwangsi faction retained the semblance of power south of the Yangtse River, though Yunnan had broken away and Szechuan was in no mood to assist the Canton government either with ammunition or soldiers; and when the Kwangsi faction made an incursion into Fukien in order to eliminate Chen Chiung-ming's forces, Sun Yat-sen issued orders to Chen Chiung-ming and Hsu Chung-chih to oust the rival forces from Kwangtung. With the slogan "Kwangtung for the Kwangtungese," the forces of Chen Chiung-ming advanced against the enemy, and by November 1920 the whole of Kwangtung had been recaptured. Sun Yat-sen and Wu Ting-fang immediately returned from Shanghai, and a military government was set up.

By March 1920 conditions in Kwangtung had reached a stage when the military government could be converted into a constitutional government without any danger, and on April 7, Sun Yat-sen was once more elected president. He was inaugurated on May 5, and shortly afterward Chen Chiung-ming was given the post of governor and commander-in-chief of Kwangtung province, and also minister of war.

The Kwangsi faction, however, was still in existence, and immediately began an invasion of Kwangtung territory. General Chen Chiung-ming was again dispatched against them. Toward the end of June, Wuchow was captured by the Kwangtung army, and in the following month Shen Hung-ying, a divisional commander of the enemy's forces, surrendered with 20,000 men. By the end of July the whole of Kwangsi was in the hands of the constitutionalists. The success of this expedition once again turned Sun Yat-sen's thoughts to an expedition against the North, a venture against which Chen Chiung-ming violently objected. Sun Yat-sen was determined to carry out his project, but when he reached Kweilin in October 1921 at the head of the punitive expedition, he was met with the news that Chen Chiung-ming was sabotaging him in the rear. Sun Yat-sen found himself wedged between the Hunanese forces in the north and the mysteriously hostile presence of Chen Chiung-ming in the south. There was therefore no alternative except to continue marching north. Sun Yat-sen opened negotiations for a free passage through Hunan and reached Chuanchow near the Hunanese border in March 1922. The news of the sudden murder of Teng Keng, Chen Chiung-ming's chief of staff, at the railway station in Canton gave rise to the thought that the rear might be completely cut off, and Sun Yat-sen reluctantly decided to return to his base. By the end of April he was once more in Canton. The mysterious activities of Chen Chiung-ming in the rear were carefully examined, but no direct proof of sabotage appears to have been available, and though he was removed from his position as governor of Kwangtung and commander-in-chief of the Kwangtung army, he retained the office of minister of war.

Chen Chiung-ming troops had been in occupation of Canton. He now withdrew his troops on the advice or order of Wu Ting-fang, the new governor of the province. His presence and the presence of his army in the neighborhood of the capital was a source of danger which was perceived by Chiang Kai-shek, who wrote a brief memorandum outlining the possibilities of a sudden descent by Chen's troops on Canton, and advising an immediate and swift expedition against the man who still retained the title of minister of war—advice which Sun Yat-sen unwisely rejected. When the northern expedition was resumed a few weeks later, and Sun Yat-sen's troops were fighting in Kiangsi, a flanking movement by fifty battalions of Chen Chiung-ming's forces under the command of General Yeh Chu cut off his retreat, and Canton was occupied by the enemy in the rear. Accompanied only by his bodyguard Sun Yat-sen set out from Shaokuan and entered Canton on June 1.

Unexpectedly, on June 16, Yeh Chu's troops rebelled. Five hours earlier, at ten o'clock on the night of the fifteenth, Sun Yat-sen received a warning by telephone to leave the presidential palace at once. He refused to take the news seriously. Two hours later his secretary, Lin Chin-mien, and State Councilor Ling Tsu-wei drove independently to the palace and begged him to leave immediately. They said there were 25,000 troops in the city, who at any moment might break out into open revolt. Sun Yat-sen still refused to leave. He said it was his duty to remain at his post and suppress a riot if it occurred, and if he failed to use the requisite amount of force, he would incur the ridicule of foreigners and Chinese alike. The two visitors left.

At two o'clock in the morning they returned. Gunfire could be heard. Looting was going on near the port. Some of the houses of Kuomintang members were already in flames. The military officer who reached the palace at the same time insisted upon immediate departure, and refused to take responsibility for the President's safety unless he fled to a gunboat moored along the river. There were less than five hundred loyal soldiers in the city. A hurried conference was held and Mme. Sun Yat-sen was awakened. It was decided that she should remain with a bodyguard of fifty soldiers while Sun Yat-sen set out with only three members: his secretary, the military officer, and Dr. Ling Tsu-wei.

It was nearly three o'clock in the morning. Sentinels were posted on all the roads and no passengers could pass without being questioned. Once, when they stopped at the point of the bayonet, one of them pretended that his father was sick and they were sending for a doctor. The ruse succeeded, and a little later, when a column of rebels was looting the Ministry of Finance, they succeeded in mixing with the rebels so successfully that they passed unrecognized. A little later they reached Naval Headquarters on the banks of the Pearl River and were ferried across to the government cruiser *Yung Feng,* which was to be their home for the next fifty-six days.

Since ten o'clock on the night of the fifteenth the presidential palace had been surrounded. The rebels expected the President to escape by motorcar, but when, at three o'clock the next morning, it was discovered that no motorcar had left the palace, they decided to take the palace by storm. A price of two hundred thousand dollars was placed on Sun Yat-sen's head, and three days' "holiday" would be granted immediately after his capture. The sinister implications of the holiday did not fail to intimidate some of the party members remaining in the city, but Sun Yat-sen was already safely on board the *Yung Feng,* and he ordered the cruisers *Yu Chang* and *Chu Yu* to get up steam and to sail from Whampoa to bombard the rebels at Pai Yuan San (White Cloud Mountain). After a short bombardment the warships returned to their base, and on the next morning delegations of sailors, who had come to confirm their loyalty, were received by Sun Yat-sen. The same day, Chen Chiung-ming issued a proclamation calling upon Sun Yat-sen to resign. A day later Sun Yat-sen wrote a proclamation to the punitive expedition calling upon them to return from the front and put down the rebellion.

There was still no news of the whereabouts of Mme. Sun. The air was full of rumors that the commanders of the fleet were secretly negotiating with the enemy. These rumors were at first disbelieved, but at eleven o'clock on the night of July 8 three gunboats left Whampoa and set out for a secret destination. There remained seven warships—the *Yung Feng, Yung Chiang, Chu Yu, Yu Chang, Tungan, Kwangyu, Paopi*—under Sun Yat-sen's command and three under Chen Chiung-ming, the *Haichi, Haisen,* and *Chaoho*. It was reported at the time that the commanders of the rebel warships had received bribes of two hundred and sixty thousand dollars. Meanwhile rebels from Yu-ju had seized the important Changchow battery, and Sun Yat-sen decided to steam upriver in the hope of securing a base for counterattack. In his speech from the quarterdeck he said: "Today we are witnessing a fatal war between violence and law. Tomorrow we shall sail upriver to White Goose Pool, where we have no expectation of life and every certainty of death. Forward!"

On the morning of the next day, the tenth, the *Yung Feng* opened fire on the enemy battery. The fire was returned, the cruiser receiving six direct hits. There followed an interminable battle in White Goose Pool between the cruisers and the rebels, a battle which lasted nearly a month. Toward the end the enemy employed a rudimentary form of torpedo, the first exploding during the afternoon of July 19 while Sun Yat-sen was sitting down for lunch. Fortunately the torpedo failed to sink the cruiser but slightly damaged the stern plates of an American gunboat moored in midstream. Meanwhile mediators were sent by Chen Chiung-ming to ask for a truce. To a mediator who arrived on the cruiser on July 1 Sun Yat-sen declared:

"When the Sung Dynasty was in ruins there arose the patriot Wen Tien-hsiang. When the Ming Dynasty was in ruins there arose the patriot Shih Koh-fa. Now that the Republic is in ruins, shall there be no more Wens and Shihs? If I preferred life in these circumstances to death, how could I face the revolutionary martyrs and the youth of the country with equanimity? I am determined to fulfil the early ambitions which I have cherished for thirty years, and if necessary I shall die for the Republic."

In reply to the Minister of the Navy, Tang Ting-kuan, he wrote on July 10: "In the age of the tyrants Emperors could die for their country. Shall not Presidents be allowed to die for their Republic? Only if the rebels are sincerely grief-stricken shall I open negotiations with them."

On June 3 President Hsu Shih-chang of the northern government resigned as a consequence of the war between Chang Tso-lin and Wu Pei-fu. Chang Tso-lin was driven back into Manchuria; and Wu Pei-fu announced his intention of restoring the constitutional government and invited Sun Yat-sen to Peking. Sun Yat-sen felt that he was in honor bound to remain in Kwangtung, where he had been elected to the presidency by a constitutionally formed parliament. As he explained to an American correspondent who visited him on board the cruiser on June 24: "I was elected by the members of parliament and I am responsible only to them. If I did not perform my duty, I would be betraying both them and my country; and even if Chen Chiung-ming calls upon me to resign, I can only tender my resignation to parliament which elected me. Nearly ten days have passed since Chen Chiung-ming began the rebellion, but I am responsible to Parliament and to the country and must fulfil my duty by keeping the law, and therefore I have never slackened in my efforts to quell the rebellion. If I were to surrender and escape simply for the sake of saving my life, I would be betraying my whole life-work. I have sworn to put down the revolt, and I have no intention of disobeying the law."

He was still hoping for news from the northern expeditionary force. A few days later he learned that they were advancing successfully against Nanchang, the provincial capital of Kiangsi; but meanwhile the rebels were moving north along the Canton-Hankow railway in an effort to capture Shaokuan. Only July 8 it was learned that revolutionary troops were concentrating on Nanhsiung near Shaokuan and had captured several key positions in preparation for a final assault on the city. A few days later the carefully fostered rumor that Sun Yat-sen was dead led to the loss of Nanhsiung and the temporary demoralization of the revolutionary army.

No punitive expedition against the North had suffered a worse fate. It had seen its rear cut off, its supply columns disorganized, and its morale shaken by rumors. The Hunanese stood firm on their frontiers; the revolutionary forces were surrounded on all sides. Meanwhile, in the sultry heat of summer, Sun Yat-sen paced the quarterdeck of the cruiser *Yung Feng* and looked out upon the white skyline of Canton. He gave orders, made negotiations, threatened, cajoled, a president in direct command of less than two hundred sailors. During those fifty-six days spent on the cruiser, provisions were always scanty, water was always running short, millions of mosquitoes and midges settled on the deck, and floating mines and torpedoes were sent from shore. His chief of staff, General Chiang Kai-shek, sometimes swept the decks and sometimes slipped ashore in disguise in search of provisions. The two men, who together revolutionized China, were living a life which beggars would have despised and jailbirds would have found less consoling than their prisons.

The rebels won. There came a moment when Sun Yat-sen realized the futility of carrying on a war of one armed warship against a city, and at three o'clock on the afternoon of August 9, with the assistance of the British consul at Canton, he was taken aboard the gunboat *Moorhen*, accompanied by General Chiang Kai-shek and Admiral Chen Chak. At four o'clock the *Moorhen* left her moorings and steamed down-river. They reached Hong Kong early the next morning, where the refugees were transferred to the S.S. *Empress of Russia*, a fast mail packet steamer which arrived in Shanghai four days later. As soon as he landed, Sun Yat-sen issued a manifesto revealing Chen Chiung-ming's betrayal and announcing his determination to continue the struggle.

Mme. Sun Yat-sen's escape was still more dramatic. Sun Yat-sen left the presidential palace at three in the morning, but his wife remained until daybreak. The palace was halfway up the hill and connected with the government offices by a covered passage. The enemy on the crest of the hill kept up an intermittent fire all night. There was little ammunition in the palace, and by eight o'clock most of it was exhausted. Taking only the most necessary supplies, accompanied only by a foreign adviser, Colonel Bow, and two guards, they crawled along the bridge passage and made their way under fire to the government offices. They had left at the last possible moment, for a few minutes later a concerted attack on the palace resulted in the deaths of nearly all the guards. Some hours passed before they could reach the government offices. At four o'clock in the afternoon, after the enemy had sent an officer to negotiate terms for a truce, even the offices were attacked, and they escaped once more only by mingling with the crowd.

Canton was on fire from the shells of the warships. The dead lay everywhere, some with their chests caved in and their legs severed, others blown into fragments by hand grenades. Mme. Sun was in such despair that she begged the guards to shoot her. At one time they could hear a mob moving up a side street. They lay down, pretending to be dead, in the middle of the road. Half an hour later, when the firing had come to an end and looting began, they reached a farmhouse. As soon as they reached the farmhouse, Mme. Sun fainted, only to be awakened a moment later by cold water and the drumming of rifle shots. The rifle shots came to an end shortly afterward—one shot had killed an incautious bodyguard—and a few hours later they made their way in disguise through the outskirts of the city. Two days later they reached the waterfront and succeeded in being taken on board the *Yung Feng*, where Sun Yat-sen was directing operations or quietly reading in the wardroom, to the sound of high explosive shells and the continual fusillade of rifle shots from the shore.

In later years he would speak of the Canton rebellion as the most terrible in all his career. His private bodyguard was massacred; his old friend Wu Ting-fang died brokenhearted on June 23; all his books and manuscripts were irretrievably lost; and the city he had done so much to build was once more shattered by gunfire. Chen Chiungming's treachery was partly the result of Sun Yat-sen's trusting affection for his young lieutenant. He had offered him the governorship of the two Kwang provinces (Kwangtung and Kwangsi), and on the last day of the conference held on the eve of the northern expedition, Sun Yat-sen said: "We are marching against the north. If the punitive expedition succeeds, we shall move the capital to Nanking. We shall not return. Meanwhile we entrust you with the two provinces and ask you to act as our rearguard. If on the other hand the northern expedition fails, we shall not have the courage to return, and whatever you do, you will be in a position to safeguard your own interests, and even if you throw in your lot with the north, we shall never criticise you." Sun Yat-sen attached so much importance to this conversation that he included it in *The Three*

Principles of the People. He appears to have trusted Chen Chiung-ming until the last moment.

In a private letter, Chiang Kai-shek bitterly assailed Chen Chiung-ming; but the President accepted the danger, he recognized Chen Chiung-ming's brilliant qualities, he was determined to march to the north, and he failed because he placed too much trust on a subordinate who had acquired immense prestige after the reconquest of the two southern provinces. For years Chen Chiung-ming had dreamed of fame. In an early poem he wrote: "Failing to grasp the sun and moon, I have been untrue to my youth," and in the margin of the poem, in the fashion made acceptable by centuries of tradition, he added a gloss describing a dream in which he grasped the sun in one hand and the moon in the other. He was so overwhelmed by the dream that he changed his name to "Chiung-ming," two characteristic epithets to describe the sun and the moon.

But there were other forces at work, besides dreams, to enlarge his ambitions. Shortly after being dismissed from the governorship he opened negotiations with Wu Pei-fu. The Fengtien wars were over, the second president of the republic Li Yung-hung had been reinstated in office, there was talk of a new constitution, and Wu Pei-fu began to believe that a united and constitutional government of China might be brought about by discussions between the warring groups. The fly in the ointment was Sun Yat-sen, whose expeditionary army was still on the borders of Hunan. There was little sympathy between them. A Buddhist scholar, elegant and morose, he had little in common with the devout Christian who regarded the scalpel as a revolutionary weapon.

Like Chen Chiung-ming, and unlike Sun Yat-sen, Wu Pei-fu was a *hsiu ts'ai*, the holder of the first degree of the triennial examinations held under the monarchy, and though this degree corresponded to little more than a bachelor of arts, it was nevertheless held in great respect by the people. The two scholars were known as "the two *hsiu ts'ais*," and they were in complete agreement upon the necessity of defeating Sun Yat-sen. The revolution flared up; Sun Yat-sen fled; but the battle for the law was not yet over. A great Chinese philosopher wrote: "There are men that govern, but there are no laws that govern." The coming years were to prove that law itself could govern, but only after a revolution which shakes the country to its foundations.

As in a Greek drama, where the chorus speaks now for the people, now for the assembled hosts of the gods, now praising the lawgiver, now inviting or inveighing against catastrophe, the history of China was unfolding toward a new climax. The sense of strain had reached a new limit; and human suffering in starvation, floods, and massacres was not less unbearable because it was silent. It is the custom to regard civil wars in China as comparatively bloodless. They are not; nor are any civil wars bloodless.

From Shanghai the dispassionate eye of the surgeon could look back over more than twelve years of destruction which had brought no profit to the country. He was now powerless. He could do no more than raise a standard. "Let us raise a standard to which the wise and the honest can repair," said Washington to the Constitutional Convention. "The event is in the hand of God." Now, from the study of the rue Molière, in the interval between wars, Sun Yat-sen spoke to the whole of China in a clear voice, though it was no longer easy for him to speak aloud:

"We have destroyed too much. We must be rigorous, stern and unsentimental. It is time that we should make a plan for the future and carry it out to the end. We must begin the great task of reconstruction, or perish from the map of the world."

III. THE PRINCIPLES OF A PEOPLE

I

FOR nearly three thousand years China had been dreaming within her frontiers. The codes of law, the behavior of emperors, the creations of the poets and artists were divorced from life, and while the Chinese people retained the same sturdy qualities of independence and industry which they possess today, the tide of the legislators, the emperors, and the artists flowed over them and made little more impression than a wave will make on the fishes stirring beneath the surface. Chien Lung and Kang Hsi, those brilliant interlopers, left no deep impression on the people. The emperors and empresses of the Ch'ing dynasty performed their functions well; they prostrated themselves at the Altar of Heaven at the proper season, gave orders, dismissed officials, executed the corrupt, and announced in the thundering voices which were peculiar to emperors when speaking from the Dragon Throne the dictates of the supreme ruler in Heaven. And yet the emperor was less powerful than those "homeless men among the rivers and the lakes" who ruled in the subterranean kingdom over which the princes possessed no control.

The secret societies had been ruling China quietly ever since the fall of the Ming dynasty. During the reigns of Kang Hsi and Yung Cheng, efforts had been made by the imperial government to rewrite and distort history, and everything pertaining to the relationship between the

Sung dynasty and the Mongols was deleted: a heavy censorship, no less oppressive because it was often exercised benevolently, turned scholars into court flatterers and librarians into pimps. But history is heredity; it doesn't die; like human life, at times of great turmoil it goes underground. Of the real history of the Chinese people during the Ch'ing dynasty we know little except from the songs and the novels which escaped the censorship, but we know enough to understand the smoldering violence of the struggle which was waged relentlessly between the people and the empire.

To Sun Yat-sen, in his struggle with the emperor, the greatest source of power lay among the secret societies; and without the help of their organized resistance, his implacable hostility to the reigning dynasty would have ended, as it ended with so many before him, in bitter regret and unavailing effort. The faith of a writer is known by the things of which he writes best; and it is perhaps no accident that Sun Yat-sen wrote best of the secret societies, of primitive man, of love, and of livelihood. In the *San Min Chu I (Three Principles of the People)* there is a passage on primitive man which describes by implication the kind of life which was lived under the dictatorship of the emperor:

"As to the original birthplace of man, some say that the human species originated in only a few places, but geologists assert that after man once appeared on the globe he was to be found everywhere, for whenever we dig into the earth we find human relics. The struggle between man and savage creatures has not yet ceased. If we penetrate among the wild mountains or go out into the great deserts, where no man and no smoke is to be seen, we can find once more the kind of environment in which men and animals existed in old times."

But how could he be sure that the old times had not

returned? "China is a sheet of scattering sand," he had written years before; and is a sheet of scattering sand so different from a "desert where no man and no smoke is to be seen"? He, who had demanded rigor from himself and from others, found himself at last in the position of a philosopher who has forgotten to define his most precious beliefs. And now, only a few months before his death, he began to set about compiling a manual of these beliefs.

It is one of the misfortunes of history that this book was never completed. Of the lectures which afterward became known as the *San Min Chu I*, he wrote toward the end of March 1924: "I have had no time to finish these lectures. I can only mount the platform and speak extemporaneously." Time was running out; the manuscript of some previous lectures had been lost in the bombardment of the Canton residency, and already the air was full of plots and counterplots. These lectures were given at a time when he was "eating bitterness." Again and again he refers to the defections of the war lords. Tang Chin-yao had seized Yunnan, Chao Heng-tih had seized Hunan, Lu Yung-ting had seized Kwangsi, and Chen Chiung-ming had seized Kwangtung. Sun Yat-sen himself possessed no power outside the city gates of Canton, yet it was precisely because he no longer possessed any great power that he was able to speak clearly and dispassionately in the *San Min Chu I*. He was merciless against the Chinese who by maintaining their belief in individual liberty had allowed the war lords to achieve power:

"To talk to the Chinese about liberty is like talking to the aboriginal Yao tribes deep in the mountains of Kwangsi about making a fortune in money. The Yaos frequently come down from the heart of the mountains and bring bear galls and deer horns to exchange for other articles in the open market. At first the traders in the market wanted to give the Yaos money for their things; the Yao always refused money and were perfectly content to bear away a piece of rock salt or some cloth. We think nothing is better than to make a fortune in money, but the Yaos are content to have usable things. . . . The liberty which Westerners talk about has its strict limitations and cannot be described as belonging to everyone. Young Chinese students when they talk about liberty break down all restraints. That foreigners should not be familiar with Chinese history and should not know that since ancient times the Chinese have enjoyed a large measure of liberty is not strange, but that our own students should have forgotten the song of liberty of the ancient Chinese—

> When the sun rises, I toil;
> When the sun sets, I rest;
> I dig wells for water;
> I till the fields for food;
> What has the Emperor's power to do with me?

is surprisingly strange. We can see from this song of liberty that China, while she has not had liberty in name, has had liberty in fact from days of old, and so much of it that she need not seek for more."

But since there was too much liberty—and there was evidence enough in China, as in the French Revolution, to place liberty on trial for the crimes committed in her name—he was pledged to discover and define the terms by which the revolution might yet succeed. Once again, like a man who returns in his old age to his birthplace, he found the answer in the secret societies, for it was the secret societies who, throughout the tribulations of the dynasties, had kept alive the ideas of brotherhood and livelihood. At the end of the same chapter in which he bitterly assailed the Chinese for their increasing love of liberty, he made a comparison between the tenets of the French Revolution and the Chinese revolution, which was still unborn. In the place of liberty he substituted the freedom of the nation; in the place of equality he substituted the principle of the people's sovereignty "which aims to destroy autocracy and make all men equal"; in the place of fraternity—but here he paused, since the Chinese term *T'ung-pao* was so familiar that he could barely withhold his agreement from an idea which he held inherently sacred; but he paused only long enough to observe that fraternity was included within the larger scope of the people's livelihood "which aims at the happiness of our four hundred millions."

Min-tsu, Min-chuan, Min-sheng (People's Nationalism, People's Sovereignty, People's Livelihood) are terms which he never accurately defined, for in their essence they elude definition. Under People's Nationalism were included a whole complex of ideas concerning the position of China in relation to foreign countries. The economic oppression under which China had been exploited by the powers was perhaps the main incentive for his bitter diatribes against foreigners and for his determination to raise China to a higher status in the comity of nations. He was relentlessly determined to free China, not only from foreign domination in the places where foreign domination had occurred, but also to free the country from the threat of invasion—a threat which may well have been imaginary but which nevertheless existed in the hearts of millions of Chinese. The proximity of Annam, the presence of the leased territories all armed and fortified with the most modern equipment, the exasperating behavior of the powers, who were themselves exasperated and bewildered by interminable civil wars, made it necessary that China in order to gain her freedom of action should become conscious of nationhood and resolute to defend herself. With the customs in the hands of foreigners, with large-scale economic exploitation, and with a great increase of imports over exports,

China was in the position of a suppliant whose prayers were left unheard. A strong, united China might be able to free itself from foreign bondage; but how could China be strong and united?

In answer to this question Sun Yat-sen proceeded to tell the story of a Chinese stevedore whom he had met in Hong Kong. The stevedore saved ten dollars, invested it in the Luzon lottery, and hid the ticket inside his bamboo carrying pole. When, some weeks later, he discovered that he had won the first prize, he was so overcome with joy that he threw the pole into the sea. And Sun Yat-sen continues:

"The coolie's bamboo pole may represent nationalism—a means of existence; the winning of the prize may represent the time when China's flourishing imperialism was evolving into cosmopolitanism and when our forefathers, believing that China was the world's great state—that 'Heaven has but one sun, people but one king'; that 'gentry of all nations bow before the crown and pearls'; that universal peace would henceforth prevail and that the only thing necessary was a world harmony in which the world would bring its tribute to China—threw away nationalism as the coolie threw his bamboo pole into the sea. Then, when China was overcome by the Manchus, she not only failed to become master of the world, but even failed to keep her small family property intact. The national spirit of the people was destroyed just as the bamboo pole was thrown into the sea."

For Sun Yat-sen, as for many Chinese, there remained the terrible fear that the coolie, having thrown his lottery ticket into the sea, might suddenly decide to throw himself after it.

"But if we Chinese can find some other way to revive our national pride, if we can discover some other bamboo pole, then no matter what foreign political power op-

THE PRINCIPLES OF A PEOPLE 179

presses us, we will survive through the ages. We can overcome the forces of natural selection; Heaven's preservation of our four hundred millions of Chinese till now shows that it has not wanted to destroy us; if China perishes, the guilt will be on our own heads and we shall be the world's great sinners. Heaven has placed great responsibilities upon the Chinese: if we do not love ourselves, we shall be rebels against Heaven."

But the problem of nationalism is not solved by an invocation to Heaven in the mood of his famous invocation at the Ming Tombs, and he continued to elaborate the nature of Chinese nationalism throughout the remainder of the book. When the revolution was brought into being, a wave of iconoclasm had swept the country: the old gods were dethroned, and no others were restored in their place. After thirteen years of civil war, it became necessary to discover whether the gods were indeed dead; and the rather surprised members of the Kuomintang sitting in Canton heard their leader invoking the ancient virtues of the Chinese race, discussing the validity of Mo-tsu's "love without discrimination" and the religion of Jesus, repenting because the old ancestral temples had been desecrated and the character for "loyalty" which was traditionally inscribed on the left hand of the altar had been defaced, because "in former days loyalty was shown to princes, and because we have a republic we need not speak of loyalty." How mistaken was the view of the iconoclasts he proceeds to elucidate in a sermon on the eight cardinal virtues of the Chinese race.

"When we undertake a task we should not falter from first to last until the task is accomplished; if we fail, we should not begrudge our lives as a sacrifice—this is what we mean by loyalty. The ancient teaching of loyalty meant sometimes death. And if we say that the ancient conception of loyalty refers only to loyalty to the throne, and that now we have no need for loyalty, then we are committing a great crime. In a democracy we should still show loyalty, and loyalty to four hundred millions must naturally be on a higher level than loyalty to one individual."

But loyalty, like patriotism, is not enough; and he examines carefully the meanings of the old virtues: filial devotion, kindness, love, faithfulness, justice, harmony, peace, in an effort to convince the Chinese that though China has suffered innumerable setbacks, the main task of the revolutionary, as of the scholar, is "to regulate the mind, make sincere the purpose, search into the nature of things and extend the boundaries of knowledge." Against the impact of the West, China had failed to put up a sufficient defense. The powers had gambled on China's nonresistance, and proved only too successful.

The reason was not far to seek. The formalism of the Sung dynasty had penetrated the mentality of the latter Ch'ings; Chinese thought and aspirations were remote from life. The greatest, the most urgent task of reconstruction lay ahead; and reduced to its simplest terms this task might be construed in the words of Mencius as "to rescue the weak and lift up the fallen." The idea of livelihood, therefore, is included within the idea of nationalism; for how otherwise than by becoming conscious of their interrelations with other Chinese can the superior men rescue the weak and lift up the fallen? And in the peroration to the last lecture of nationalism, Sun Yat-sen insisted that the members of the party should take a binding oath to succor the distressed:

"Let us today, before China's development begins, pledge ourselves to lift up the fallen and to aid the weak; then when we become strong and look back upon our own sufferings under the political and economic domination of the powers and see weaker and smaller people undergoing similar treatment, we will rise and smite that imperialism.

Then will we be truly 'governing the state and pacifying the world.'"

II

IN THE *San Min Chu I* the doctrine of the revolution is divided into three stages: first, the emancipation of the Chinese nation from the domination of the powers and of the war lords; second, the realization of a democratic program leading to a constitutionally elected government; third, "the nation to be the possession of the people, governed by the people, with benefits for the people equally divided." He insisted that from the very beginning this third stage was to be kept consistently in view.

Under the terms of the revolutionary program, the political system was to be essentially democratic, the greatest possible power being concentrated in the hands of the people in the duly elected National Assembly. The hsien was to become the unit of government, and every hsien would elect a delegate to the National Assembly. The provinces, in all matters that concerned the provinces alone, were to be self-governed; they would partake of a degree of autonomy which would make them almost federated states. The details of the desired government, its status, its degrees of power and dominion, its five powers (executive, legislative, judicial, censorship, and examination) were minutely studied, not only in the *San Min Chu I*, where indeed the details are often lost in the broad sweep of Sun Yat-sen's plan for the regeneration of China, but in countless speeches and articles written at the time. Even the time of election of the National Assembly is given in the *Outline of Reconstruction of the National Government* issued during the period when Sun Yat-sen was making his historic speeches on the Three Principles of the People. "When more than half the provinces have reached the stage when local self-government has been completed throughout the province, then a National Assembly shall be elected to promulgate a constitution." (Art. XXIII.)

The new government would rise from the broadest mass of the people. It would be equipped with vast powers, but a complex system of limiting control, partly in the hands of the censorship and partly arising out of the delicate balance between provincial and government powers, would prepare the way for a "coherent state," possessing many of the advantages of the traditional Chinese government, but possessing also (and perhaps this is more important) sufficient elasticity to meet the strains of the industrial revolution which Sun Yat-sen expected to see in his own lifetime. And since the larger aim of the revolutionary society was to make the hsiens self-governing, the upper structure of society could not but be democratic.

The virtues of this system must not blind us to its weaknesses. Though the exact definition of powers could be analyzed in the study, they referred to a period so far in the future that many students were convinced that Sun Yat-sen was impractical. Accused of utopianism, he could reply sincerely: "At least we have made a start. We have decided that the unit is the city community or the *hsien*. The new government, arising out of the broadest mass of the people, with its duly elected representatives in the National Assembly, will exercise representative power in a way which China has never experienced before. The State will take over all the large enterprises; we shall encourage and protect enterprises which may reasonably be entrusted to the people; the nation will possess equality with other nations; every Chinese will be equal to every other Chinese both politically and in his opportunities of economic advancement. When we have done this, when the benefits of society are enjoyed by all equally, then and only then can we lay our hands on our hearts and say that the revolution has begun."

The problems facing the legislator in China are vast and sometimes overwhelming. In a population containing a quarter of the inhabitants of the globe, where ignorance and squalor are the traditional accomplices of the highest scholarship and the greatest art, where the provinces differ in customs and dialect almost as much as the separate states of Europe, the lawgiver must show an understanding compliance with the effects of his laws among the illiterate and the ill-favored. "To be fair to all" might mean, and usually does mean, "to be unfair to the few."

In a period of military domination, it is not always possible to maintain a purely democratic attitude; and though habeas corpus goes by default, and "the agreed laws of the period of military government" are not always effective, a start has been made, in the semiparliamentary council known as the People's Political Council, to wield democratic powers through the representatives of the people. The people's voice is not silent. It can be heard in the Legislative Yuan, in the newspapers, in the universities and middle schools. The People's Political Council is empowered to demand from each ministry of the government a report of its activities; it can make suggestions and inaugurate reforms. The doctrine of the revolution remains, and if the details have sometimes been obscured by the nature of an implacable war, it nevertheless remains true that power in China devolves from the broadest mass of the people.

In the lectures on Min-chuan (the People's Sovereignty) Sun Yat-sen found himself in the extraordinary position of a convinced democrat who feared for the survival of European democracy on Chinese soil. He insisted that the Chinese democratic government should have its roots in Chinese history and assume a purely Chinese complexion:

"Statesmen and students of jurisprudence are now speaking of government as a machine and of law as an instrument, and our modern democratic age looks upon the people as the motive power of government. But if we follow the dust of the West, will not each generation be more dissatisfied than the one previous, and will we not finally have to stage another revolution? If another revolution becomes necessary, then it follows that our own revolution is a failure. What can we do to keep this revolution of ours from being a futile waste of energy? What plans shall we lay in order to secure a permanent government and a lasting peace—'enduring repose after one supreme effort'—and prevent calamities in the future? If we fail to follow the advanced systems of the West in their entirety, then we must think out new and better procedures ourselves. Are we capable of doing this? If we want to answer this question, we must not continually despise ourselves as small and mean. The stream of democracy has flowed into China and we welcome it for the reconstruction of our nation, but can we ourselves find a new and better way to make use of it? For thousands of years China has been an independent country. In our former political development, we never borrowed materials from other countries. Only in recent times has Western culture advanced beyond ours, and the passion for this new civilisation has stimulated our revolution. But since the ideas of democracy are still fluid and by no means perfect, if we imitate the West, then we shall find that the systems may already be out of date and we may find ourselves in a dead-lock."

This danger, more commonly understood by military strategists, is both a warning and an incentive to further action. The "pure cast of Chinese democracy" is essentially eclectic and opportunist: the problem of the legislator is to discover the best laws, not those which are theoretically most useful. "China has now the idea of democracy, but no perfect machinery has been invented in the world to express this idea." In the West the unit is the single individual with his vote; in China the unit was to be the hsien with its elected representatives in the provincial council or assembly. In England until recently the town boroughs were empowered to elect representatives to Parliament, but under the Chinese system the hsiens would possess still greater powers; they would elect their representatives to the assembly, but they would also possess the four rights of election, recall, initiative, and referendum.

The foreigner may be allowed to observe that this is a dangerous burden to place on the city magistrates and has usually given rise to disunity in Europe; but there is no reason why a similar system in China should not succeed. In a country of four hundred million inhabitants, it is almost inconceivable that the individual can be regarded as a unit of government. The hsien, like the Russian soviet, represents an ultimate nucleus of the people which (since we have developed no scientific method of measuring political forces) may be far more representative of the popular will than the vote cast in a ballot box.

The significance of Sun Yat-sen's proposed reforms is perhaps greater today than it has ever been. Compelled to regard the government of a country in continental terms, he was unconsciously providing the basis for an interpretation of the kind of government which must follow the Second World War. He had made a particular study of French and American democracy, and though he understood their limitations, he was candidly sincere when he wrote that of all the inventions of mankind, they seemed to be among those which were destined to endure. The tide of democracy had overflowed the shores of China; it was necessary above all to canalize the flow and to insure that the greatest number should benefit.

In 1889 Prince Okuma sought an audience with the emperor Meiji and said:

"No government, monarchical or otherwise, is as strong as a government that rests on the people, and enables those in authority to know what the people wish and what is best for them. An assembly will have to be established in this country sooner or later, and therefore the Government ought to hold out to the people this idea, and educate them to the fact that in due time such an assembly will be established for them. The people shall know that it is coming, and they should be educating themselves for this responsibility. But we must also remember that privileges like this can never be recalled. When you give suffrage and representation, you give them for ever."[1]

It was the genius of Sun Yat-sen that he recognized the weight of his responsibility in introducing democracy to China and that he was sufficiently clear-sighted to see its dangers and its great virtues.

III

IN THE year 1896 a book entitled simply *Learn (Chuen Shueh Pien)* was sent by the viceroy of Hupeh and Hunan to the chancellor of the Hanlin Academy in Peking with the request that it be laid before the young emperor Kuang Hsu. The slim book, bound in red silk, was carefully read by the Emperor, who wrote a commentary upon the book for the use of his ministers of state and who added the imperial rescript to the editions which were published in the provinces:

"We hereby command that the forty volumes which have been sent, be handed to the Grand Council of State,

---

[1] *Conversation between General Grant and the Emperor Meiji*, ed. Sahuro Yoshido, Tokyo, 1937, p. 17-18.

which shall distribute a copy each to the Viceroys, Governors and Literary Examiners of China in order that they may be extensively published and widely circulated in the Provinces.

"And these high officials are enjoined to use their sincere endeavors and exhort the people to hold in reverence the Confucian Religion and suppress all baseless rumours. Respect this." [2]

The book was a call to arms and a warning against republicanism; it was also a considered statement, by one of the most brilliant of the imperial viceroys, of the dangers facing China as a result of the invasion of the West. To those who hesitated before accepting Western scientific knowledge, he answered that the court itself insisted upon a widespread knowledge of the West:

"Our own holy dynasty, while possessing works on mathematics, astronomy, geography and agriculture, has provided for the translation of foreign books, established manufactures, arsenals and naval boards, and has frequently sent students to America, England, France and Germany to study common law, mining, naval and army tactics, railroading etc. The Tsung-li Yamen has printed books on law, science and other subjects, and the Shanghai office has issued over seventy different works that have been translated from foreign sources and that embrace in themselves a library of universal knowledge.

"The Court has ever been desirous of breaking the spell of ignorance by which the people are bound, and hopeful that the officials would themselves learn something that would benefit the country; but these have looked upon the new learning with contemptuous disgust and refused to modify their old ideas. Many of our Chinese extol foreign learning to the skies, and even go so far as to assert that

[2] *China's Only Hope*, An Appeal by Her Greatest Viceroy, Chang Chihtung, translated by Samuel I. Woodbridge, New York, 1900, p. 3.

the government and customs do not possess one redeeming feature. What! cast reproach upon our fathers and grandfathers? During all these generations has there not been one general, one minister, one scholar who deserved the name? And pray what education could Western countries boast of two thousand years ago? And what system of government?"

The trap is laid in the last word of the peroration; the old Viceroy knew the strength of the traditional government, as he knew the weaknesses of Chinese technological development. To the revolutionaries he could be bitterly contemptuous, believing that the great traditions would be overthrown and nothing would replace them. Like Sun Yat-sen in another age, he recognized the faults of the democracies; unlike Sun Yat-sen he was blind to their redeeming virtues.

"We confess that China is not a powerful nation, but the people under the present government get along very well by themselves; if this republic is inaugurated, only the ignorant and the foolish will rejoice. For rebellion and anarchy will come down upon us like night, and massacre will seal our eternal grave. Even those who establish the republic will not escape. Murder and rapine will hold sway in city and village. The burning of churches will follow, and under the pretext of protection, the foreigners will send troops and men of war to penetrate the far interior of our country. This talk about a republic is very agreeable to the adversaries of China.

"Years ago the Government of France was changed from a monarchy to a republic. The common people rose against the upper class, because the rulers were vicious and the government cruel. Our Emperor is exceedingly humane, our laws are not oppressive, and it is folly to introduce these democratic ideas to bring manifold calamities upon China. We have studied the philosophy of these republics, and find that translators of foreign books have wrongly interpreted the word 'republic' by *Min-chuan,* which is literally the 'popular sovereignty.' For the people in the republics of the West have only the right to *discuss* measures, and not to carry these measures into execution. . . ."

The Three Principles of the People were still unknown, but Chang Chih-tung elaborated three things necessary in order to save China from revolution. They were first, to maintain the reigning dynasty; second, to conserve the holy religion; third, to protect the Chinese. For Sun Yat-sen the first proposal could have little meaning, and the second was perhaps outside his field of knowledge until later times. But the revolution which he accomplished was founded upon an understanding of the third proposal, and the spirit of earnest inquiry with which Chang Chih-tung elaborated his command to *learn* is not very far removed from Sun Yat-sen's prevading desire to *change*. Though they were irreconcilable, they were not enemies; and more than once Sun Yat-sen was heard to remark that Chang Chih-tung, though misinformed, had provided the groundwork of the revolution. It was ultimately in their attitude to the people's sovereignty that they differed. Chang Chih-tung despised a popular assembly, believing that the Chinese officials in the Assembly would be obstructive through ignorance:

"The people know nothing about the affairs of the world at the present time, are utterly ignorant of the details and intricacies of civil government, they have never heard of the demand for foreign schools, government, military tactics and machinery. Discussion or non-discussion would be all the same, for these members of parliament would be ignorant of the matters in hand; they would have no knowledge to carry the appropriation bill, and no money to pay the appropriation if the bill were carried. A useless institution indeed!"

To Sun Yat-sen this "useless institution" was the saving hope of an empire which was growing dangerously autocratic. To the end of his days he believed that no other solution was possible. To the irreconcilable and unconciliatory spirit of the Ch'ing viceroy he opposed the will of the people and the urgency of reform. Chang Chih-tung believed honestly that in the "Middle Kingdom" everyone was directly responsible to Heaven and that Heaven was eternally benignant. He had forgotten that Heaven does not insure for everyone equally the good things of the earth; above all he had forgotten that Heaven was supremely indifferent to the people's livelihood.

IV

THE most controversial, and the greatest of the Three Principles is usually assumed to be the People's Livelihood. On this subject only four lectures were delivered by Sun Yat-sen, but he refers to this principle constantly in his writings. Today, when China is regarded as an equal among the great nations, with democracy already on her doorstep, the first two principles of nationalism and sovereignty may be assumed to have been solved. The importance of livelihood, therefore, is paramount among the younger generation of Chinese thinkers and intellectuals.

It is not altogether clear whether Sun Yat-sen envisaged a socialized community, and there is evidence that his views shifted between an extreme form of state control and a looser, and perhaps more tolerable, "orbit of social reconstruction." Within certain definite limits, he appears to have approved of Marxism and its underlying spirit of deliberate and unyielding conformism. "Class war is not the cause of social progress," he wrote, "it is a disease developed in the course of social progress, and the cause of the disease is starvation, and the result of the disease is war." He regarded Marx, as he would sometimes regard himself, as a "social pathologist," and he invested Marxism with all the attributes of the surgeon's knife, which will fail to make a clean incision unless handled delicately. In the last instance there was no real difference between the principles of the Kuomintang and the principles of the Russian Revolution; the difference lay in the methods with which they were applied.

It is impossible to understand livelihood without understanding the stages of the revolution. The third and final stage was essentially a stage to be reached when communication and industrial progress had led to a state when "the greatest benefits could be shared equally among the people." "The state is to be possessed by the people, governed by them and dedicated to their benefits." In this sense the task of the revolutionaries may appear to be utopian; but it is precisely the utopian character of the Three Principles which has made them valid and acceptable.

The industrialization of Chinese mineral resources, nationalization of banks, large enterprises, and the complex of transport and communications, the socialization of distribution and the system of direct taxation which he hoped to introduce are to be regarded only as the symptoms of the patient's good health; they are means toward a certain definite end, just as in war similar measures are introduced by all governments as a means to victory. He believed that surplus values in land could be excised by the introduction of a taxation measure by which the landowner could choose to assess himself. If his valuation was high, he would be taxed on it; if it was too low, it could be compulsorily purchased by the government. In this way he hoped to reach an authentic level of taxation fair to all; and though the system differs in some essentials from the methods employed in the West, it was one which could readily be appreciated by the practical Chinese.

In the lecture on nationalism Sun Yat-sen spoke of the ignorance of the masses, who are "born in a stupor and die in a dream," and it was precisely to their ignorance that he ascribed the decline of Chinese power—"a fall of ten thousand feet in a single drop." In later years he was to produce large-scale plans for reconstruction, as in *The Principles of Reconstruction,* where plans for railways, harbors, grain elevators, dockyards, and highways are set down in a blueprint for the future; for he saw that the race is not always won by the generation which first sets out on the journey, and the industrialization of China was still to come. The ignorance might disappear with education and improved communications. And what then? The Japanese had begun their race in 1870, and even if the Chinese did not begin their race till a hundred years later, their immense resources would allow them to outstrip the enemy. A united, strong democratic China might grow even out of the cesspools of Peking; and with the decline of the old traditional methods and the revival of the scientific spirit he could look forward to a regenerated China.

Livelihood is another word for the future, and all that the future would hold of promise and recompense for the suffering. In the name of livelihood, rather than liberty, he threw his gauntlet to the world, for the surgeon who had experimented with the same ideas as the Encylopedists found himself at last in the position of a doctor who recommends for the disease of starvation an increase of food and does everything in his power to supply it. And while corruption and extreme poverty flowered in Peking, the voice from the rich province of Canton spoke far more authoritatively upon the needs of the Chinese, since livelihood means also the prospect of a richer and more conscious life.

He was already dying when he gave the lectures on the Three Principles. His voice trembled with indignation when he spoke about the sufferings of China, but it was noticed that when he spoke on livelihood he was most at ease, and he is reported to have said that if one only of the Three Principles was allowed to survive, he prayed that it would be livelihood—the people's health. According to the old Chinese proverb, "The nation looks upon the people as its foundation; the people look upon food as their heaven." Where the emperor had failed, he was determined to succeed—the distribution of the good earth must be equalized among the people who were its owners. It was as simple as that; yet the road was almost inhumanly difficult. He was old; time was running out; even the members of the party listening to him were not always in agreement. To coat the pill he would tell stories, even stories against himself.

"I remember, when I was a student in Canton thirty years ago, how the sons of wealthy families in Saikwan would put on their fur-lined garments as soon as winter came. The winters in Canton are not very cold, and furs are not really necessary. But these wealthy young men had to wear their fur-lined garments every winter to exhibit their wealth; when the first cold came, they wore their light furs, and when it became a little colder, they wore heavy furs. In the middle of winter, no matter what the weather was, they always dressed in heavy furs. And one day, when they went to a meeting with their heavy furs, and the weather suddenly turned warm, they complained: 'Unless the wind changes, the people's health will be impaired!'"

It was a quiet obsession for "the people's health" which drove him along the long, dangerous road. There are other obsessions, but a revolutionary concern for health is usually characteristic only of doctors, and those who are suffering from ill health. He had failed to diagnose his own disease, but he succeeded perfectly in diagnosing the disease of his country. "This illness must cease!" he said, but he was no longer the doctor exploring a tumor with a scalpel: he was the doctor who patiently assists the birth of a child.

The child was to grow; it was to grow in spite of the Peking militarists, the corrupt officials, the inadequate training of the students and the technicians. It was to grow with amazing rapidity, because it possessed a faith in the future in livelihood—the people's health—and a doctrine of rigor. The people's health! Rigor! These were the two watchwords. Henceforth they were never to be separated.

IV. THE SENSE OF GLORY

I

THE rule of the war lords was dying. The visible signs of its death lay in the corruption surrounding Peking. The old city had watched innumerable conquerors with the passivity which comes from old age, but now at last it was dying. For a little while longer parliaments were felt to be desirable, cabinets were manipulated, presidents were elected or arbitrarily chosen, but in the interval a third and final militarist revolution was taking place. In March 1918, when Tuan Chih-jui returned to the premiership, he dispatched two generals to conquer Hunan. Wu Pei-fu and Chang Chin-yao were totally dissimilar. Wu Pei-fu, the Buddhist scholar, wrote a bitter epigram describing his rival as "one whose fatty remains will serve only to fertilize a few yards of Chinese soil." The appointment of Chang Chin-yao at the conclusion of the expedition to Hunan as governor of Hunan only embittered him still further, and a few months later he made a strategic retreat to the north and captured Peking with the co-operation of Chang Tso-lin.

The fruits of victory were sour. Chang Tso-lin, after walking into Peking on the heels of Wu Pei-fu, assumed supreme command and relegated Wu Pei-fu to the subordinate position of vice-inspector of the armed forces of Chihli, Shangtung, and Honan. Wu Pei-fu thereupon retired with his troops to Luyang. A few months later the Washington Conference was to introduce a new note of confusion into the already complicated structure of

Chinese politics. In November 1921 the Premier, Liang Shih-yi, instructed the Chinese delegates to yield to the Japanese, hoping that Japanese financial interests would reward the republic with much-needed financial assistance. Wu Pei-fu thereupon started a telegraphic campaign against the Premier, accusing him among other things of betraying the country. Chang Tso-lin, convinced that Wu Pei-fu was interfering in affairs that did not concern him brought a hundred thousand well-equipped troops through the Great Wall. Wu Pei-fu and Feng Yu-hsiang combined together against the Old Marshal, and in a series of battles which broke out in April 1922 Chang Tso-lin was forced back into his native Manchuria.

The news of Chang Tso-lin's retreat was greeted by Sun Yat-sen as yet another defeat for his cause. Wu Pei-fu's responsibility for the Canton rebellion, though never openly admitted, was sufficiently evident to make Sun Yat-sen feel that an alliance with Chang Tso-lin might yet save a desperate situation. In one of his letters at the time he wrote: "General Chang and I have the same enemies, and I will take him or anyone else who will help me in a combination to overthrow Peking."

At the same time he was becoming increasingly bitter at the attitude of the foreign powers, who appeared to be conniving at the ceaseless struggle for power among the war lords. "The foreign powers have given Peking moral prestige by their actions," he wrote. "They have intervened in China's internal affairs by practically imposing upon the country a government which is repudiated by it. They have supported a government which cannot exist for a single day without their support, and they have hindered China from establishing an effective and stable government."

The one government which had not interfered diplomatically in China's internal affairs was Russia, and he began to turn eyes increasingly to Moscow. In 1918 on the anniversary of the Russian Revolution, he sent Lenin his fervent congratulations, and a month after his inauguration as president of the southern republic he met the Soviet envoy Malin. While in Shanghai after the Canton rebellion in 1922 he wrote to General Chiang Kai-shek on August 30: "Recently a letter came from a special envoy sent to enquire about the Far Eastern situation and the means of solving it. I have given my replies in detail and kept in touch with him, and we may easily consult him on various matters as they arise. I hear that he will bring a military officer with him and I have asked him to send this officer to Shanghai as soon as possible, so that I may be informed about the military situation in detail. Pray come here as soon as you have recovered from your illness."

Adolf Joffe arrived in Shanghai in January 1922 with plenipotentiary powers to discuss diplomatic relations between the two governments. He was an envoy with an extraordinary prestige, for he had represented Russia at the peace conference at Brest Litovsk and was later appointed ambassador to Berlin. He had spent some months in the north, but his conversations with Sun Yat-sen proceeded as though Sun Yat-sen were still president of the provisional government. On January 26, 1923, an important agreement was signed between them:

"Dr. Sun Yat-sen holds that the communistic order, or even the Soviet system, cannot actually be introduced into China because there do not exist the conditions for the successful establishment of either communism or Sovietism. This view is entirely shared by Mr. Joffe, who is further of the opinion that China's paramount and most pressing problem is to achieve national unification and attain full national independence; and regarding this great task he has assured Dr. Sun Yat-sen that China has the warmest sympathy of the Russian people and can count on the support of Russia.

"On the basis of the proposals mentioned in Russia's message dated September 27th 1920, Mr. Joffe assured Dr. Sun Yat-sen that the Soviet Government was prepared to annul all the treaties concluded by Tsarist Russia with China (including the treaties concerning the Trans-Siberian railway) and to negotiate anew with China. Mr. Joffe gave the formal undertaking that the Soviet Government would not attempt to enforce an imperialistic policy in Outer Mongolia or to sever it from Chinese authority."

This undertaking came at a time when Sun Yat-sen was in great need of allies, but its significance lies in the broad policy of the Soviet government to surrender all the Russian concessions and the unpaid balance of the Boxer indemnity. For the first time for many years China was being treated in terms of equality by a foreign power. When Adolf Joffe disappeared to Japan to recuperate his health, he took with him a young follower of Sun Yat-sen named Liao Chung-kai, an authority on peasant agriculture, who was later to become a leading collaborator for Sino-Soviet rapprochement.

From this moment Sun Yat-sen was irretrievably committed to a policy which would be favorable to the Soviet government, not because he was inherently in sympathy with Russia or even familiar with its problems, but because he realized the importance of the spectacular advance of the Soviet system. "Our faces are turned towards Russia," he wrote at the time. "We no longer look to the Western Powers." And though he still looked in fact more to the Western powers than to Russia, because his education and background were preponderantly Western, it is significant that he could make this admission.

Even before the meeting with Adolf Joffe he had been working on the theory that Russia and Germany had more to offer the new republic than the Western powers. In September 1922 the *Hong Kong Telegraph* began to publish a series of his private papers, which had been stolen from the archives of the President's Palace by Chen Chiung-ming. These papers showed that he had been in secret correspondence with Russian and German advisers, and even contemplated an alliance. To many of his followers the papers appeared to have been forged, for no public announcements had been made on the subject of an alliance and nothing could have been more clearly calculated to disturb the powers. But the papers were genuine; Sun Yat-sen publicly acknowledged them, and Chiang Kai-shek was to write in the colophon of his account of the Canton rebellion:

"At the end of September, when I read in the newspapers the secret negotiations between Dr. Sun Yat-sen and Germany, my hair almost stood on end and my eyelids nearly froze to my eyes. I felt that Chen Chiung-ming was more malevolent than any serpent. . . . If countries like England, France, America and Japan are anxious for the restoration of friendship and mutual assistance, why should not China conclude agreements with Germany and Russia? Or should China be permanently cut off from diplomacy and reduced to a state of isolation?"

The beginning of 1923 saw still another bewildering turn of fortune. Toward the end of the year 1922 Sun Yat-sen learned that sufficient funds had been raised to provide for a punitive expedition against Chen Chiung-ming. Armies from Yunnan and Kwangsi thereupon converging upon Canton on January 15, 1923, Chen Chiung-ming fled along the East River to Waichow and disbanded his army. In this breathing space Sun Yat-sen returned to Canton, appointing Chiang Kai-shek chief of staff and Sun Fo mayor of the city.

He was aging now. The effects of the Canton rebellion

could be clearly seen in the lines of his face and the physical weariness which he made no efforts to hide: the old dynamo was showing signs of strain. But though he was ill, and the first symptoms of cancer were beginning to show in the whiteness of his face and in sudden spasms of incurable pain, he could still think in terms of the whole of China. As soon as he arrived, he issued a declaration proposing "the disbandment of the superfluous soldiery and the establishment of a united and efficient government."

Shen Hung-ying was repulsed, but Chen Chiung-ming dug himself into the banks of the East River and offered a rugged resistance. When autumn came, the architects who were rebuilding Canton heard the sound of gunfire in the hills—Chen Chiung-ming was coming to avenge his defeat.

The weather was sultry, full of storms and squalls of rain. For more than two months a battle raged in the mud. Sun Yat-sen commanded the armies in person, a frail figure in a trench coat and a topee, sick with weariness but more hopeful than he had ever been. If peace could be maintained in the south for a few years, he could look forward to a time when the whole of China would be following the Three Principles. And when Chen Chiung-ming was finally defeated and he returned once more to the task of reorganizing the party, the old rigor was tempered by understanding and there was less bitterness. "The revolutionaries should sacrifice themselves first and should absolutely obey the party rules and instructions," he wrote in a memorandum to party officials.

The example of Russia, whose revolution had taken place seven years after the Chinese revolution, was a continual warning. In November 1923 he organized the party once more. In a letter to Chiang Kai-shek he wrote: "Henceforth our revolution can never succeed unless we take the Russian revolution as our model. . . . If the present situation verges upon collapse, we shall be compelled to resort to drastic measures according to the Chinese proverb 'to cut the entangled hemp with a sharp knife.' Today our revolutionary committee is prepared to take these measures." And in the manifesto which followed the reorganization of the party, he laid special emphasis on the necessity of purging undesirable members: "Today misgovernment and economic bankruptcy augur ill for the Chinese Republic. The disease of penury has grown still worse; the cure lies in our political reorganisation. . . . Our party has struggled for years with the Three Principles of the People as our aim, and though the names have been altered at intervals, the goal and the principles are the same. The reason why we have not yet succeeded lies in our failure to reorganise the members. There must be communication between the members of high rank and those of low rank, and we must purge the party of all undesirable elements."

Early the next year, on January 20, 1924, the first National Congress of the Kuomintang opened at the National Higher Normal School in Canton. A hundred and sixty-five representatives from the provinces and from overseas came to attend the conferences given by the Generalissimo during the seventeen meetings. Once again he criticized the behavior of party members in the past:

"After the revolution was accomplished, we were at a loss to discover a suitable basis for reorganisation. But now we have found a suitable basis, and we have assembled the comrades from the different provinces in order that they can pass resolutions on our new proposals. . . . We shall examine the new methods daily while the conference lasts. They are not free from imperfections, and this is precisely why it is necessary to hold these conferences, so that you may study them and improve upon them. . . .

The two important things concerning the reorganisation of the party are: firstly, it must again become a powerful political party, and secondly, we must use the power of the party to reconstruct the country.

"The party lacked solidarity in the past, not because we were faced by a powerful enemy, but because we destroyed ourselves from within. It is of the greatest importance that all members of the party should be united in a spiritual unity. In order that all members may be united spiritually, the first essential is that they should sacrifice their freedom, the second is that they should offer their ability. The past failures of the party are due to the fact that while the individual members had freedom the party as a whole possessed none, and while the individual members had ability the party as a whole was powerless. Herein lies the failure of the Kuomintang in China. Our reorganisation today is planned to abolish these shortcomings. . . . The former revolution was brought about by the momentarily conscience-stricken attitude of those who knew that only by a revolution could China be saved, but no one knew when a revolution could be accomplished. Moreover no one worked out a complete plan of action for the time after the revolution. The effort was individual, not disciplined, and though the Manchu regime has been overthrown, we are still after thirteen years in a state of becoming, and nothing has been accomplished. Yes, we are still in a state of revolution."

In the closing speech he stressed the necessity of careful preparation for united action:

"It is thirteen years since the establishment of the Republic, but we have still not realised the aim of the Three Principles of the People. Why? In the first place there was no complete control over party members. In the second place our comrades have not exerted themselves to the uttermost. We are holding this First National Congress in order to put forward a complete method of controlling our members and in order to define the discipline of the party, so that we may put into effect the Three Principles of the People."

Finally he compared party members with soldiers at the front:

"As soldiers fight in the field, so party members must struggle for the cause. During a battle, soldiers will obey their commanders even if the order is wrong, since even by obeying a wrong order, they may win the battle. If some of the soldiers think the order wrong, and act separately, the whole army will be embroiled, and the enemy will defeat them piecemeal. Our members were accustomed to act separately, each one considering that he alone was right. In consequence the whole party lost its spiritual unity and the revolutionary aims never materialised. Henceforward the success of the revolution lies in united action and solidarity."

In the proclamation issued at the conclusion of the conference, the war lords and the imperialists were attacked with undisguised bitterness:

"The warlords, who can hardly stand on their own legs and do nothing but wag their tails, have won the support of the imperialists who finance them handsomely with the sinews of war in order to stir up a succession of civil wars. Meanwhile the imperialists take the opportunity of increasing their spheres of influence and controlling Chinese interests. The chaos in China has been caused by the imperialists, who achieve huge profits through the warlords' bloody hands. Moreover the internal disorders prevent industry from forging ahead, and even now Chinese industry cannot cope with foreign capital. Since the failure of the Chinese revolution, the middle classes in China have suffered repeated reverses and been plunged into penury. The peasants can no longer plough their fields, but must sell their property at a low price. Day after day the cost of living increases, and misery stalks through the land."

The second part of the proclamation defined the Three Principles of the People. The nationalism of the Kuomintang is defined as the self-emancipation of the Chinese nation and the equality of races within China. By democracy is meant that the Chinese people should have not only the right of election but also the power of initiative, referendum, and recall. Livelihood, a more complicated topic, was defined under the headings of the equalization of land value and the regulation of capital. Henceforward the party was to concentrate on these three issues, but the last —and to the eyes of the Chinese peasants the most important—received additional emphasis in the proclamation: "The Nationalist party makes a bid for the support of labourers and peasants. According to our doctrine of livelihood the State will provide land for cultivation to those farmers who have been deprived of their land or to those who have suffered from their landlords. Irrigation systems will be provided and colonisation schemes will be devised to help those farmers who are without land of their own. . . ." The farmers, the most powerful and the least vocal elements in China, were to come within the scope of the party for the first time, for the revolution had been largely proletarian and derived its strength from the great industrial towns of Canton, Hankow, and Shanghai. Banks were to be provided, laws would be passed to facilitate the commerce of agricultural supplies, and in every way the party promised to pursue a policy which would be favorable to the farmers.

The third section of the proclamation referred largely to external affairs. The party demanded the abrogation of the unequal treaties, the repayment of foreign loans, the abolishing of foreign concessions, extraterritoriality, and foreign control of the customs, and the salt gabelle. "Those of the powers which voluntarily renounce all special privileges and voluntarily abrogate the treaties which infringe on the sovereign rights of China shall be considered the most favoured nations." The section concluded with resolutions upon the adoption of the hsien as the unit of local self-government, the introduction of universal suffrage and complete freedom of association, speech, faith, and place of abode.

The methods of revolution had changed; the organization of the party changed also. Where previously there had been a supreme leader and a host of small committees, the new organization involved a complete structural alteration of power centered upon the standing committee of the Central Executive Committee. This standing committee, which met once a week, would share the responsibility of leadership with the chief executive, who would possess, during the first stages of the governmental program, undisputed authority. With a new program, a new organization, and a new discipline, the party was stronger than it had ever been. Communists were admitted to membership as individuals, not as collaborators—the first Communist to be admitted being the distinguished intellectual Li Ta-chao.

The presence of Communists in the new party was probably influenced by the arrival in Canton in October 1923, a month before the reorganization, of Mikhail Borodin, who came ostensibly as a representative of the Rosta News Agency but in practice to advise on the newly established government. He had served the Communists in Turkey and Persia, and his powers as a negotiator were sufficiently impressive to suggest his appointment as Sun Yat-sen's personal adviser, an appointment which was to create increasingly vast changes in the revolutionary struggle. He was short, suave, and self-confident. As an agent of the Third International he combined immense revolutionary fervor with a command of the Chinese situation which was itself perhaps the most impressive thing about him.

Sun Yat-sen's determination to make Borodin his high political adviser may have been influenced by an incident which occurred in December. The Chinese Customs Service in Canton was held under an international administration with headquarters in Peking. All revenues received in Canton were accordingly remitted to Peking and a considerable part of this revenue found its way to the northern government. To Sun Yat-sen it seemed grossly unjust that funds received in Canton should go to Peking, and in December he threatened to seize the Customs House unless the moneys were handed over to the southern government. Immediately landing parties were put ashore to protect the Customs House, and a display of naval force by foreign ships took place in the harbor, while guns were directed upon the city. Sun Yat-sen stood firm. In refusing to yield he was backed by all the members of the party and the majority of Chinese in the port, and the deadlock which might have lasted indefinitely came to an end when a compromise was effected through the mediation of the British and American consuls.

But the southern government was powerless, not only against foreigners but also against Chen Chiung-ming. China was weak for lack of a disciplined army. The revolution had exhausted the best energies of the people, and the survivors were not always capable of fighting for a cause. The age of the war lords was passing, but graft and bribery remained. Whole armies could be won over by a checkbook, and no leader could rely implicitly on the loyalty of his troops.

A revolutionary army, trained by revolutionaries, with a strict moral code, might yet save the situation; and when Chiang Kai-shek returned from Russia in 1923, his first task was to set about the organization of the Whampoa

Military Academy. From Russia came the first foreign military adviser to the reorganized party. General Ga-lin, later to achieve a still greater fame as General Blücher, was placed in command of the training of cadets in military affairs. Liao Chung-kai, who had accompanied Joffe on his tour of Japan, acted as party representative. During the following six months more military advisers were sent from Moscow—at one time it was reported that there were more than thirty Soviet officers in Sun Yat-sen's army—and by June 1924 the Whampoa Academy, so long a dream, had become a reality. On June 16 Sun Yat-sen addressed the five hundred cadets who attended the opening ceremonies:

"At the beginning of the Revolution in 1911 many members of the party lost their lives in their heroic struggle in all the provinces. The most well-known among them were seventy-two martyrs of 'The Yellow-flower Mound.' Therefore, when the revolution actually broke out, all the provinces participated, and the Manchus were overthrown and the Republic came into being. The revolution is now only partially accomplished, and this is entirely due to the fact that we had no revolutionary armies to carry out the final aim of the revolutionary party. As we had only the revolutionary party struggling for revolution and no revolutionary army, the Republic has been and still is controlled by the war lords and politicians who overran it, and so there was no democratic foundation, and thus our revolution can never be realized. What I expect from this school is a rebirth of the revolutionary spirit with the cadets of this school as the nucleus of the revolutionary army. With a well-trained and disciplined army, we have every reason to believe in the future success of our revolution."

The school was a success. By September the first cadets were being sent out, and new cadets were being enrolled.

General Chiang Kai-shek assumed the presidency of the academy. Two training corps, where revolutionary officers and soldiers could be trained, were established by General Ho Ying-ching. In October, four months after the establishment of the academy, the cadets were already in the firing line.

A revolt, organized by the Merchants' Volunteer Corps, a semifascist organization raised by the Canton merchants, with Chen Lien-pai, the compradore of the Hong Kong Shanghai-Banking Corporation as the commandant, broke out after a long period of disturbances. By August 15 the southern government received reports suggesting that an outbreak was imminent. Nine thousand machine guns, ordered by Chen Lien-pai, were known to be on board a Norwegian steamer bound for Canton. It was known that the vessel had reached Amoy, and Sun Yat-sen telegraphed to General Hsu Chung-chih to detain them. The guns were confiscated. The Merchants' Volunteer Corps demanded their return and threatened a strike of businessmen. Meanwhile the British consul communicated with the Chinese Ministry of Foreign Affairs, threatening reprisals. Sun Yat-sen immediately lodged a protest in London and received assurances that the British consul had no power to protect the merchants' organizations in Canton in defiance of the legitimate government, and with some satisfaction Sun Yat-sen heard that the consul had been summarily dismissed from his post.

The end was not yet. The merchants still possessed hidden stores of arms and ammunition, and on October 10, the anniversary of the revolution, a procession of students, laborers, and peasants was fired on by the Volunteer Corps. The Whampoa cadets were called out. The merchants were disarmed. And with the defeat of a faintly sinister fascist organization, the government could once more attack the problems of a united China.

The way was hard, as it is hard for all governments in a state of transition from one civilization to another. The Three Principles of the People were pledges yet to be fulfilled. With little money, a small army of cadets, and inexhaustible hope, a new way might be found; but the leader was aging and there was as yet no sign of his successor. In the hearts of the Chinese the austerities and mortifications of revolution had worked a miracle. All ardently desired union; none knew how it could be accomplished. "Without bloodshed, by an act of faith," Sun Yat-sen had written in Shanghai. But the faith that can move mountains cannot move a nation of four hundred and fifty millions at once.

Time was needed, and everyone knew there was no time. In Canton people were accustomed to talk of the race against death. Sun Yat-sen alone seemed to be the personification of revolution; he alone could bring unity about. But already he was dying and no one knew how long he could live or whether he could survive into the new year. An old man, surrounded always by students, smiling and yet somber, wearing a gray military coat and a felt hat, he seemed to be the embodiment of the two worlds, the one which was passing and the one which was yet to be born.

II

"THE expedition to the North . . ." More and more often the words came to his lips. In the earliest days of the revolutionary struggle, forty years previously, he had hoped to unite China under a republic by attacking the North from Canton as his base. Peking was under the control of Wu Pei-fu. Accordingly he had allied himself with Chang Tso-lin and the Anfu group, but in May 1922 Chang Tso-lin's army collapsed, and his forces had turned bandits and were swarming over the countryside. Wu Pei-fu was at the height of his power. Li Yuan-hung was president of the northern republic, a post long coveted by Tsao Kun, whose protracted intrigues compelled the President to take flight in June 1923. An unsatisfactory situation was made still more unsatisfactory when, in October, Tsao Kun was officially elected president as the result of bribery unparalleled in a city where bribery was commonplace. According to the popular opinion of the time, five thousand dollars was paid for each vote.

In September of the next year internal strife broke out in the Yangtse Valley when the war lords of Kiangsu and Chekiang came to blows. During the same month fighting broke out once again between the Chihli faction (under Tsao Kun and Wu Pei-fu) and the remnants of the Anfu clique (under Tuan Chih-jui) and the Fengtien faction (under Chang Tso-lin). Sun Yat-sen took this opportunity to launch his final northern expeditionary force, and on September 18 he issued a manifesto calling upon the provinces to assist in the expulsion of the Chihli regime. He sent General Hsu Chung-chih with the Kwangtung army to the north, General Chiang Kai-shek led the cadets along the East River in a final purge of the remnants of Chen Chiung-ming's forces, and at the same time Hunan and Hupeh troops under the command of General Tan Yen-kai penetrated into Kiangsi.

China was once more in a ferment. Wu Pei-fu, accompanied by "the Christian General," Feng Yu-hsiang, marched across the Great Wall against Chang Tso-lin. The battle against Chang Tso-lin was successful, but Feng Yu-hsiang had been in alliance with the revolutionaries for some time, and instead of following Wu Pei-fu, he suddenly turned back, occupied Peking, imprisoned Tsao Kun, and banished the young emperor from the Summer Palace. This eager giant, with the manners of an aristocrat and the appearance of a Laughing Buddha, held all the strings in his hand and played them all at once. He was sublimely unconscious that forever afterward his enemies would refer to his "betrayal." He had saved the revolution. Now at last the emperor was decisively removed from the throne. Wu Pei-fu's army was in flight. Chang Tso-lin came to Peking, but this time he did not make the mistake of sending the chief architect of his power on a mission of inspection. Feng Yu-hsiang remained in Peking. Tuan Chih-jui was appointed "provisional chief executive functioning as the President of the Republic," and with the defeat of the Chekiang and Kiangsu war lords the way was open for the unification of China.

A few weeks later Feng Yu-hsiang invited Sun Yat-sen to Peking. Fears were expressed for Sun Yat-sen's safety, but once more he scouted them. "If you regard me as the Generalissimo," he is reported to have said, "then perhaps I shall be in peril, but if you regard me simply as a party member, it is nothing serious at all." Accompanied by Mme. Sun Yat-sen and a supporting staff, he left Canton on a government cruiser on November 12, 1924. Two days earlier he had issued a proclamation saying that he was making the journey to the north in the hope of convening the national assembly, to abolish imperialism, to solve the problems of the people's livelihood, and to surrender the southwestern federation for a united China.

No man has ever made a journey with such high hopes. On the morning of the seventeenth he landed in Shanghai, only to discover that the International Settlement authorities had failed to provide him with a landing permit on the grounds that his political activities were undesirable. To a Japanese pressman who visited him on board the cruiser, he said that since Shanghai was Chinese territory and he was the very landlord, he could do anything he pleased provided he obeyed the general laws of conduct.

The International Settlement relented. Northern representatives came to visit him, a tea party was held in his honor, and in his own house in No. 29 rue Molière he gave a tea party to newspapermen.

He would have liked to stay longer in Shanghai, but the northern representative urged him to visit Peking at the earliest moment, and on the twenty-first he sailed for Peking by way of Japan. He reached Nagasaki on November 23. On the S.S. *Shanghai Maru* he was treated with every care, but the sea journey was already taxing his strength. At Kobe, which he reached on the afternoon of the twenty-fourth, there were more ceremonies, more speeches, thousands of Chinese students would rush forward and clasp him by the hand. He smiled, waved his hat, made speeches to the Chinese in which he insisted upon the convocation of the national assembly, and to the Japanese in which he insisted that they should help China in a spirit of benevolence, for China's prosperity would pave the way to lasting peace in the Far East. From November 25 to the thirtieth he was continually making speeches, which were fully reported in the Japanese press; and it seemed as though all the years of struggle had not been in vain, and as though the respect which was paid to him came from the heart of the Japanese people. The air of Kobe invigorated him. He complained of sleeplessness, but otherwise he was well. Long years of suffering had made inroads in his health; his cheeks were lined, and now more than ever he resembled a prophet; but on the *Hokuryo Maru,* in which he left Kobe for Tientsin, his vitality returned for a few days: he dictated letters to his secretary and spoke often of how much he looked forward to the meeting in Peking. In November the Sea of Japan is often violent; cold winds blow from the Arctic, and inevitably he caught cold. His cook had been left behind at Shanghai; he complained that he could not take his food comfortably, and when he reached Tientsin on the fourth of December, he was already a dying man.

III

THE landing stage and the jetty were crowded with people waving to him, and as soon as he landed he was surrounded by cheering crowds. Once more he took the opportunity to announce that nationalism and livelihood, the two most important of the Three Principles, were to be restored to the people. "I have come to convoke the People's Convention and to abrogate the unequal treaties," he said decisively, and as he looked round at the assembled journalists, the flags and the cheering people, it was noticed that he was shivering and did not always answer the questions put to him. As though the northern government had not rejected all his recommendations, as though he were still in the safety of Canton, he began to talk slowly and forcibly of his plan to organize the country on a co-operative basis, with representation from all the progressive movements, a country in which the people would have complete power to decide their own fate. As he spoke, several journalists noticed that he was in great pain, and once or twice his hand moved quickly to his hip, and drew back again. But as he stood in the light of the arc lamps, his face was impassive, dead white, the white hair brushed straight back from his forehead, the long black padded gown hanging in folds to his feet, the image not of a suppliant but of an old conqueror who had come for the last time face to face with his foes.

It was once of those gusty mornings when the wind comes from the north across the plains, a day of frost and mildew, the cold air penetrating the bones. As he stood shivering in the cold, it was noticed that he smiled rarely, and for the first time people realized that he was growing old.

He motored to the Chang Garden Hotel, which for the next three weeks was to be his headquarters. In the afternoon he called on Chang Tso-lin, who entertained him at a banquet, but a three-hour conference with the Old Marshal overtaxed his strength. Not accustomed to the cold weather in the north, and worn out by the long, desultory journey from Canton, he took to his bed. The doctors diagnosed influenza and a relapse of the liver disease.

He was not a good patient; Dr. Schmidt complained that he was restless, tormented by inactivity—and though the influenza was cured in ten days, the relentless nagging pain in the liver remained. One day, a fortnight later, when he was still in bed and Dr. Schmidt was still trying to seek the cause of the swollen liver, there came two representatives from the North bearing the basis of representation as worked out by the Peking government: every one of his recommendations had been rejected.

There was worse to come. The chief executive had actually sent notes to the foreign legations acknowledging that the northern government would faithfully observe all extraterritorial rights. Appalled by the news, Sun Yat-sen is said to have staggered out of bed and shouted: "I am determined to abolish all unequal treaties! Then why do you observe them? Why did you invite me to the North? Do you fear the powers?" And though at last his rage subsided, and he was put to bed with a temperature of a hundred and a pulse of 120, he determined to see the matter to an end. Ten days later, in a special coach, surrounded by his entourage, he set out for Peking, where he arrived on the last day of the year, dangerously ill and in a state of collapse.

He no longer smiled. The effort of speaking wearied

him, and those who remained by his bedside in the Hotel de Pékin were conscious that he was continually thinking and making plans for the future. He still dreamed that the North would collaborate with the South and form some kind of corporate state where the voices of all classes would be heard in the parliament. But it was too late, the hands on the counterpane remained still, and the old leonine head sank back on the pillows, while the doctors watched him through a hole cut in a screen. He was conserving his strength.

For ten days he lay quietly in the hotel, attended by Russian and German physicians; and for the first time the dread rumor of cancer crept into the press reports.

The new president of the reorganization conference to be convened by the chief executive was Chao Ehr-sun, an old monarchist, a devoted follower of the Manchus and a staunch supporter of Yuan Shih-kai's monarchical regime; and the cabinet was composed almost entirely of followers of Wu Pei-fu, war lords and supporters of the monarchical restoration movement. The wheel had turned full circle. In a final outburst of fury the sick man gave orders that no members of the Kuomintang party should take part in the reorganization conference—his last official order to party members.

On January 22 the disease took a turn for the worse: his temperature varied between 41°C. and 27°C.; the pulse began to beat so fast that it seemed impossible that any heart could withstand the strain. On the afternoon of the twenty-sixth, at the suggestion of Dr. Krieg and after consultation with the hospital doctors, he was removed to the Peking Union Medical College Hospital in the city. At half past six in the evening, he was operated upon by Dr. Adrian Taylor, a former missionary and head of the Department of Surgery and it was discovered beyond all doubt that the disease was cancer—the liver was hard like a stone. When the wound was closed, a treatment of ultraviolet rays was employed as a last resort, but on February 18, when nearly all hope was abandoned, he was removed to Wellington Koo's Chinese home in Tieh Shih Tse *hut'ung* in the northern part of the Tartar City. There he spent his last days.

Chinese doctors were called in, but they proved as unsuccessful as the rest. Worn out by the disease, appalled by the wave of reaction, and conscious of being surrounded by enemies, he lingered for another six weeks, rarely speaking, preferring the grasp of a man's hand to the voices of consolation. At night he wept bitterly. During the day his white face lay impassive on the pillows.

On the afternoon of February 24, at three o'clock, the nurse came from the sickroom to report that he was sinking. His wife, his son, and his eldest grandson hurried into the room, followed later by Dr. and Mrs. H. H. Kung, T. V. Soong, Tai En-sai, his son-in-law, and several others. At that moment it seemed that the sick man was about to die. There was a whispered conference and Wang Ching-wei was asked to draft a will. No one knew whether the sick man would be able to speak, or even whether he could sign a document. Because time was running out, and because it was necessary that the party should have instructions to follow after his death, Wang Ching-wei approached the bedside and explained that though everyone knew the sick man would recover, it would first be necessary for him to enjoy a long convalescence, and meanwhile the party would be without his leadership. Sun Yat-sen listened, paused for a long time, and then said: "I have nothing to say now. If I recover, I shall move to Tang Shan (a watering place in the Western Hills) and recuperate, and then I shall have plenty of time to talk with you. But if I am going to die, it is useless to say anything." [1]

One by one they implored him to leave a message for the nation. Once again he was silent, and at last, speaking slowly and enunciating with difficulty, he said:

"I see that you are in real danger. After my death, our enemies will either weaken or destroy you. And if you escape from danger, you will still be weakened, so why should I say anything?"

There was a long pause. The man who was dying seemed to believe that everything he had worked for had been lost irretrievably. Once again Wang Ching-wei implored him to speak. In those intervals, heavy with danger, no one realized that he would soon crown his work by assenting to a statement in which everything he believed and fought for would receive a final, uncompromising seal.

"We have followed you for many years," Wang Ching-wei whispered. "We have neither feared danger nor been weakened by the enemy. Whom should we fear, and by whom shall we be weakened? If you leave us a message, it will serve to guide us in our national life."

"What do you want me to say?"

"We have written a message and we are now going to read it to you. If you agree, we shall ask you to sign—but we would prefer a message from your own lips."

Sun Yat-sen nodded; Wang Ching-wei produced a statement and began to read slowly and quietly. Sun Yat-sen cried: "All right! I quite agree!" and then the family implored him to say some words for them; he agreed, and the second statement was read out to him. He would have signed the two documents immediately if he had not discovered his wife leaning her head against the door and weeping.

[1] The following conversation was taken down verbatim and signed by Sun Fo, Kung Hsiang-hsi, Soong Tse-ven, Tsou Lou, and Wang Ching-wei.

The first document read:

"I have devoted forty years to the work of the National Revolution with the aim of securing for China a position of freedom and independence. After forty years of experience I am profoundly convinced that in order to achieve this aim, we must call up the masses of the people and unite with those peoples of the world who will treat us on terms of equality and who will struggle together with us.

"At present the revolution is not yet completed. All my comrades should work unceasingly according to the General Principles of Reconstruction, the Outline of Reconstruction, the Three Principles of the People written by me, and the declaration issued by the First National Congress of the Kuomintang, until this aim is achieved. The convocation of the People's Convention and the abolition of the unequal treaties that I have advocated recently must be carried out with the least possible delay. This is what I wished to call your attention to."

The second will read:

"I have been so devoted to national affairs that I neglected to manage my property for my family. My beloved wife Soong Chingling shall have my possessions—my house and my books—as souvenirs. My son and daughter are now grown up and can live by themselves. Let them take care of themselves and carry out my wishes."

During the following days the disease began to show alarming symptoms. The patient could not excrete; he could not drink water; and the body began to swell. In an effort to prolong the life that was already flickering out, Dr. Krieg was summoned back to the bedside, and a little later Dr. Wang-lan, a Japanese-trained physician, began a series of injections. The injections, though they appeared to have some effect, could not remove the deep-seated cause of the illness, and by March 9 he was beyond all help. The rate of pulse increased to 160 beats a minute, while the rate of breathing decreased to eighteen respirations an hour.

Though he was so close to death, and knew that he was about to die, his mind wandered back to the East River in Kwangtung, where the revolutionary forces were still fighting against Chen Chiung-ming. He was relieved when dispatches were read to him proclaiming that the war was well in hand under the command of the young general Chiang Kai-shek and General Hsu Chung-chih. Swatow was recaptured. Hu Han-min was in Canton supporting the revolutionary troops with money and ammunition. Order was being maintained in the reoccupied areas. As the long roll of victories reached the Tartar City, Sun Yat-sen begged them to send an urgent telegram to Hu Han-min that "on no account should the citizens of Canton be disturbed by our military forces."

This was the last telegram he sent. On the afternoon of March 11 his breathing came with even greater difficulty, and seemed indeed to stop. Toward evening he called for the documents of his will, and with the help of his wife, who lifted up his hand, he signed his name to them. A few minutes later he said slowly:

"When I left the two provinces of Kwangtung and Kwangsi, I thought I would come here and further our national unity and peace. I proposed to convoke the People's Convention and to put into practise my Three Principles of the People and the Five-power Constitution for the reconstruction of a new China; but I have been seized with a stupid disease and now I am past all cure. Really, to live and to die makes no difference to me personally, but to leave unrealised the principles I struggled for for so many years grieves me deeply. Strive for the early convocation of the People's Convention and try to realise the Three Principles of the People and the Five-power Constitution. If you do this, I shall 'close my eyes after my death.'"

Shortly afterward he grasped the hand of his brother-in-law H. H. Kung and said: "You are a Christian; I too am a Christian," and later he added: "I am a messenger of God to help men to obtain equality and freedom."

Already he was sinking. During the whole of that afternoon, those who were present at his bedside listened for his last words. In China the last words of a good man have a particular significance; they are engraved on wood and inscribed in the family records. But the doctor ordered him to remain silent; he fell asleep, and at half past six in the afternoon, when he awoke, his hands and feet were already cold. During the night he was heard to say: *"Ho ... Ho ... Ping, fan-dao, chiu ... chiu ... chung-kuo."* "Peace ... struggle ... save China."

He lingered on until the next morning; at half past nine he was dead. His wife, his son, and his grandson Sun Tse-ping, were by the bedside when he died. It was March 12, 1925.

IV

"ALL greatness," said a Chinese poet, "has fallen from the clouds," meaning perhaps that the element of water is the more splendid, or that the conjunction of fire and water has made all greatness visible. But the great rains of the revolution had not fallen from a sunlit sky, and so much had been swept away in those fourteen years that people blinked in the sunlight on the roads of Peking and wondered whether it was indeed true that the revolutionary who had conjured up the lightning, and brought down the dissolving rains, was dead.

Already he had become a legend. Old peasant women,

in hobbled feet, would touch his clothes and call him "Emperor." He who had hated the empire became on his deathbed enthroned. He was powerful throughout his life, but in death he was still more powerful. The young boy who had thrown pebbles in the flames and watched them explode; the doctor who diagnosed under the microscope the diseases of human beings; the revolutionary leader whose success lay in continual defeat—all were remembered and all were dead. Almost singlehanded he destroyed a monarchy which was in existence when the Sumerian kings were still worshiping on stone towers, and created a republic for four hundred million people with a handful of students, a gunboat, and a passionate belief in the divine right of men to possess sovereignty and a livelihood within a democratic community. With three words he overturned a kingdom.

He lived for the future and seems never to have envied the past. The old Chinese virtues—justice, truth, acceptance of every conceivable hardship—he retained to the end of his days; but he had destroyed the old order more fundamentally than the emperor Meiji destroyed the shogunate. And now he was dead, and though the voice engraved on the gramophone records was heard by the numbed crowds in the old Imperial Park in the Forbidden City, and thousands of people came to see the white waxen face under the glass cover of the coffin, and thought he was dead, he was more alive than he had ever been.

Three weary years were to pass before the whole of China was united, years of war and bloodshed and harassing armies moving swiftly from the south; and only ten years later, again China was to begin her long war with the Japanese. But during these gusty days of March in Peking, among cryptomerias and acacia trees, while the coffin lay in an imperial pavilion under the blue and white flags of the Kuomintang, the hush that had descended upon China during his protracted illness seemed to lift, and more than one commentator reported that there was a greater feeling of unity in the country than anyone could remember before.

He had asked for Christian burial. On the day when the body was removed from the hospital, the cortège was followed by a surpliced choir, carrying candles. There were soldiers with black armbands, students in blue gowns, ministers with silver swords, all the consuls, diplomats, mayors, and officers of the city; and following them came the people shouting and crying and setting off fireworks and beating their breasts. Inside the small pavilion were wooden boards painted red and inscribed in gold. Unlike the majority of these inscriptions they did not describe his virtues. The board above his head read: "Those who strive will achieve." On the two boards beside the coffin were the inscriptions: "The Revolution has not been achieved," and "Comrades, we must struggle harder." He had been rigorous in life; in death he was mercilessly stern. But no one among the thousands who came to pay their last respects, not even Karakhan, the Soviet ambassador, who had assumed the role of chief mourner, knew how stern he could be.

Meanwhile the press all over the world was pouring out eulogies of the dead man. The American press described him as being among the five or six pioneers and leaders of the world: Wilson, Lenin, Gandhi, Kemal, and Clemenceau. The Japanese press hailed him as a man who had lived and died for a cause; the English praised his rigor and unselfishness, the French his revolutionary acumen. But it was left to Tai Chi-tao, one of his closest friends and his lieutenant during many of their rebellions, to pronounce the most genuine as well as the most generous of the funeral orations:

"What I held most in esteem was his deep tenderness.

Mencius has said that only those who are averse to killing may succeed in unifying a country. In saying this, Mencius did not mean that those who aspire to unite a country or even the whole world should not kill a single person, but that they should be averse to killing. Sometimes men have to be killed; sometimes men have to struggle; but whoever is given to killing will fail. The statesmen who win our worship are those who are given to tenderness. Those who are lacking in ability or intelligence cannot succeed in uniting a country, but the greatest requisite of all in order to unite a country is tenderness.

"For many years I have been one of his followers. I never heard him speak about himself. He gave everything to others and received nothing for himself. Living the life of a revolutionary, he never amassed any property, he had no selfish desires, no thought of personal revenge. We may possibly be as learned as he was, but we can never be so full of tenderness."

On April 2 a long funeral procession marched from the old imperial park through the west gate of the city to the Western Hills. Once more there were students and banners and high officials in mourning, but now the peasants and farmers from all the districts around, and representatives from Canton, came to join the procession. At Pei Yuan Szu, a small elaborately carved marble temple in the hills, where peonies grew in the courtyard under the shade of drooping acacias, the heavy wooden coffin halted and the last funeral orations were made. The sun shone, and already in the distance Peking was disappearing under a bluish-gray carpet of leaves. As the monastery bells and gongs beat a salute, the coffin was taken up the long winding steps and installed in a high chamber overlooking the city he had failed to conquer in life and succeeded in conquering triumphantly in death.

On June 10, 1929, in the presence of the greatest in the land, among soldiers and scholars, peasants and diplomats, the gold encrusted coffin with the head facing the east was taken down the stone steps of the monastery and deposited on a special train in Peking. In a vast mausoleum constructed at fabulous cost on the slopes of the Purple Mountain, within sight of the tombs of the first Ming emperors, he was laid to rest in the presence of his son by his first marriage, Dr. Sun Fo; Mme. Sun Yat-sen, and the leaders of the Kuomintang. Among cypresses and marble steps, under the blue-tiled roof of the mausoleum, he lies like the old Chinese god who "seems at rest, but whose boundless, restless spirit moves eternally."

It is doubtful whether he would have entirely approved of this marble monument. His tastes were simple, and all his life he had been only the small rain falling pitilessly on a rock which crumbled in the end to reveal the granite beneath; and on this granite was inscribed the name "Sun," meaning descendant and "Wen," meaning the arts. And indeed the names were not fortuitous—he loved literature, and books were never far from his keeping. He built up a private library which was generally considered to be the best in the land, and his reverence for the classics is witnessed in constant quotation. Above all, he was a scholar. He possessed the scholar's love for reticence and quiet contemplation, and the scholar's habit of careful analysis.

In his hatred of torture, love for children, and reverence for peace (the word that was most often on his lips), he was not very far removed from his favorite poet, Tao Yuan-ming. In one of his speeches toward the end of his life he said, speaking slowly and gravely:

"I have done my work; the wave of enlightenment and progress cannot now be stayed, and China—the country in the world most fitted to be a republic, because of the industrious and docile character of the people, will in a short time take her place among the civilized and liberty-loving nations of the world."

He was a man who had lived a long time away from his native land, and had examined it attentively, and from afar it appeared always brighter and more beautiful than it was. This exile from another world prayed above all that the four hundred millions of Chinese peasants should be assured of livelihood; and this was his strength, for the inarticulate millions found in him the substance of their dreams. The vision he created is still a vision, but at last the lion was fully awake, and in the fullness of its youth, a youth which Sun Yat-sen had restored to them in double measure, the lion roared and thundered at the Japanese.

APPENDIX A

A NOTE ON SUN YAT-SEN'S ANCESTRY

Since the Revolution many scholars have attempted to discover the sources of Sun Yat-sen's ancestry. The task was supremely difficult, for the southern provinces have so often been overwhelmed by invaders from the north that all traces of family genealogies have often been lost. Luck, and great patience among Chinese scholars, have combined to form the main outlines of Sun Yat-sen's descent.

The earliest known ancestors of the Sun family have been traced to the district of Chenliu, near Kaifeng, in Honan. Sun Li, one of his earliest ancestors in the Tang dynasty, is known to have led the imperial troops in the suppression of the Hwangtsao rebellion * on the borders of Fukien and Kiangsi. The rebellion lasted ten years. During this period Sun Li emigrated to Ningtu in Kiangsi, and after the suppression of the rebellion he was honored by the emperor with a dukedom and a grant of lands. Through the Five Dynasties and right up to the Sung dynasty, the Sun family remained in Kiangsi. Gradually, as the descendants grew numerous, they began to spread widely over south Kiangsi and Fukien until finally, in the early Ming dynasty, they were found in Kwangtung.

* The Hwangtsao rebellion, named after the rebel leader (Hwangtsao means "yellow nest") occurred in the reigns of the emperors Shih Chung and Chung Ho. It began at a time when the country was given over to warring factions, and the authority of the emperors was being questioned by the people. It was a popular rebellion, the troops of the rebel invading Honan, Kiangsi, Fukien, Chekiang, and several other provinces. Sian and Loyang were captured by the rebels, the emperor Shih Chung fled to Szechuan, and Hwangtsao proclaimed himself emperor with the dynastic title of Chi. The rebellion was finally quelled by General Li Keh-yung in 884 A.D.

The first emigrant from Fukien to Kwangtung was a certain Sun Yu-sung, whose traces have been found along the borders of the East River in Kwangtung. During this emigration the family altar, which is still the altar of the Sun family, was erected at Kun Kung village on the East River. Sun Yu-sung emigrated during the reign of the emperor Yung Lo of the Ming dynasty. Here the Sun family lived for eleven generations. In the Ch'ing dynasty the twelfth descendant, Sun Lienchang, is known to have lived in the village of Ch'ung K'oumen in the district of Heungshan (Chungshan), Kwangtung. His father, Sun Ting-piao, took part in the wave of resistance against the Ch'ings in the south, and appears to have suffered during the enforced migration which accompanied the quelling of the rebellion. For three generations the Sun family remained in the village of Ch'ung K'ou-men: it was the fourteenth ancestor, Sun Tien-chao, who removed his family to Choyhung in the middle of the reign of Chien Lung (about 1766). Sun King-yin, Sun Yat-sen's grandfather, married a daughter of the Huang family, who lived until 1870. Sun King-yin is reputed to have been prosperous, but was later reduced to penury by a too strict observance of the laws of *feng-shui,* or geomancy, which prescribes that children should search for the most auspicious places of burial for their ancestors. After spending most of his money building graves for his ancestors, he retired to his village and gave himself up to farming. Sun Yat-sen's father also believed in geomancy, and it is said that after his father's death a geomancer predicted that a great man would be born from the family ten years hence. Sun Yat-sen was born thirteen years after his grandfather's burial. His father, Sun Tao-chuan, married the daughter of a certain Yeong Chun-chang when he was thirty-three and the bride eighteen. A painting of a family group which has been preserved shows his mother as a delicate and beautiful woman surrounded by three of her six children. Her husband is short and dark, swarthy like many Cantonese, with the typical broad shoulders of a farmer.

APPENDIX B

CHRONOLOGICAL TABLE

1866 Sun Yat-sen born November 12 (the sixth day of the tenth moon of the fifth year of the Emperor T'ung Chih).
1871 His eldest brother, Ah Mei, sailed for Honolulu.
1878 Ah Mei returned from Honolulu.
1879 Sun Yat-sen sailed for Honolulu and entered Iolani School.
1882 Sun Yat-sen graduated from Iolani School.
1883 Returned to China. The idol-mutilating incident, and the escape to Hong Kong.
1884 In April entered Queen's College, returning to Choyhung for his marriage May 7. Sailed for Hawaii in response to his brother's invitation in October.
      The Sino-French War broke out.
1885 Returned to Choyhung in March and resumed his studies in Queen's College in July.
      The Sino-French War ended.
1886 Entered Pok Tsai Medical School, Canton.
1887 Transferred to Alice Memorial Hospital, Hong Kong.
1888 His father died on February 12.
1891 Sun Fo born October 18.
1892 Graduated from the Medical School of the Alice Memorial Hospital. Founded a hospital in Macao.
1893 Removed the hospital to Canton.
1894 The Sino-Japanese War broke out, July 1.
      Sun Yat-sen visited Tientsin with Lu Ho-tung to interview the viceroy Li Hung-chang, later returning to Canton and sailing for Hawaii, where a chapter of the Hsing Chung Hui was inaugurated. Returned to Hong Kong in December.

1895 The first revolutionary attempt occurred September 9. Left for Hong Kong about ten days later, and then sailed to Honolulu via Japan.
1896 Remained in Honolulu for six months, leaving for San Francisco in June. Sailed from New York on September 23, arriving in Liverpool on the thirtieth. Detained in Chinese Legation on October 11 and released on the twenty-third.
1897 Made an extensive tour of Europe. The Three Principles of the People formulated.
1898 Left London for Japan in July. *Coup d'état* in China in August.
1899 In Yokohama.
1900 Boxer uprising occurred in the summer. The second revolutionary attempt occurred in Waichow, Kwangtung, on August 13.
1901 In Japan.
1902 In December traveled to Hong Kong.
1903 Sailed from Hong Kong to Annam. Returning to Japan, sailed for Honolulu on October 5, beginning the second world tour.
1904 Arrived San Francisco, April 6.
1905 Left New York for Europe in the spring and held his first convention in Brussels, second in Berlin, third in Paris, returning to Japan in July. Tung Meng Hui inaugurated August 20.
1906 An uprising occurred in Hunan, October 19.
1907 Left Japan for Annam. The third unsuccessful revolutionary attempt occurred on April 11 at Kwangkong, followed by a fourth attempt on April 22 at Chi-niu Hu, Waichow. The fifth attempt occurred on July 24 near Chinchow and the sixth at Chen-nan-kuan on October 26.
Left Annam for Singapore.
1908 The seventh unsuccessful revolutionary attempt occurred on February 25 at Chin and Lien, followed by the eighth on March 29 at Hokou.
The dowager empress Tzu Hsi died on November 15

APPENDICES

        preceded by the emperor Kuang Hsu. Prince P'u Yi enthroned.

1909 Sun Yat-sen set out for his third and last world tour.

1910 The ninth unsuccessful revolutionary attempt occurred at Canton on January 3.

        Sun Yat-sen returned from San Francisco to Penang. Resumed his third world tour toward the end of October.

1911 The tenth unsuccessful revolutionary attempt occurred at Canton on March 29.

        The Revolution broke out on October 10 at Wuchang.

        Sun Yat-sen arrived in Paris on November 11 and in Shanghai on December 24. The peace conference opened on December 15. The representatives of all the provinces which had declared their independence met in Nanking on December 29 and elected Sun Yat-sen provisional president.

1912 Inauguration of the republic on January 1.

        Emperor abdicated on February 12.

        Sun Yat-sen resigned on February 14.

        National Assembly at Nanking elected Yuan Shih-kai provisional president. Yuan entered office on March 10.

        Sun Yat-sen arrived in Peking in August.

        The Kuomintang inaugurated in Peking on August 25.

        In October, Sun Yat-sen set up the Bureau of Railway Development in Shanghai.

1913 Sun Yat-sen sailed for Japan in February.

        March 20. Sung Chiao-jen assassinated in Shanghai.

        March 25. Sun Yat-sen reached Shanghai from Japan.

        April 8. National Assembly opened.

        April 27. Yuan Shih-kai formally negotiated with the Five-Power Consortium for the loan of £75,000,000.

        In July, Hsiung Hsi-ling became premier.

        July 12. Second revolution began.

        July 20. Chiang Kai-shek and Chen Chih-mei attacked Shanghai.

        July 23. Sun Yat-sen deprived of his post as director-general of railway development.

October 10. Yuan Shih-kai formally assumed presidency.
November 3. Dissolution of Kuomintang party.

1914 January 10. Parliament suspended.
July 8. Inauguration of Chung Hua Ke-min-tang.
October 25. Sun Yat-sen married Soong Ching-ling.

1915 January 18. The Twenty-one Demands presented to Yuan Shih-kai by the Japanese minister.
May 9. Yuan Shih-kai accepted the demands.
December 5. An abortive attempt was made by the revolutionaries to attack the Shanghai arsenal.
December 25. The third revolution, led by Tsai Ao, broke out in Yunnan.

1916 January 1. Yuan Shih-kai became emperor.
March 22. The monarchy was renounced and Yuan Shih-kai restored the republic.
June 6. Yuan Shih-kai died, succeeded by Li Yuan-hung.
In June, Sun Yat-sen returned to China.
In August parliament was convened again.

1917 March 14. China broke off diplomatic relations with Germany.
May 8. Bill promoting China's participation in the World War presented to parliament.
May 23. Tuan Chih-jui deprived of premiership by President Li Yuan-hung.
In June parliament was dissolved by Chang Hsun, military governor of Anhui.
July 1. P'u Yi restored to the throne.
July 14. Tuan Chih-jui quelled the movement for the restoration of the monarchy, and China returned to a republican form of government. Li Yuan-hung refused to resume presidency.
Sun Yat-sen left Shanghai for Canton on July 17.
August 1. Feng Kou-chang succeeded Li Yuan-hung in presidency.
In August Tuan Chih-jui returned to premiership.
August 14. China declared war against Germany and Austria.

APPENDICES

August 25. An extraordinary convention held by parliament in Canton.

August 30. Military government set up in Canton.

September 1. Sun Yat-sen elected generalissimo by parliament.

November 22. Tuan Chih-jui resigned from premiership.

1918 January 3. Sun Yat-sen led two cruisers to bombard the yamen of the Kwangtung military governor.

March 23. Tuan Chih-jui returned to premiership.

May 4. Sun Yat-sen resigned from the post of generalissimo and left for Shanghai.

October 10. Hsu Shih-chang succeeded Feng Kou-chang as northern president. Tuan Chih-jui resigned.

1919 May 4. Student's movement.

Sun Yat-sen remained in Shanghai, writing *Plans for National Reconstruction*.

1920 In July war broke out between the Anfu clique headed by Tuan Chih-jui and the Chihli faction led by Tsao Kun and Wu Pei-fu.

In August, Sun Yat-sen instructed Chen Chiung-ming and Hsu Chung-chih to oust the rival forces from Kwangtung.

October 10. Chung Hua Ke-min-tang became Chung Kuo Kuomintang. In November, Kwangtung was recaptured by Chen Chiung-ming.

1921 In April parliament elected Sun Yat-sen president.

He was inaugurated on May 5.

In July, Chen Chiung-ming recaptured Kwangsi.

In October Sun Yat-sen led a military expedition against the North.

1922 April 1. War broke out between the Chihli clique and the Fengtien faction.

Sun Yat-sen returned to Canton in the latter part of April

May 6. Sun Yat-sen resumed the northern punitive expedition and reached Shaokuan, returning to Canton on June 1.

June 2. Hsu Chih-chang resigned and Li Yuan-hung restored to the presidency.

June 16. Revolt in Canton.

August 9. Sun Yat-sen left Canton for Hong Kong, and sailed for Shanghai the next day. Issued a proclamation from Shanghai on August 15.

1923 In January, Sun Yat-sen interviewed Adolf Joffe.

January 15. Sun Yat-sen instructed Sun Fo to raise funds for the Yunnan and Kwangsi troops in order to expel Chen Chiung-ming.

He returned to Canton in February.

During the summer he sent Chiang Kai-shek to Russia.

In June, Li Yuan-hung was forced to flee from Peking by Tsao Kun, who in October was elected president.

In November the Chung Kuo Kuomintang party was reorganized.

Chiang Kai-shek returned from Russia in December.

1924 January 20. Convention of the First National Congress opened.

June 16. Whampoa Military Academy opened.

In September war broke out between Chekiang and Kiangsu.

In October a second war between the Fengtien and Chihli factions broke out.

October 15. The revolt of the Merchant Volunteers was suppressed.

October 18. Sun Yat-sen launched northern punitive expedition.

November 2. Tsao Kun forced to retire from presidency.

Sun Yat-sen left for the North on November 12, arriving in Shanghai on November 17. On December 4 he landed at Tientsin, interviewing the representatives of the northern government on December 18. Started for Peking on December 31.

1925 February 24. The documents of his will were drafted.

March 12. Sun Yat-sen died at the age of sixty.

BIBLIOGRAPHY

(Books in Chinese are marked with an asterisk.)

Cantlie, Sir James, and C. Sheridan Jones, *Sun Yat-sen and the Awakening of China.* New York, 1912.
Cantlie, Neil, and George Seaver, *Sir James Cantlie.* London, 1939.
Chao, Chu-wu, *The Nationalist Revolution in China.* London.
* Chen, Chin-ch'ih, *A Table of the Principal Events in China.* Shanghai, 1935.
* China Cultural Society, *Biography of the Martyrs.* Chungking, 1942.
* Chiang Kai-shek, *An Account of the Troubles in Canton.* Nanking, 1927.
* Ching, Hsu-hsih, *A History of China.* Chungking, 1940.
* Feng, Chih-yu, *Anecdotes of the Chinese Revolutionaries.* Chungking, 1941.
Hahn, Emily, *The Soong Sisters.* New York, 1941.
* Kuomintang Historical Sources Commission, *Chronological Table of Sun Yat-sen's Life* (unpublished).
* Li, Pan, *The Principal Events in Chinese History since the Birth of Sun Yat-sen.* Shanghai, 1929.
* Lin, Sou-fu, *A History of the Chinese Revolution.* Foochow, 1942.
Linebarger, Paul, *Sun Yat-sen and the Chinese Republic.* New York, 1925.
Linebarger, Paul, *The Gospel of Chung Shan.* Paris, 1932.
* Lo, Hsiang-lin, *A Study of the Heredity of the Father of the Republic.* Chungking, 1942.
* Lu, Hung-hua, *A Biography of Dr. Sun Yat-sen.* Chungking, 1942.

* Lu Tsou, *A History of the Chung Kuo Kuomintang.* Changsha, 1941.
MacNair, Harley Farnsworth. *Modern Chinese History.* Shanghai, 1933.
Price, Frank, *San Min Chu I* (English translation). Shanghai, 1927.
Restarick, Henry B., *Sun Yat-sen, Liberator of China.* Yale University Press, 1931.
Sharman, Lyon, *Sun Yat-sen, His Life and Its Meaning.* New York, 1934.
* Sun Wen. *Complete Works.* Shanghai, 1937.
Tong, Hollington, *General Chiang Kai-shek.* London, 1936
Woo, T. C., *The Kuomintang and the Future of the Chinese Revolution.* London, 1928.
* Wu, Cheng Huan (editor), *The Complete Works of Sun Yat-sen.* Shanghai, 1927.

INDEX

Ah Mei, 10-11, 12-13, 15, 17, 19, 23, 29, 36, 144
Ai Kuo Hsueh She, 63
Alice Memorial Hospital, 25, 39
Amoy, 1, 21, 58
Anfu faction, 154, 162, 209, 210
Anhui, 128, 129
Anking, 86
Annam, 21, 22, 37, 65, 76, 79, 80, 81, 82
Association of Elder Brothers, 53
Aveling, 48

"Black Banner Regiments," 22
Blücher, General, 207
Blue Thriving Village, 3
Borodin, Mikhail, 205-206
Bow, Colonel, 169
Boxer Indemnity Fund, 158
Boxer uprisings, 54-57, 60, 68

Cabinet, Chinese Republic, 115
California, University of, 144
Cantlie, Dr. James, 25, 26, 34, 36, 39, 42, 43-44, 62, 126
Canton, 1, 4, 7, 24, 25, 28, 30, 31, 58, 82, 83, 84, 85, 130, 140, 155, 158
Cap Suy Mun, 17
"Castle," Kafka's, 3
Chang, 8
Chang Cheng-wu, 115, 117, 124
Chang Chih, 74
Chang Chih-tung, 50, 52, 60, 76, 77, 189, 190
Chang Chin-yao, 195
Chang Garden, 63
Chang Hsun, 152, 153
Chang Ming-chi, 97
Chang Piao, 76
Chang Po-wan, 62

Chang Tai Yen, 63
Chang Tso-lin, 154, 162, 167, 195, 196, 209, 210, 211, 214
Changsha, 94
Chao Ehr-sun, 215
Chao Heng-tih, 175
Charge to Learn, 60
Chekiang, 210, 211
Chen Chak, 169
Chen Chi-mei, 95, 115, 121, 125, 129, 130, 132, 139, 140, 148, 149, 151
Chen Chiung-ming, 130, 155, 156, 162, 163, 165, 169, 170, 171, 175, 199, 200, 206, 210, 219
Chen Ju-sheng, 148
Chen Lien-pai, 208
Chen-nan-kuan, 22, 80
Chen Shao-pai, 25-26, 31, 34, 35, 52, 58
Cheng Shih-liang, 24-25, 30, 33, 34, 35, 52, 58, 59
Chiang Kai-shek, 31, 95, 129, 140, 149, 151, 163-164, 168, 169, 171, 199, 210, 219; organization of military academy, 206-208
Chiating, 7
"Chien Hung Store," 31
Ch'ien Lung, 2, 173
Chihli faction, 154, 210
Chin, 80, 82
Chinese-Annamese frontier, 37
Chinese Nationalist Party, 157
Chinese Revolutionary Alliance, *see* Tung Meng Hui
Chinese Revolutionary Party, 135-136, 157-158
Ch'ing dynasty, 1, 2, 7, 36, 173, 174
Ching-hsing Kuan, 6, 18
Ching-ming, 5
Chingtien, 6

237

INDEX

Chiniu Lake, 79
Chiu Chin, 86
Chou An Hui, 149
Chow Yung, 63
Choyhung, 1, 3, 6, 8, 10, 36
Chu Chin-lan, 155
Chu Yuan-chang, 110
Chung, Consul-General, 67
Chung Hua Ke-min-tang, see Chinese Revolutionary Party
Chung-kuo Ke-ming Tung Meng Hui, see Tung Meng Hui
Chung Kuo Kuomintang, see Chinese Nationalist Party
Chung Kuo Pao, 52
Chusam, 21
Clemenceau, 98
Clive, Robert, 62
Communications, in China, 120, 191-192
Communism, 197, 205
Confucius as Reformer, 47
Cool Mountains, 22, 81
Council of Seven, 156

Dairen, 37, 139
Darwin, 61
Das Kapital, 48, 61
Descent of Man, The, 61

East River, 58, 199, 200
Eki, Mr. Hioki, 147
England, wars against, 1-2
"Essay With Eight Legs," 60
Evolution and Ethics, 61
Ewa, 13

Fang Wei, 115, 117, 124
Fascism, 208
Feng Kuo-chang, 94, 95, 154
Feng Yu-hsiang, 153, 196, 210, 211
Fengtien group, 154, 171
"Five Objects of Knowledge," 50-51
Five-Power Constitution, 69, 219
Fontainebleau, 2
Foochow, 1, 130
"Four Big Brigands," 26, 31, 52
Formosa, 21, 28, 58
Franco-Chinese War, 21-22, 37

Fuchow, 22
Fukien, 21, 58, 129, 148, 156, 162

Ga-lin, General, 207
Gentaro, Kodama, 58, 59
George, Henry, 48
Goodnow, Dr. Frank, 149
Gordon, General, 7
"Great Peace" Emperor, 7, 138
Green Society, 24-25

Hakka, 6
Haleakala, 36
Han Dynasty, 52, 62
Hangchow, 95
Hankow, 27, 76, 77, 90, 91, 92, 94
Hanoi, 65, 79, 81
Hanyang, 90, 92, 94, 95
Harbin, 140
Haxell's Hotel, 39
Hawaii, 65
"Heavenly Prince," 2, 3
Heaven's Reason Society, 53
Heilungkiang, 140
Ho Ying-ching, 208
Hokou, 81, 82
Honan, 90
Hong Kong, 1, 17, 24, 25, 30, 31, 32, 33, 52, 82, 83, 99, 169
Honolulu, 65
Hopeh, 90
Hotel Street Theater, 65
Hsing Chung Hui, 28-29, 35, 38-39, 65, 69
Hsiung Ping-kuan, 91
Hsu Chung-chih, 129, 162, 208, 210, 219
Hsu Hsih-lin, 86
Hsu Shao-tseng, 96, 115
Hsuan Tung, 84
Hsu Shih-chang, 167
Hsueh Shih-chu, 79
Hu Han-min, 71, 73, 78-79, 80, 83, 129, 155, 219
Hu I-sen, 80
Hua Hsing Hui, 77
Huang Ming-shuh, 148
Hukwang, 93

INDEX

Hunan, 50, 52, 71, 76, 78, 79, 93, 140, 155, 175, 210; independence declared, 129
Hung Hsien, 150-151
Hung Men, see "Triads"
Hung Shiu-ch'uan, 1, 6, 7-8
Hungkiang, 77
Hupeh, 50, 52, 55, 76, 78, 92, 93, 210
Hupei, 27
Huxley, 61
Hwang Hsing, 71, 76, 80-85, 92, 94, 97, 102, 115-117, 124-125, 129, 139, 141, 151
Hwang-Kong, 79
Hwang Ming-tung, 81
Hwang Yung Hsueng, 31

I Ho Tuan, 54
Ilto, 59
Imperial School of Interpreters, 37
Industry, Chinese, 191-192
Inukai, 51
"Iskra," 73

Joffe, Adolf, 197, 198, 207
Jung Lu, 56

Kai Hokai, Sir, 25
Kalakaua, King, 15-16, 66
K'ang Hsi, 2, 53, 60, 173
Kang Yu-wei, 47, 50, 51, 58, 64, 65, 70, 153
Kansu, 56
Karakhan, Ambassador, 222
Kerr, Dr. John, 24
Kiangsi, 78, 129, 164, 168, 210
Kiangsu, 7, 210, 211
Kiaochow, 37
Kidnapped in London, 42, 46
Kingfishers, 4
Kobe, 34, 35, 52
Kojimachi Fujiro, 70
Korea, 28
Kowloon, 144
Krieg, Dr., 215, 218
Kuan Ti, 6
Kuang Hsu, 20, 47, 64, 88, 186
Kung, H. H., Dr., 216, 220
Kung Hsiang-hsi, 145

Kuomintang, 48, 116, 121, 122, 125, 130, 155, 157, 160, 164, 179; dissolved, 132; inefficiency of, 136; First National Congress, 201, 218
Kwang Yu-wei, 37, 64
Kwangchow-wan, 144
Kwangsi, 4, 6, 37, 56, 80, 150, 155-156, 162, 175
Kwangtung, 1, 4, 8, 24, 29, 32, 37, 56, 58, 79, 80, 90, 94, 97, 125, 129, 150, 155, 175, 210
Kwangtungese, 3, 39
Kweichow, 150, 155
Kweilin, 155, 163

Laotse, 161
Learn, 186
Lenin, 48, 73, 197
Li Brothers, 9
Li Hai-chin, 151
Li Hung-chang, 22, 27, 28, 41, 56-57, 58
Li Lieh-chun, 129
Li Yuan-hung, 92-93, 96, 108, 151, 154, 171, 210
Liang Chi-chao, 37, 47, 50, 64-65, 73, 74, 95, 115, 150, 152
Liang-Hu College, 77
Liang-pi, 105
Liang Shih-yi, 196
Liao Chung-kai, 76, 198, 207
Liaotung, 28
Lien, 80, 82
Lillin, 77
Lin Chin-mien, 164
Ling Tsu-wei, 164, 165
Liu Ying-fu, General, 23
Liuyang, 77
Love Country Academy, 63
Lu Ho-tung, 19, 21, 26-27, 30, 31, 32-33
Lu Yu, 87
Lu Yung-ting, 155, 175
Luanchow, 93, 95
Lunghua, 130
Luyang, 195

Macartney, Sir Holliday, 41, 43-44, 45, 46
Macao, 1, 4, 11, 21, 25, 26, 33

Malin, 197
Manchu dynasty, 9, 17-18, 24, 26, 27, 29, 31, 32, 34, 35, 37, 43, 53, 77
Manchuria, 70, 139, 140
Manson, Sir Patrick, 39, 41, 42, 44, 62
Marx, Karl, 48, 61
Maui, 36
Meheule, Rev. Solomon, 14
Meiji, 38, 186
Merchants' Volunteer Corp, 208
Min River, 22
Ming dynasty, 7, 24, 53, 110-113
Min Pao, 73 74, 79; suspended, 83
Mou Fo-I, 77

Nagasaki, 52
Nanchang, 168
Nanhsiung, 168
Nanking, 76, 80, 94, 95, 96, 102, 105, 129, 130; treaty of, 1
Nantao, 149
Nanyang Technical Academy, 61
Napoleon, 2
National Party of China, *see* Kuomintang
Nienfei, 1-2
Ningpo, 1

Okuma, Count, 51; Prince, 186
Opium War, 1
Osaka, 52
Outline of Reconstruction of the National Government, 181-182, 218

Pai Yuan San, 165
Pao Huang Tung, 51
Pao Wen-hui, 129
Pearl River, 33, 82, 165
Pei-ti, 19
Pei Yuan Szu, 223
Peiyang, 50
Peking, 2, 3, 4, 10, 29, 30, 35, 42, 56, 57, 61, 74, 81-82, 88, 95, 105, 153, 158, 162, 195
Peking National University, 63
Penang, 83

People's Gazette, *see* Min Pao
People's Political Council, 183
Pescadores Islands, 28
Ping-hai, 58-59
Ping-hsing, 77
Piracy, 8-9
Plan Safety Society, 149
"Po-hsueh Hung-tzu" examination, 53
Pok Tsai hospital, 24, 25, 30
Portsmouth, Treaty of, 70, 71
Principles of National Reconstruction, 160, 192, 218
Pu Lun, Prince, 66, 88, 117
P'u Yi, 87, 153

"Railway Defense Societies," 90
Railways, Chinese, 88-90, 119-120, 122, 124
Reau, M., 91
Red Society, 24-25
Red Spears, 52-53
Reform China and Save Her, 37
Revive China Society, *see* Hsing Chung Hui
Russo-Japanese War, 70
Ryosaku, Yamada, 59

Saigon, 57, 58
Salisbury, Lord, 45
San Ho Hui, *see* "Triads"
Sandalwood Mountains, 10
Schmidt, Dr., 214
Secret Societies, 7, 22, 24-25, 28-30, 31, 33, 35, 38-39, 52-54, 67, 69, 71, 77, 78, 173, 174, 176
Seoul, 28
"Shang Ti," 7
Shanghai, 1, 29, 61, 63, 95, 96, 129, 140, 156
Shangtung, 37, 54, 154, 158
Shansi, 56, 57
Shao Ho, 148-149
Shaokuan, 164, 168
Shen Hung-ying, 163, 200
Sheng Hsuan-huai, 89
Shih Chien-ju, 52, 58, 59, 60
Shih Huang Ti, 22
Shih Koh-fa, 167
Shimonoseki, 28, 47

INDEX

Shogunate, Japanese, 2
Shun-chih, 53
Sianfu, 57, 94
Singapore, 81, 82, 99
Sino-Japanese War, 28, 57, 58
Society of Heaven and Earth, *see* "Triads"
Soong, Charles, 144
Soong, Ching-ling, 143, 145, 218
Soong, E-ling, 144
Soong, T. V., 216
Soong Yao-ju, 30
Ssu Ma Chien, 54, 62
Sugano Choji, 80
Sugiyama, Mr., 56
Sun Fo, 26, 144, 199, 224
Sun Mei, 5
Sun Tao-chuan, 4, 5
Sun Tao-jen, 129
Sun Tse-ping, 220
Sun Yat-sen: ancestry, 227-228; birth, 4, 5; brothers, 5, 10-11, 12, 15, 17, 19, 23, 29, 144; burial, 222-224; childhood, 6-16; daughters, 36, 145, 218; death, 220; director-general of railway development, 119, 129; elected president, 102; exiled from Japan, 78; father, 4, 5; Generalissimo, 155; illness, 214-220; kidnapped, 39-47; marriages, 21, 26, 143-144; mother, 4, 5, 36; other names, 41, 41 fn.; rebellion, 16-20; resignation, 109-110; schooling, 8, 13-16, 21, 24; sisters, 5; sons, 26, 36, 140, 144, 216, 218, 220; travels, 36, 38, 66-67, 68-69, 83-84; ultimatum to Yuan Shih-kai, 128-129; wife, 21, 26, 143-144, 164-165, 169-170, 216, 218, 219, 220, 224
Sun Yen, 145
Sung Chiao-jen, 71, 73, 90, 122, 124, 125, 126, 127
Sung Dynasty, 173, 180
Swatow, 219
Szechuan, 1, 76, 78, 90, 129, 132, 150, 155, 162

"Tai Cheong," *see* Sun Yat-sen
Tai Chih-tao, 139, 222
Taiping rebellion, 1, 2, 6, 7, 24, 27, 38, 53, 74
Taiyuanfu, 56
Taku forts, 55, 57
Talienwan, *see* Dairen
Tan Yen-kai, 129, 210
Tang Chih-yao, 155, 175
Tang Shan, 216
Tang Shao-yi, 96, 155
Tang Ting-kuan, 167
Tao Kung, 1
Tao Yuan-ming, 224
Taylor, Dr. Adrian, 215
Teh Chang, 5
Teh Sai, 59
Teh Yu, 5
Teng Keng, 163
Three Character Classic, The, 8
Three Principles of the People, 27, 53, 67, 69, 133, 170-171, 174-175, 181, 189, 190-191, 193, 200, 202, 204, 209, 213, 218, 219
Thirty-year-old Flower Fades Like a Dream, 73
Thucydides, 62
Tientsin, 22, 27, 55, 56, 61, 76
Ti-ho, 19
Ting Kung-liang, 140
Tong Kaks, 28
Tongking, 22
Torazo, Myazaki, 58, 71, 73
Toyama, 51
"Triads," 7, 24, 25, 54
Tsai Ao, 150
Tsai Chih-ming, 91
Tsai Yuan-pei, Dr., 63, 115
Tsao Kun, 162, 210
Tseng Kuo-fan, 7, 27
Tsingtao, 147, 154
Tsitsihar, 140
Tsu Hsi, 50, 87
Tsungli Yamen, 56, 57, 76
Tuan Chih-jui, 106, 115, 152, 153, 154, 162, 195, 211
Tung, 42
T'ung Chih, 4
Tung Cho, 77
Tung Fu-hsiang, 56
Tung Meng Hui, 69, 71-73, 74, 75, 77, 78, 80, 84, 86, 87, 116, 122

Tung Wen Kuan, 37
Tung Yui-nan, 30, 31, 58
Twentieth Century Chinese Society, 71
Twenty-one Demands, 147-148, 152

Vatican City, 156
Versailles, Treaty of, 158
Victoria Hospital, 24

Waichow, 58, 79
Wang, Dr. C. T., 125
Wang Ching-wei, 71, 73, 79, 87, 139, 141, 216, 217
Wang Chuan-hui, 115
Wang-mo, 19
Wars of the Three Kingdoms, 137
Wen Tien-hsiang, 167
Wesleyan College, 143
West River, 4, 21
Whampoa, 165, 166; Military Academy, 206-208
White Cloud Mountains, 165
White Cloud Societies, 53
White Goose Pool, 166
White Lily, 53
Wilson, Woodrow, 126, 151
World War I, 146, 153, 158-159
Wu Chih-hu, Dr., 63, 65
Wu Pei-fu, 156, 162, 167, 171, 195, 196, 209-211
Wu Ting-fang, 96, 110, 156, 161, 163, 170

Wu Yueh, 86
Wuchang, 28, 76, 77, 80, 90, 92, 94, 96
Wuchow, 162-163
Wuhan, 90, 97
Wusung, 76

Yang Hao-ling, 25-26
Yang Sao-jen, 85
Yangchow, 7
Yangtse Valley, 7, 21, 80, 140, 210
Yao tribes, 175
Yeh Chu, 164
Yellow Eyebrows, 52
Yellow River, 3
Yellow Turbans, 52
Yeong, 4
Yin Chang, 93
Yo Fa Hui, 132
Yokohama, 34, 51, 64
Yu Hsien, 54-55, 56
Yu-ju, 166
Yu Shao-huan, 25-26
Yuan Ke-ting, 149
Yuan Shih-kai, 28, 50, 54, 88, 93, 94, 95, 96, 104, 108, 124, 158; death, 151; elected president, 131; elected provisional president, 110; self-appointed emperor, 149
Yung Cheng, 173
Yunnan, 1, 2, 4, 21, 22, 37, 81, 82, 129, 150, 155, 162, 175
Yunnanfu, 4